√ Aug '91

African Saga

MIRELLA RICCIARDI

African Saga

COLLINS
8 Grafton Street, London W1

William Collins Sons & Co. Ltd
London · Glasgow · Sydney · Auckland
Toronto · Johannesburg

BRITISH LIBRARY CATALOGUING IN PUBLICATION DATA

Ricciardi, Mirella
African saga.
1 Ricciardi, Mirella
I. Title
967.6'203 0924   TRI40.R4/

ISBN 0 00217512 6

First published 1982
Reprinted 1982
This edition 1985
Reprinted 1987
© Lipat BV 1982

Set in Monophoto Ehrhardt and printed by
BAS Printers Limited, Over Wallop, Hampshire

I dedicate this book
to my brother Dorian,
to Lorenzo,
my magnificent obsession,
and to George, my "wife".
Also to Adrian House
for his unflinching belief in me.

Contents

Prologue

Lorenzo and I left the others in the car. We took off our shoes, rolled up our trousers and started down the road, trudging ankle-deep through the slushy mud; hand in hand we started our first romantic walk through the Queen Elizabeth National Park.

The park was full of animals, wild creatures everywhere. Elephant, rhino, lion and leopard waited for darkness to come out onto the road. The thick mud slowed us down, the muscles in my legs began to ache, and the light was fading fast. Suddenly, as happens in Africa, it was dark. We trudged on in silence listening to the forest awakening around us.

Something moved nearby. I stopped in my tracks and squeezed Lorenzo's hand. We listened, holding our breath. Wild animals, if taken by surprise, can turn nasty, but they are wary of man and usually keep away from him. I opened my eyes wide, trying to pierce the darkness ahead. A branch broke, birds rose screeching from the forest around us. Something fell with a thump, the leaves and branches moved as if pushed aside. I tightened my grip on Lorenzo's hand. A shadow moved slightly to our right, about ten yards away, we stared intently at it. Our eyes were getting used to the dark and we began to distinguish black from black.

I pulled Lorenzo down beside me and pointed into the dark; like the shadow of a cloud passing overhead we saw an opaque outline move towards the middle of the road. "Elephant," I whispered, "just let them pass."

A second shape appeared on the road. We could hear the rumbling of their stomachs and their ears smacking against their heads. They stood for a few moments, with upraised trunks lazily sniffing the air, and then moved on slowly, slithering down the opposite bank. Very gently we edged forward, and felt our way for about twenty-five yards when another elephant came crashing through the bushes onto the road. We threw ourselves over the bank flat on the ground. It crossed the road to where we lay, still unaware of our presence, followed by a tiny calf. I had never been so close to an elephant before.

Lorenzo seemed amazingly unafraid. As we picked ourselves up I stepped on a rotten branch covering a hole filled with water and fell back to the ground with a splash. The elephant swung around to face us.

"Don't move," I hissed, "she hasn't seen us." Once more we lay flat on our stomachs, staring at her, watching her trunk pick out the scents in the air around her. She let out a high-pitched scream and charged off into the trees. We had just been given a little lesson in animal behaviour.

Six and a half hours later, we arrived at the camp. It was midnight, a thin slither of a moon hung in the sky. We had met many wild creatures on our way; a pride of lions lying on the road, three water buck, dozens of baboons and monkeys and buffalo and two fat hippo on the edge of a pond. They had all quietly given us right of way. We woke the park ranger sleeping in his sentry box, who leapt to his feet when he saw us standing over him like muddy scarecrows. Half an hour later we were in a simple, whitewashed rondavel with a straw-thatched roof and two iron beds, freshly made up.

"Will you marry me?" Lorenzo asked suddenly. "I need a girl like you around."

*

This book is a personal story.

Families, like trees, grow and develop with their surroundings. Seeds are blown by the wind and new trees are born elsewhere. Roots sink into the ground from which the new tree draws life. Children, like branches, stretch out. Families and trees have similar destinies.

The roots of my family tree sank deep into the soil of Africa and the little kingdom into which I was born and in which I grew up with my brother and sister on the shores of Lake Naivasha, a magic lake on the floor of the Great Rift Valley in East Africa, was home. It was built on the urge that drives people into the unknown in search of the light still missing from their lives. Our lives were bathed in that light.

But the land from which three generations drew life was threatened. The winds of change were blowing. This was no longer "white man's country". But to outsiders our existence had a surreal and fairy-like quality which we never found again.

PART I

Families Like Trees

ROCCO FAMILY TREE

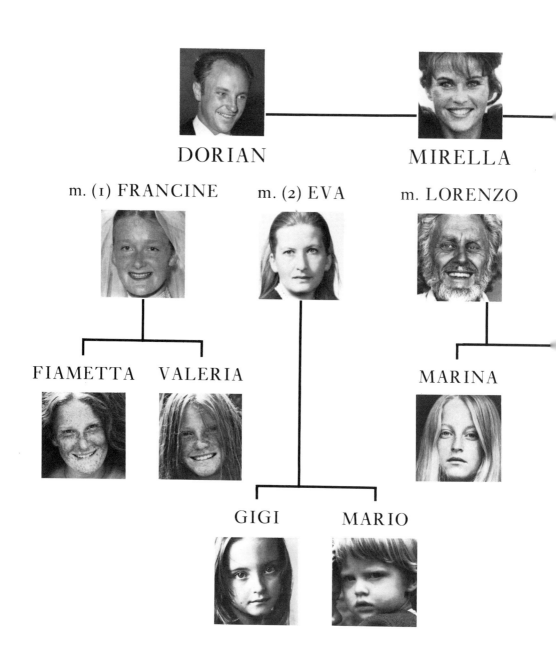

MARIO   GISELLE

ORIA

m. (1) GIUNIO   m. (2) IAIN

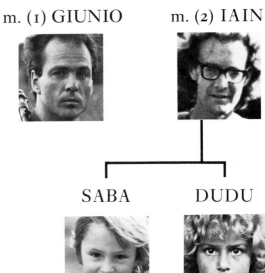

AMINA   SABA   DUDU

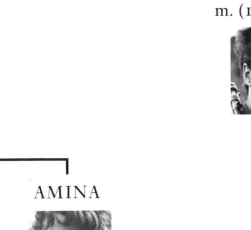

CHAPTER I

Mario

Dawn was breaking over the Baensizza Plateau in northern Italy. The Spad fighter plane, hit from the rear, went into a spin and plunged to earth. An oak tree broke its impact with the ground, and the pilot, Mario Rocco, was ejected from his seat and crashed through the branches, while his plane burst into flames in front of him. Picked up by some soldiers entrenched nearby, he was taken to the field hospital at Cividale with nineteen broken bones, but miraculously alive.

It was 15th November, 1914. Mario Rocco was just twenty-one. He had been given his wings only a few days previously and this flight was his first mission. An hour before he took off to attack the Austrian lines he had accepted a glass of milk from his old Scottish nanny. He was never to touch milk again.

Betty McPherson had cared for him since he was one day old, and when he joined the army she staunchly announced that she would follow him. In vain Mario tried to explain that nannies did not accompany their charges to war, but Miss McPherson was Scottish, and a determined lady. War or no war, where Mario went she went.

The following day the Austrian fighter-pilot who had shot him down flung a bunch of red carnations over the charred remains of Mario's plane with a note pinned to them inscribed "From Georg Braun to a gallant pilot". The flowers were picked up by the Italian soldiers below, and the Commanding Officer sent a message to Braun saying that Mario had survived the accident and that the flowers had been sent to the hospital.

It took Mario eleven months to recover from his crash. After four months in traction he left the hospital in a wheelchair. His father found him a villa in Capri, but two months later, bored with life on crutches, he rejoined his squadron in Castelfranco where, still incapacitated, he was

made mess officer. He worked beside the cook who had been the chef at the Excelsior in Rome, and discovered he had a culinary talent which he later turned into a fine art.

In October 1917 he left the air force and returned to the cavalry regiment he had joined after he left his military academy. He was present at the disaster of Caporetto, when the Austro-Hungarian armies broke through the Italian lines. To stem the tide of deserters one man out of every ten was picked out and shot. Mario was assigned to command the firing squad. He was deeply shocked by this experience, but the rigours of army discipline so impressed him he upheld them for the rest of his life.

When the war was over, Mario was posted to Vienna on a reparations mission. There he met Georg Braun who had read his name on the list of newly arrived officers. "Your flowers were sent to my mother, not to my grave," Mario told him. The two young officers struck up a friendship which was to last for many years, and Mario fell wildly in love with Georg's sister.

Mario had been much spoiled by his mother and his sisters Nina and Lisa who, in true Neapolitan style, were slavishly devoted to him. With his handsome face and Mediterranean charm he was a natural ladykiller, and many of his encounters turned into love affairs, but the first and only great love of his life was the beautiful and fiery Irene Ibsen, granddaughter of the famous playwright. Their courtship was swift and passionate and they married in the spring of 1919. A year later a daughter was born. They named her Rosetta after Mario's mother Rosa but the gulf that separated Norway from Naples could not be spanned in a single generation. Their marriage turned into a series of violent disputes and Rosetta was the victim of their emotional tug-of-war. The distraught fathers arranged a divorce and Irene was given custody of the child. She promptly changed Rosetta's name to Susannah Ibsen and broke Mario's heart by erasing him from her life for ever. In his anguish he cut his wrists. His life was saved *in extremis*. Unable to endure the commiseration of his family and friends in Naples he boarded a ship bound for China, and disappeared for two years.

From Shanghai Mario travelled to Mukden for an arms dealer who sold surplus army aircraft to the Manchurian rebels, got involved in a guerilla war, in which he flew and crashed three planes. In Peking he was befriended by King Li, a rich Mandarin who spoke beautiful French

Mario Rocco aged 19 in the uniform of the Ninth Lancers.

OVERLEAF   The only great love of Mario's life was Irene (far right, beside Mario) the beautiful and fiery granddaughter of Ibsen. Naples 1920.

and who was so fat that his silken robes rippled over him like oily waves when he moved. Mario spent hours listening to his philosophy of detachment, a philosophy which remained with him throughout his life and was to help him often in moments of adversity.

When he returned to Naples he was twenty-eight years old and a changed man. He joined the Rocco-Lacapria flour mills, the family business that turned American wheat into Italian pasta. Appalled by the working conditions in the mills, he enlisted in Matteotti's Socialist Party and soon became the spokesman for the grain millers' union, the *Uomini in bianco* ("men in white", covered in flour). He led workers' strikes and clashed with his father, the police and the Black Shirts. He was elected to the Chamber of Deputies as a Socialist MP, but because he was under thirty he was not permitted to serve. The men in Mario's family were all Fascists and he soon became the heretic among them. Inevitably he came to the notice of Mussolini, then at the beginning of his power, who had him arrested and brought to Rome. Dressed specially for the occasion in full uniform, his decorations pinned to his chest, Mario stood to attention in the austere reception quarters of the Palazzo Venezia. "Young man, you are a thorn in my side," Mussolini told him. "Change your ideas and join the Party, or leave Italy." "I prefer to leave my country, sire," Mario replied. That same night, still in his uniform, with little money as usual and unable to say goodbye to his family in Naples, he was put on a train to Paris. It was the beginning of a ten-year exile.

On arrival in Paris he made his way to the studio of Jane Avril, an American girlfriend of his and a painter. He spent several months in her studio, where his good looks, *joie de vivre*, his violin and his Latin love-songs quickly made him a favourite with the artists in her circle. In the spring of 1924, at a lunch party given by a former brother officer who was now a painter, he met Giselle Bunau-Varilla. She was a sculptress. She invited him to her studio in the rue Notre-Dame des Champs.

CHAPTER 2

Giselle

Giselle Bunau-Varilla was born into a powerful and wealthy family in Paris. Her father, Philippe Bunau-Varilla, had come to the notice of Ferdinand de Lesseps and at the age of twenty-seven was made engineer-in-chief of the Panama Canal project. De Lesseps' vision became Philippe's obsession. With John Hay, Undersecretary to Theodore Roosevelt, he eventually signed the Hay/Bunau-Varilla treaty which transferred the Canal Zone from Columbia to the United States. In their suite at the Waldorf-Astoria in New York, his wife Ida triumphantly stitched another star to her American flag.

The success of the Panama venture brought huge financial rewards. With his half-brother Maurice, Philippe Bunau-Varilla bought *Le Matin*, then a small Paris newspaper, and together they turned it into the leading daily paper in France.

With the success of *Le Matin*, Maurice became one of the stars of the Parisian political and social scene. The two brothers had been born in abject poverty from two different fathers, Jean Bunau, who came from Alsace, and Francisco Varilla, a Spaniard. Their mother, Caroline de Bois, hyphenated the names so that her sons could carry the same surname. The two boys married two sisters, Ida and Sonia de Brunoff, aristocratic girls who were no match for their dynamic husbands. Long-suffering and resigned, covered in beautiful clothes and expensive jewellery, they slipped gently into the background sighing, "*Nous autres pauvres femmes!*" So much was forbidden to the wives and daughters of their age and milieu, and Ida's daughter Giselle was expected to conform. She was to be married off pure, innocent and ignorant of life as soon as possible, "in case she falls in love with the chauffeur". Giselle's mother once managed to persuade the *Préfet* of Paris to have all the stray dogs in the neighbourhood castrated, so that her daughter should not witness them mating – or so the story goes. Her brother Etienne, to whom "all things were permitted because he was a boy", chose the books she was allowed to read. Beyond visits to the circus and daily walks in the Bois, most things were out of bounds to Giselle.

Her family position conditioned her outlook on life. Proud of the wealth and achievements of her father and uncle, she was nevertheless, contemptuous of a world in which a woman's mind was shaped to an acceptance of selfish masculine indulgence. This marked her so deeply that her attitude towards men remained one of open scorn.

Dressed in *des petites robes blanches très sages*, she wore a bored, sad expression. But her pale green eyes were alert and bright and betrayed an inner fire.

"Giselle is an obedient, docile girl on the surface," her mother wrote in her diary, "but beneath this aspect I feel there is a growing energy which is pushing her away from us. She is so like her father. I often wonder if I had anything at all to do with her make-up. She does not mother her dolls like most girls of her age, but instead lines them up on the back of the sofa and shoots at them with her brother's bow and arrow!"

When she was sixteen, Giselle was permitted to attend some lectures at the Louvre. At the insistence of the Director of the *Ecole des Arts Décoratifs*, a friend of her uncle Maurice, who recognised her artistic potential, she was also allowed to join classes in what her family referred to as "that den of iniquity where men and women posed in the nude". In a corner of the studio, sad and bent, sat her ever-vigilant governess and Giselle was mortified to discover that she was the only pupil subjected to this supervision.

In 1912, at the age of twenty, Giselle accepted her first proposal of marriage without realising that her suitor might have been more interested in her fortune than in herself. A year later she was divorced. Her father's own childhood and poverty-stricken adolescence had given him no guidance as to the education of his children. He lavished on them all the material necessities that he himself had lacked but took no interest in the formation of their minds. Immersed in his Panamanian vision he was so often absent from home that he never realised that Giselle had inherited his own personality.

In 1915 Giselle married again. Her new husband, the Marquis di Castelmarigi, left soon after for the front, and she set herself up in a

Giselle Bunau-Varilla. "I have met a beautiful and important woman who may change the direction of my life . . ."
Giselle's powerful family conditioned her for life.

Giselle studied under Auguste Rodin (*left*), then already
a very old man living alone and penniless.

studio at 9 rue Notre-Dame des Champs. At her uncle Maurice's sumptuous house on the avenue du Président-Wilson, she met Baron Empain.

Empain spoke to her of the distressing conditions on the battlefront and the desperate need for help in any form. Determined to be of some use in the war effort, she left next day for Calais, where she found the station platform strewn with the dead and dying soldiers from the Belgian front. She had stood on this same platform so many times before on her way to and from her holidays by the sea. After hearing of the dire shortage of beds, doctors and nurses, bandages, medicine and food, she returned to Paris and handed her friends at the American Embassy a long list of her requirements. These immediately began piling up at her parents' home on the avenue d'Iéna where she had commandeered her mother's staff and taken over the ground floor to receive the donations. She personally accompanied the supplies to the front, for pillaging on the trains was so bad that often only a small proportion of the supplies ever arrived.

Giselle then crossed the English Channel, contacted the Society of Friends in London, secured from them ten thousand bottles of milk and returned with these to France on a British gunboat. Later she toured America, lecturing and showing a dramatic documentary film on the war. So generous was the American response to her war effort appeal that she had to make additional arrangements for storage. The Director of the *Ecole des Beaux Arts* assigned a whole wing of the Louvre to her and the Pavillon des Fleurs became her headquarters until the war ended.

When her husband, who had been taken prisoner, returned, they found they had become strangers and soon afterwards they divorced. Giselle went back to her studio and her bohemian, bachelor life, and studied under Auguste Rodin, then a very old man living alone.

In the winter she brought him food and coal. In the spring she took him for drives in the country in her brother Etienne's bright red Bugatti. Finally she prompted her uncle Maurice into launching an intensive campaign in *Le Matin* which led to the formation and financing of the famous Musée Rodin in Paris.

With her numerous artist cousins, Giselle often travelled to North Africa, where she spent long periods in Morocco and Tunisia drawing and sculpting the people in the streets. Her clay heads and beggars'

Giselle in Morocco in 1923. She spent long periods in North Africa drawing and sculpting the people in the streets.

hands were fired in the local kilns and on one occasion she found them all smashed because her work was so realistic that the people thought she was a witch. One day in a café in Cairo she met the famous archaeologist Howard Carter who invited her to visit Tutankhamun's tomb with him before it was officially opened. This visit awoke in her a deep passion for Egyptian art which greatly affected her later work and sharpened her growing curiosity for the African continent as a whole.

Giselle was also one of the first women to fly. She went up with her brother Etienne, whose pilot's licence was No. 16, and Blériot, Santos-Dumont and Orville Wright became her friends. Independent and adventurous, she now lived alone in her studio at No. 9 Rue Notre-Dame des Champs. It was here that Mario Rocco came to visit her.

CHAPTER 3

In the Beginning

"'I am no one, just an exile. I came to Paris because everyone comes to Paris, but now I have to start my life again,' he said to me. He looked at me with coal-black eyes, his black hair wild and I have fallen in love with him, who knows, maybe for ever," Giselle confided to her diary that same night.

"I have met a beautiful and important woman who may change my life," Mario wrote to his mother the next day.

Mario stepped into Giselle's world and the doors of Paris opened to him. It was a bohemian world spiced with power and money. At her side he plunged into the social round of lunch and dinner parties and fast became a favourite everywhere. Where Giselle went he now went.

But as the affair blossomed Mario became haunted by its implications. With little money and no direction of his own he was in danger of becoming a pawn in Giselle's hands. During a sun-drenched holiday in her converted fort on the Mediterranean island of Port Cros, he decided to break away. "The lesson learned from my tumultuous existence," he wrote to her, "is never to think of tomorrow, and to forget yesterday. It is a child's philosophy, but it allows life to be lived minute by minute and makes it possible to bear all that life holds for us. I can only tell you that the two 'I's within me – *das Ich* and *der Ich* – are constantly at war. The one involuntarily succumbs to your influence and is happy to confide in you, the other instinctively tears itself away. If *der Ich* is the stronger I will not wait for you, I will immediately take the boat for the mainland. *Das Ich* will put me into your hands, your artist's hands, which will mould my raw clay and will make of me an important work. In the meantime I want you to know that the sweetness of this thought makes me drunk."

Mario gave way to his instinct for self-preservation and abandoned

Giselle on her island. He boarded a ship in Marseilles for the United States. Penniless again, he wrote almost daily to his mother in Naples.

10th October, 1926
250 Stone Street
New York City

Mother dear,

This is a country where dreams can become reality on condition that one has a strong back and does not suffer from a large appetite. I spend everything I earn just to keep alive; every day I gamble with my life and never know if tomorrow I will eat or end up in a hospital, in prison or in a madhouse, but I have quite decided to remain in America all my life.

18th October

I have just disembarked from the ferry boat that took me to Ellis Island. It is two o'clock in the morning. I was caught five days ago as I was leaving the docks where I had gone to accompany a girlfriend onto her ship. All my documents had expired and I was deported and kept in custody. I cannot describe the horror of these days. An island behind the Statue of Liberty (what irony!) ringed with iron fences and armed guards. My fellow prisoners were gathered from the dregs of the Levant, with Chinese, Negroes, Jews, Greeks and southern Italians thrown in as well – all living in unbelievable filth and stench. An existence that beggared description – hell, in short. But this morning a wire from Washington with a recommendation from Senator La Follette opened the doors of my prison and here I am back in New York, the parody of liberty, looking for a friend who will lend me a dollar for food. My last two dollars were spent on the telegraph asking you for some money.

25th October

This life of mine made of good and bad luck, rich one day, poor the next, breaks me in pieces, yet if you asked me to change to a conventional, easy life, I would probably hesitate. What would I do if I returned to Naples? Get a job in a bank or become an employee in some business. Anyone who had tasted the freedom of this life cannot look back. Forgive me, mother, you know how I love you.

Your adoring son, Mario

3rd November

Mamma Mia

I accepted your suggestion to represent Father's business in New York, but the recession is about to put an end to our venture. Two shiploads of wheat were emptied into the harbour last week, the price no longer justifying the expense of the voyage. I am living a hand-to-mouth existence once more. Giselle B-V showed me the easy way, but the Hispanic pride I have inherited from you keeps me from turning my back on my misfortunes.*

15th November

I see only a few friends. They are four or five women who hang around me and tell me they adore me. They say they will do anything for me, they do not leave me alone, they say they need me to live. I hate them. They bother me immeasurably and I have decided to suppress my relations with all women.

20th November

I wrote to you a few days ago to tell you that women are poison to me, and today I received a wire from Giselle B-V who says she absolutely wants to come to America to marry me. I telegraphed her immediately and told her she was MAD. Marry me? I don't want to marry her or anyone else. I don't love anyone.

21st November

My friend Alberto tells me I am mad to refuse a wife with a million dollars. I feel like a fool. I can't help it. The only thing I want to do is to live with you, only for you, to enjoy your love which is mine and in which I was born.

20th December

Giselle has been here for two weeks, despite the fact that I sent her dozens of letters and telegrams telling her not to come. She has taken a studio not far from mine and has declared she will not return to Paris alone. I don't know what to do. I cannot get married. I don't feel the need to and I don't want to embark on another adventure like the one

*Mario's mother was Spanish, born in Madrid.

with Irene. I don't want to live with her in free cohabitation. It would not be right for her and could have grave consequences for me. I don't know if I love her. I think I am no longer capable of love and at the same time I do not have the patience to tolerate the love of others. I am like Buridan's ass and will end up dying through being unable to make up my mind. That is all. How will it end? God only knows.

West 11th Street
14 January, 1927

I have moved into Giselle's studio. I have capitulated. My business ventures have been dogged with misfortune; they have all collapsed around me, but I will not abandon my struggle to maintain my independence, while Giselle paints and sculpts and lovingly cares for me.

28th February

Dear Mother,
    Giselle is pregnant.
Your loving Mario.

11th October

Two days ago our first child was born. We named her Sabina, but she died last night of pneumonia. My grief is immeasurable and I need to talk to you, for I know you will weep with my tears. Mother dear, what savage hand is fate holding out to me? Giselle is very strong, stronger than I am, she says she wants children more than anything on earth. I know you are near me with your sorrow.

1st November

Giselle returned to Paris yesterday. Our union has not been very successful and it is better this way. I know that ultimately I must find my own way and her presence in my life will hamper me, even if at times it renders it more bearable.

Paris
15th November

My adored Mario,

Yesterday I had dinner at my uncle Maurice's château. Baron Empain was there. He is the chairman and principal shareholder of the Katanga copper mines. He is leaving for the Belgian Congo in a few weeks, and has invited me to visit him there. The prospect of a new adventure in Africa has fired my imagination and I am asking you to come with me and accept his invitation. Telegraph your reply.

Giselle

25th November

My dearest Mother,

I am leaving New York and shall be in Naples before Christmas. I shall be able to spend four or five days with you and will then be leaving for Marseilles on the first step in my voyage to the Belgian Congo, where Giselle and I have been invited by Baron Empain. I am with the Société Congo Grands Lacs who have bought 400,000 hectares of land which it seems is even richer than the Transvaal and where the climate is spring all year. I don't know how long I will be there, but certainly not less than two years. I would like to see my little Rosetta before I leave. At least I feel that the bad days are over. I kiss you and all the family.

Mario.

Mario arrived in Naples on board the *Biancamano* on 18th December. His mother and sisters, his father and brother Renato were there to meet him with Giselle, who had come from Paris by train the day before.

In Marseilles the seamen were on strike; the departure was postponed for a week, but the adventure had started. Provisions, guns and ammunition bought in Brussels on Empain's suggestion were packed in tin cases weighing not more than twenty-five kilograms, the maximum weight an African porter could carry. On 20th January, 1928, in heavy fog and freezing weather, they sailed for Dar-es-Salaam. They turned their backs on the Northern Hemisphere, on a life to which neither had adjusted, and headed towards the Dark Continent and the unknown.

CHAPTER 4

Africa

Dar-es-Salaam
5th February, 1929

Mamma Mia,

We have finally arrived in Dar-es-Salaam, which in Kiswahili means "The Haven of Peace", and spent our first night at the New Africa Hotel, the only lodging in the tiny port. It is a land-locked, palm-fringed, natural harbour of great beauty and one of the last ports of call on the Arabian dhow route. We steamed up the bottleneck entrance into the sleepy bay where several Arab dhows lay at anchor beside our landing wharf.

Giselle and I were happy to step off the ship onto African soil at last, and we are excited at the prospect ahead.

I shall write again in a few days so you can follow us on our trip. I miss you very much and think of you always.

Your far away and loving son, Mario

Ugigi
9th February

Here we are in Ugigi, where Stanley met Livingstone. We left Dar-es-Salaam three days ago on the Tanganyika Railway built by the Germans at the turn of the century. It still retains a distinctly German look which contrasts amusingly with the surrounding country. Baron Empain arrived a few hours before we did, having walked for three days to be at the rendezvous. "Mario Rocco, I presume," he said, smiling, as he walked towards us with outstretched hand, and we enacted the historic meeting beneath the very same tree.

We continue our journey to Kigoma together and shall then leave for Uvira aboard a paddle-steamer.

Uvira
14th February

The crossing of the Tanganyika Lake was picturesque and steaming hot. Our black travel companions were very curious and stood around staring, making comments on and touching everything about us. There is no landing stage at this diminutive village of Uvira and the passengers from the steamer are carried to shore on the backs of sturdy African porters.

It was Giselle's first physical contact with black-skinned men. She did not much like those strong black hands that clasped her by the thighs. The acrid smell of African bodies brought home to her the stark reality of our adventure. We led the way and our equipment followed us in dugout canoes that moved swiftly over the muddy waters, pushed by long slender poles that plunged in rhythm with the chanting men. On every side lay Africa, mysterious, powerful, untamed and steaming.

We have been in Uvira for almost a week with Empain's party and are staying in a small boarding-house kept by a burly Englishman called Cross and his lady-friend Judy. Cross is a man whose life is one of utter monotony relieved only by drink. His sallow complexion is characteristic of the European who has lived many years in Africa where the hot damp climate and strong sun have taught him to seek the shade. Empain, too, is a heavy drinker and we are beset by drinking parties, but we have not come to Africa to drink and I think we are going to part company with him.

15th February
We have contacted the Belgian District Commissioner and told him of our problem with Empain and our desire to continue on our own; he has offered to help and will secure sixty African porters for us at a salary of one franc per man per day plus rations.

Our northward-bound caravan will be leaving in two days and we shall commence our foot safari without any fixed destination or limit of time. Giselle and I have chosen to live a life without restrictions of any kind and we are placing ourselves in the hands of God.

OVERLEAF   Arriving in Uvira in 1929. Africa lay
all around, powerful, steaming and untamed.

Six hours' march
north of Uvira
16th February

We are now part of the Dark Continent where time and money, direction and communications hold no more meaning. The giant trees of the forest, the mountains and the valleys, the great white plains have become our world, the distant horizons and misty mountain outlines our only focal points.

Last night we unpacked our safari cases, so neatly packed and labelled, for the first time. I explained to one of our porters that he should sweep out the floor of the tent before bringing in the two camp beds. When I went to inspect the job an hour later I found the man kneeling on the floor, a rag in his hand, carefully mopping the canvas. The container carrying our precious drinking water lay beside him on its side, empty . . . I was so furious I punched the man on the jaw and he collapsed on the ground. Giselle and the other porters came rushing to the tent. "There's going to be a riot," Giselle hissed at me. I reached for my shotgun expecting trouble, but the men suddenly burst into peals of laughter and advanced to shake my hand, and pat me on the back. The prostrate porter opened his eyes and looked up at us. I bent down to help him to his feet and apologised for having hit him. His large round face just beamed back at me and he laughed with his companions who led him away, but we had no more drinking water for twelve hours after that!

When we returned to the camp fire we noticed something move in the undergrowth. A bird took flight and screeched in the dark. Little black faces, half-hidden by the leaves, began appearing all round. They were the pygmies of the forest. Their village was not far from where we had stopped for the night. Like shy animals they had come to investigate our presence on their territory. Hesitantly, they advanced into the firelight. Quite naked and very small, the men carried bows and arrows; the women had babies strapped with leather thongs to their backs. We watched each other for a while and then the little people disappeared back into the forest.

Later in the night another sound, another movement, stirred Giselle from her sleep. When she opened her eyes she saw a gentle undulation in the canvas. She stretched out an arm and woke me. "Look at the side of the tent; it is moving." Moments later, framed in the entrance I saw the mottled, heavy-set head and shoulders of a leopard in the bright moonlight. A hunk of meat hung from its powerful jaws. Slowly I reached for my rifle. We stared at each other for a brief moment as I aimed to fire, but the animal turned and leapt into the night. Next morning we discovered that the antelope carcass we had left hanging high in a tree had been stripped of its two hind legs.

The little people returned the next day. An old grizzly-haired man with a shaggy beard ventured forward to speak to one of the porters. His fears dispelled, he moved towards us and squatted at a safe distance while the others remained sheltering in the bushes. We looked at each other and then I smiled and stretched out my hand to him. He took hold of it, contact was made, and the others moved into the camp and swarmed around us.

Next day they brought us berries and manioc roots wrapped in leaves. I shot some game for them and within a few days they told me I was their "white chief", a great honour for me. They said I had a magic weapon and touched my rifle with awe and in return proudly showed me their bows and arrows, and invited me to come into the forest with them to hunt elephant. On the next day we set out before dawn. The little men, moving silently and fast, cut their way with primitive knives along hardly discernible tracks. We followed them. As the sun rose the heat became intense. The insects lifted like steam and buzzed around us; our tender European skins began to itch and welts appeared on our uncovered hands and faces. We stumbled on behind the little naked men who moved with speed and agility, careless of the heat. Suddenly they stopped, stood motionless to listen. The bush ahead had been flattened. Fresh elephant dung lay about; the hunters stuck their toes into it to gauge the temperature . . . Secrets of the forest . . . Dusk found us within earshot of the herd. The forest was alive with the rumblings of the elephants' digestive systems and the tearing of branches. The hunters fanned out in a semi-circle, careful to remain downwind, and settled at a safe distance for the night, hunched together for warmth. Giselle and I ached all over. It had been our first tough African experience. We slumped down exhausted onto the damp earth and slept beneath the canopy of forest leaves.

The sound of the hunters moving woke us. It was still dark. Groggy with sleep we watched them gather up their bows and arrows and fasten

OVERLEAF Pygmies: "Wherever we go and whenever we stop we seem to be surrounded by expectant little black men who appear from nowhere."

their knives around their naked waists. We got up, stiff and cold, and watched the pygmies hard at work already digging a trench across a clearly marked track. When it was deep enough, one of them crawled inside and the others covered it with a web of branches and leaves and then dispersed and hid. As dawn broke the forest began again to move. The elephants stood among the trees still unaware of our presence. A young male appeared on the track and came in our direction, lazily flapping his ears and ripping the vines with his trunk. As the great hulk moved over the camouflaged trench, the little man inside rose up and slashed the tendons of the hind leg just above the hoof as it passed over him. The sharp blade sank deep and effortlessly through the thick hide. A stream of blood gushed out as the animal fell screaming to one side. The waking forest exploded.

The whole herd crashed through the undergrowth, trumpeting in alarm, trees swayed in their wake, branches broke, invisible birds and monkeys took screeching flight. The hunters rushed from their hiding-places and plunged their poisoned spears and arrows into the smitten beast, now back on his feet and limping heavily after the herd. The poison did not take long to work. When Giselle and I arrived on the scene we found the excited hunters hacking at the still quivering carcass.

The inhabitants of the nearby village, alerted by the beating drums, arrived with their wooden containers and knives and joined the hunters in their gruesome work. They removed the tusks and slit open the belly. Strong black fingers like claws emptied the carcass. The huge intestines spilled wet and gurgling onto the ground and the still undigested contents of the stomach steamed fresh and green in the dark red blood. The heart and liver were cut out and carefully placed on leaves. They worked without pausing until the lacerated carcass lay like a blood-soaked island in a lake of strong, sour-smelling slush.

A ring of small fires was lit around the beast. After the ivory was carried to one side they moved in like ants and, in a chorus of excited chatter, began cutting and hacking and pulling. Three of them crawled inside the carcass and worked outwards. Within minutes the majestic elephant was transformed into a scattered, dismembered mess soaking into the hot African earth. Pieces of meat were stuffed onto the tapered ends of sticks stripped of their leaves and placed over the crackling fires. When it was raw on one side and charcoal burned on the other, the pygmies tore hungrily at it with their strong white teeth and fingers.

Giselle and I were offered the elephant's temple, a delicacy considered tender enough for the white man's teeth. As the ribcage came apart the animal was wholly destroyed and carried away piece by piece. Only the blood and the intestines remained to dry in the sun and be blown away by the wind.

Will write more later, Mario.

Kalembelembe
10th April

We have been walking for two months and have now become well accustomed to our new strenuous physical life. Our skins and feet are hardened by the sun and the rough terrain we have crossed. Guided only by our whims and instincts we followed a vague route with sketchy maps and a good compass. We stop sometimes for several days when a suitable camp site with water presents itself to us. I have been on several good hunting expeditions with my first-class trackers, while Giselle sketches the natives who are forever gathering around our camps. We feed on a variety of antelope and wildfowl. With my "magic weapon" I have become quite a celebrity in the area. The natives, always in search of meat, follow my movements with great interest. Arrivals and departures are signalled on the "bush telegraph", drums that echo across the valleys to the surrounding villages. Wherever we go and whenever we stop we are quickly surrounded by expectant natives who seem to appear from nowhere. They have named me Lukwakwa (he who walks fast), and Giselle is known as Potopot (she who works with clay).

Don't be too anxious if you receive no news of us for long periods, we are a long way from any post office and can only give mail to passing travellers who carry our letters to nearby towns. We are far from civilisation and we like it this way.

God bless you, Mother dear, I think of you all the time.

15th April

At Kalembelembe we met Captain Bird, the first white man we have talked to since we left Empain at Uvira. He is a former English pilot hunting elephant and selling ivory in Elizabethville. Bird is a laconic man who answers questions in monosyllables. He tells us nothing of himself and I know better than to ask a man who hunts ivory in Africa for a living to speak about his past.

The other day he told me he had been forced to hawk his rifles as he had run out of money. He was travelling to the Majemba district where he had news of a large herd of elephant. He asked me if he could borrow one of my rifles. Reluctantly I lent him my Rigby and he left the same day with his two trackers, taking with him only a small mountain tent rolled in a bag, some biscuits, some tins of condensed milk and some tea leaves.

A few days later a runner arrived in our camp with a message from Bird. "Dear Rocco," it read, "I am sitting beside a wounded elephant and we are both crying, he for his wounds and me for not being able to put him out of his suffering for want of one bullet. Please send me same by bearer and I shall return the gun immediately with the man after killing the beast. Thanks. Bird." I sent him the bullet, and the rifle was brought back the next day . . . I was sorry to learn this week that Bird had taken his life. I had grown to respect this lonely adventurer with his pale blue eyes and sun-streaked hair.

Majemba Valley
25th June

Mon cher oncle Maurice,

I am sure you will be happy to know that the encounter with Empain has led us to the centre of a deep forest in the middle of the Belgian Congo. Mario and I are now one with the Dark Continent and I feel I could quite easily go on living this life of wandering without direction or purpose for the rest of my life. I will be forever grateful to you for having made it possible. With Mario, who is now the sole reason for my life, I feel I have found eternity.

We have been walking for almost five months, stopping only to sleep at night or to rest for a few days by the side of a river. We are at present encamped at the bottom of a valley beside a little *village indigène*. It has no name, and consists of half a dozen mud huts with palm-frond roofs set out in a clearing in the forest. The friendly villagers came out to welcome us; many had toes and fingers missing and nasty bush sores on their legs and arms. We thought they were suffering from malnutrition and gave them all the meat we were carrying. They returned the gesture with gifts of potatoes and manioc from their meagre plantations.

The night we arrived Mario went to bed early complaining of severe headache. I gave him a glass of whisky and some aspirin and put him to bed in the tent. I remained outside beside the fire and let the night creep over my tired body, glad of this momentary respite to savour in full the wonders of this Africa which I have learned to love so well.

When I went back to the tent I found Mario unconscious on the bed covered in sweat, moaning incomprehensibly and crying out for his mother. He seemed to be suffocating. He gasped for breath and clawed at the sides of the tent as if he wanted to tear it from around him. I was seized with panic and, not knowing what else to do, scribbled a note asking for help and handed it to one of the porters urging him not to return until he had found another white man.

He ran off into the forest and was gone for five days. Mario got no better. I thought he was going to die. On the sixth day a gaunt white man wearing a pith helmet and carrying a gun appeared with my runner. He introduced himself to me as Dr del Gao, a Portuguese doctor studying leprosy in the area, and said that he had walked for three days to answer the call of a fellow white man in distress in the African jungle.

He examined Mario, who was still delirious, and asked me what I had given him. "Aspirin," was all I could answer. "I had no idea what to give him." "You did the right thing," he told me, and then added in a matter-of-fact way, "It is sunstroke. If they don't die in six days they usually pull through." He inspected Mario's helmet and found it cracked. "He will recover, don't worry," he told me reassuringly. "But get him another helmet." I asked him to spend the night with us, but he declined. He bade me farewell and vanished back into the forest whence he had come.

Would you ever have believed, *mon cher oncle*, that your little Giselle would have ended up like this? Please tell Maman and Papa not to worry about me, for I am very happy this way.

Je vous embrasse très fort, Giselle.

Near Majemba
6th July

Dear Sister Lisa,
Ten hours hunting, another elephant down. Six hundred kilos of meat

for my men. Thirty kilos of ivory per tusk. My tenth elephant to date. God knows what has come over me to write this letter to you. Is it the solitude or the hum from the small stove heating the kettle for tea? A thousand thoughts dance in my brain – a bit of nostalgia for the family and many other things prevent me from sleeping. The tent is an oven. The Maniema plains boil even at night.

I shot with my Express at twenty metres, a low hit; the elephant, screaming with pain, turned and came at us like a locomotive. Another shot and the bullet entered the stomach, but no result. It kept coming and crashed past us. As I was reloading, another crash to my left. Two buffalo, evidently frightened by the passage of the elephant, were coming towards me at full speed. *Il cuore mi saltò in bocca.* (My heart jumped into my mouth.) I didn't even have time to lift my gun, the beast passed scarcely a yard from me. The buffalo is the *most dangerous* animal in Africa. Most hunters prefer to confront two lions than one buffalo. Having pulled ourselves together we continued to track the wounded animal, following the blood trail. We crossed the Luanda river in water up to our waists, avoiding the hippo, and, *after another three hours*, caught up with the elephant still in the papyrus marsh. One more shot in the head from three paces and I downed him for good. I had to put another five shots into him to end the agony. An elephant mortally wounded cries like a baby. The spectacle of its pain is awful to witness.

It is seven o'clock, the cook is preparing dinner, I shall sit down at table in the company of the tsetse flies. In one month I shall be leaving this area and we shall head for India, Malaya and the Philippines and then, who knows, maybe for the moon.

I think of you all very often and kiss you and the children.
Your loving brother, Mario.

Luanda River
22nd July

Mon cher frère,

Maybe I should have been born the boy instead of you. Here I am in Africa, every day living a new experience, the sort of experience which few if any girls ever have.

A few days ago I told Mario I wanted to shoot an elephant. He has already bagged ten and he agreed that the next one should be mine. Not

Giselle and her one-tusked elephant in the Congo.

long after, an opportunity presented itself. We caught sight of a large lone male standing on a ridge across the valley about an hour's walk from us. Through the binoculars we watched it standing in the midday sun, motionless but for the flapping of its ears, its long trunk hanging heavily to the ground in a gentle curve.

We made our way downwind across the valley. The trackers, bent double, moved lightly from tree to tree. The wind shifted and we stopped, our eyes never leaving the animal. All around was silence. Mario handed me his gun. "This is yours," he whispered to me. I lined up the sights, a fly buzzed maddeningly in my ears, perspiration ran down the side of my face, down my neck. I bore down on the trigger. The animal lurched forward, sank to its knees and fell over. Immediately I felt a surge of guilt. Why had I done this, what had I wanted to prove, that I was equal to a man? And the animal had only one tusk . . .

I suppose one has to do everything once before a curiosity is satisfied. I hope you don't think too badly of me.

Giselle

Somewhere near Ruanda
30th July

Dearest Sister Nina,

Six months have slipped by since we left Uvira. Giselle is pregnant but she does not let her condition interfere with our adventure. She feels fit and well, and we have almost forgotten the world we left behind, although my thoughts are always with you all in Naples.

The other day I asked Giselle what she wanted to do – continue the life we were leading or have a family? She hesitated a moment and then said she would choose the latter.

We are heading northwards to Usumbura in the Ruanda district of Lake Kivu, and will attempt to reach the British colony of Kenya in time for the birth of the child. British hospitals and nurses have a good reputation and we are still within walking distance of the colony.

A big kiss to Mamma and tell her the next letter is for her.

Your distant brother, Mario.

Bujumbura
10th August

Mamma Mia,

At Baraka on Lake Tanganyika we boarded a river steamer that took us to Bujumbura, the tiny capital of the Urundi district on the north-eastern shore of the lake.

We have been here four days resting and getting cleaned up before we move on. For the first time in many months we indulged in the luxury of a warm bath and in a few days we shall be among the Watussi on Lake Kivu.

Your son, Mario.

Lake Kivu
20th August

We halted in front of a row of stately trees leading to the King of Ruanda's palace. Several tall men dressed in long flowing togas came out to meet us and greeted us with great courtesy and warmth. Having asked if we needed anything they extended an invitation from the king to visit him next day.

King Musinga is a man in his early fifties. He is seven feet tall and, like his courtiers, is dressed in a long, flowing, white toga knotted on his left shoulder and falling in great folds to his sandalled feet. He has a beautiful, ugly face with a large beak nose and fiery black eyes. The hair on his head is combed upwards and parted in three crescents adding several inches to his height. He has one hundred wives who all live with their children in separate houses in the royal compound where Giselle and I were brought to meet him.

Soyez les bienvenus, he said in greeting as he bent to kiss Giselle on the hand. He has adopted the continental way of greeting when he receives European ladies.

The royal compound covers approximately three hundred square metres and is surrounded by a fence of interwoven split bamboos. The palace stands in the middle. The dark earth around it is beaten down hard and kept damp to avoid the dust. It is a large circular construction of mud walls covered by an immense pale yellow straw roof held up in the centre by a single long pole. King Musinga lives in it with his old

OVERLEAF Musinga, King of the Watussi, was
seven feet tall and had one hundred wives.

mother, three of his unwed sisters and his latest wife.

Musinga led us into the cool dark interior of his palace and introduced us to his mother who sat on a wooden stool to one side. She was very fat and spoke no language other than her own. She welcomed us with a smile so warm that it felt like a caress. We carried on a rather halting conversation in Swahili and broken French through her son, and sat together cross-legged on the straw mats on the floor. We were later joined by the three sisters who had been shyly watching us through the slits in the walls. Strong cinnamon tea in little porcelain bowls was brought in on a copper tray by a short squat Huto. The sisters were shy and did not talk to us but smiled and giggled a lot. They are very beautiful and wear many bracelets and have long strands of beads falling from their necks and hips.

We have been here for more than two weeks now. I have shot two more elephants and Giselle has made several clay sculptures and drawings of the members of the Royal Family whose exquisite looks have driven her to a creative frenzy. They pose for hours and are always obliging, smiling and patient almost as if they considered it an honour. These people are the aristocrats of the African continent.

God bless you, Mother dear.

Mario

Bukavu
30th August

In Bukavu we visited one of Musinga's daughters who is married to the chief of this region and we were received with the customary courtesy and gracious hospitality.

Giselle presented our hostess with a box of chocolates we purchased from a Greek shopkeeper in the nearby town, but she smiled shyly and gently refused the offering. Slightly embarrassed, Giselle placed the box on the floor beside her. As I struggled in broken French with my disjointed conversation with her husband, we several times caught the young woman eyeing the box of chocolates. She moved imperceptibly towards it until she finally hid it beneath her skirts. When she thought no one was looking she picked a chocolate from the box and popped it into her mouth. Within half an hour she had emptied the box! When she got up to leave she left the empty box behind her in full view of us.

We shall be leaving Bukavu and Lake Kivu, the most beautful lake in the world, in a few days and shall be heading for Lake Victoria. Our journey is nearing its end.

Nairobi, Kenya
15th September

We left the Ruanda district and moved eastwards to Bukoba on the western shores of Lake Victoria where we boarded a steamer of the East African Railways and sailed to Kisumu on the opposite side of the lake.

Eight months have gone by and we have covered many hundreds of miles on foot. We have lived the greatest adventure of our lives and had experiences which will never be repeated. Even if I should die tomorrow I shall feel I have lived life in full, and I thank Giselle for this.

The rail journey from Kisumu was a fitting end to our Congo safari. The train rattled noisily across the silent land and screeched to a halt every few hours to load and unload goods and passengers at the tiny stations along the route. The platforms were always crowded and full of activity. Bundles of bananas and pale green sugar cane, bales of cotton and over-loaded baskets covered in coloured cloth, chickens and goats came on and off in a buzz of excited chatter. Stately Buganda women, dressed in long bright robes, rose like trees from among the mottled shorter tribes along the route. With regal grace they carried baskets and bananas and earthen pots on their heads. Many had babies strapped to their backs or on their hips suckling an uncovered breast.

The arrival of the weekly train was an occasion never to be missed; it brought news from places too far to walk to and broke the monotony of the days. The station master looked like a black Englishman in his dark blue uniform and shiny peak cap.

The Africans travelled in the third-class compartments, sitting on wooden benches. The comfortable first-class coaches are reserved for Europeans and provide white crisp sheets and bedding for overnight travellers. Meals are served in the dining-car which is also reserved for Europeans. The food was tasteless, despite the French names on the menu. The soup looked like dishwater with bits of vegetables floating in it, the meat dish was served in thick brown sauce with soggy potatoes. Lemon blancmange, soft, yellow and rubbery invariably capped the meal, followed by cheese and biscuits and watery coffee. Fresh white bread and yellow rolls of butter were served on stainless steel dishes with the K.U.R.H. (Kenya, Uganda Railways and Harbours) initials stamped below the crown reminding passengers that they were now under British rule.

I will write again soon.

Your loving son, Mario.

PART II

Kenya

CHAPTER 5

Naivasha

When Mario and Giselle reached Kenya in the autumn of 1929 its capital, Nairobi, was the largest town in British East Africa. It had already approximately twenty thousand white inhabitants and several thousand Indians who had remained after the completion of the railway from Mombasa. It boasted three hotels, two hospitals and a stately Government House overlooking a beautifully kept, English-style garden. The European residential area of Muthiaga, with its English homes and gardens, was aloof and segregated. Its country club and golf course were strictly out of bounds to Africans and Jews. It was here that the white residents gathered at the end of the day to sip their sundowners and dine and dance into the night. Collar and tie were *de rigueur* in the dining-room and a pious hush hung all about. Conversations were conducted in low voices, punctuated now and then by a loud guffaw from the bar. The silent, barefoot servants were well trained by English staff and moved mute and respectful about their business.

In contrast, the town centre, with its quaint wooden buildings and corrugated iron roofs, was shabby. The main street was tarmac'ed and named after Lord Delamere, one of the country's prominent pioneers. Mauve jacaranda trees provided shade and colour to the dusty brown sunbaked surroundings; barefoot Africans, in dishevelled European cast-off clothes, and rickshaw boys jostled for space among the Model T Fords and Chevrolets. Sparsely clad, ochre-coloured Maasai warriors strode like arrogant peacocks hand in hand down the porticoed sidewalks, gaping wide-eyed and amused at the motley array of foreigners and at the shop windows filled with the white man's trinkets, and departed before dusk to rejoin their *manyattas* (villages) and herds on the outskirts. Nairobi was a colourful frontier town, alive with prospects and expectations.

Mario and Giselle spent their first weeks in Kenya at a small boarding-house in Nairobi kept by John Hunter and his wife. John was a big game hunter who had lived in the country for many years. Through him they became acquainted with their new surroundings and the white community of farmers, hunters and tradesmen, many of whom had come to Kenya as civil servants, adventurers or black sheep of aristocratic families. The land was still uncultivated and sparsely populated by nomadic tribes. With its grassy savannahs and heavily wooded mountain slopes, the British colony was waiting to be developed. Blessed with a good climate, friendly natives and rich fertile earth, it was fit to be a white man's country.

A letter from Naples, bringing with it the news of the death of Mario's mother at the age of fifty-three, finally caught up with Mario and Giselle shortly after they arrived in Kenya.

"What do you want me to say to you?" Mario wrote bitterly to his father. "To thank you for holding back the news from me for seven months? That I am grateful you did not cable me to give me the possibility to receive one last kiss from her? Your letter did not provoke any tears. Weeping relieves pain, but I do not want to alleviate the pain that will accompany me all my life – it is the last thing she has left for me.

Your heartbroken son, Mario.

P.S. The hunting trophies intended for my mother must not be sold. They should remain in the family to avoid being turned into billiard balls for a stranger. Have them mounted at my expense and place them on either side of her coffin in the family chapel."

The death of his mother severed Mario's last links with Naples, and when, on 19th January, 1930, Dorian was born at the Maia Carberry Hospital, Mario's life took a final turn away from Europe. While Giselle was recuperating in the nursing home, he hired a single-engined Tiger Moth, and set his course for Lake Naivasha and the home of Ivy and Stephen Carnelly, whom they had met on the train journey from Kisumu.

Within minutes of take-off, the arid brown and golden African landscape lay like a great carpet beneath him, spreading to the five Ngong Hills on his left and the Aberdare range to his right. He floated over the steep edge of the escarpment, and dropped to the bed of the

When Dorian was born in 1930, Mario's life took a definite turn away from Europe . . .

Great Rift Valley. The Longonot volcano rose straight ahead of him and beyond it Lake Naivasha shone like a piece of discarded glass. As he approached Longonot, rising with elegant lines from its flattened surroundings, the plane bucked nervously; he peered down into the tree-covered crater, its flanks scarred with deep ravines cut by the lava flow many centuries before and suddenly the lake was in front of him. Pale grey shadows from the clouds moved across it. The Eburu Hills rose ahead, green and brown, and on either side the grey misty Mau and Aberdare ranges cut a great semi-circle around its northern end.

A dense band of papyrus, like yellow and green stitches in a giant tapestry, floated along the lake edge, and as he dropped the plane the ribbon came alive with feathery papyrus heads waving delicately in the breeze. On the other side of the lake, beneath the Eburu range, the land was flat and dotted with small huts and flocks of sheep and goats tended by chocolate-coloured children.

As he searched for the Carnelly's black and white Tudor-style house, the engine of his plane missed a stroke; the oil pressure had suddenly dropped. He scanned the terrain beneath him in search of a suitable place to land, turned and glided downwards. The flocks and their shepherds beneath him dispersed. As he touched down to a bumpy landing the native children raced towards the huge red and white bird. Scanty clothes knotted on one shoulder flapped like tiny wings behind their naked bodies. They swarmed around the plane and as Mario jumped out of the cockpit moved shyly backwards. He smiled and waved at them.

"It's all right, I'm not going to bite you," he told them in Swahili. An old man with long pierced ear-lobes and a toothless, friendly grin, wearing a brown and white cowskin around his shoulder, pushed forward and shook him by the hand. Pointing with his lips to a little house beneath some tall fever trees, he explained to Mario that he was on the farm of Bwana Harvey. They secured the plane to some rocks and walked together towards the house followed by the whispering, giggling children.

Harvey was standing waiting for him at the front door of his African abode; a series of rondavels with mud walls and thatched roof joined together by a portico erected on poles. He made Mario warmly welcome, and over lunch and iced beers, told him that his father, a South African, had come to Naivasha in 1905. He had died not long ago and left the five-thousand-acre farm to his seven sons. It was up for sale, he informed him offhand.

"I'll buy it," Mario told him. "How much do you want?"

"Ten thousand pounds." Harvey answered him in the same tone.

"I'll give you five but in cash."

"It's yours," Harvey answered, laughing and raising his glass. A little taken aback by Harvey's instant reply, Mario lifted his glass. "It's a deal; let's drink to it." Together they walked back to the plane to investigate the problem. Tiny particles of dust had clogged the fuel pipe. It was swiftly mended and Mario headed back across the lake, leaving behind him a map of upturned faces and waving arms.

Mario never found the Carnelly's house; he flew straight back to Nairobi and Giselle's bedside. "I've bought you a piece of Africa," he announced triumphantly as he burst into her room. They named it Dominio di Doriano after their newborn son. Thus the seed of our family tree fell on a piece of Africa filled with untamed people, game and goats.

It took Mario three years to evict the squatters living on the farm. They put up a strong passive resistance, cheerfully agreeing to leave but never doing so. Mario finally enlisted the help of his friend and neighbour, Gilbert Colville. A solitary man, Colville had come to Kenya in 1900 when he was nineteen. He had first worked for Lord Delamere where he learned a lot about the indigenous cattle and later acquired twenty thousand acres of land in Naivasha. He now ranched large herds of native Boran cattle tended by Maasai warriors; he had learned to speak the Maasai's language fluently and became a blood brother to the tribe through the ritual wrist-nicking ceremony. Colville and his naked warriors came to Mario's aid. They descended on the huts one night and seized the sheep and goats, refusing to return them until all the squatters had left the farm. It was clear within a few days.

On July 14th, 1931 "I" was born. On that same day, 142 years before, the Bastille fell and started the French Revolution. For one week I was called Bastiglia, in honour of that famous event. Then my parents changed my name to the less eccentric one of Mirella. When I married, twenty-five years later, my husband told me that the only thing he didn't like about me was my name. In Italy all the maids are called Mirella, he explained grandly.

Naivasha became our home, and for the first years we lived in the mud

OVERLEAF "A vast pink Italian castello rose on the edge of the lake."

thatch house that Harvey had built. My sister Oria was born eighteen months after me. With each new child, a new rondavel was added and the rambling little homestead was modernised with inside plumbing and running water. But the thatched roof always leaked, and in the rainy season basins, buckets and pans were dotted around to catch the water. They gave out different-sounding pings as the raindrops fell.

In 1936 the foundations of a new house were laid. My mother had been attracted by the West African pavilion at the Colonial Exhibition of 1932 in Paris. Inspired by its massive elegance, its long slender lines and sweeping roof, our African home was born against the brown hill that marked the boundary of our domain in Naivasha. The foundations were set on land that had been raised fifteen feet to protect the house from the capricious rise and fall of the lake water. With the help of some fifty African labourers, half a dozen Indian *fundis* (masons) and a Jewish architect called Zucherman, the massive construction was started and a vast pink Italian castle rose on the edge of the lake.

The stone for the high walls came from a red murram quarry at the back of the farm where it was hacked and shaped by African hands. Forty-foot cedar trunks from the Aberdare forests cut into long octagonal pillars supported the sprawling roof, which was thatched with long golden grass from the hills, and a wide, curved stairway led up to the front door. Pale pink chalk from a deposit my father found at the foot of the hills, mixed with the white stucco plaster of the outside walls, gave it a Mediterranean flavour. The English neighbours in their pretty little conventional colonial houses watched the creation grow, wondering perhaps about the sanity of those "foreigners" who had come to live beside them. When the house was completed, my father placed the Star of David, in homage to Zucherman, on the teak-lined tongue and groove ceiling of the overhanging roof. But this was later dismantled by my mother who did not want her home to be mistaken for a Jewish one.

The decoration of the high-ceilinged rooms on the ground floor was an exhilarating challenge to my parents. They pooled their creative talents and together produced an unusual design shaped by their Afro-European fantasies. Large glass-paned rectangular doors and windows let in the strong African light that filled the rooms with a soft, golden glow. The library, lined with Indian teak panels and inlaid book-shelves that held thousands of books in several languages, had a matching herringbone teak floor. The living-rooms, divided by a large, almost

ABOVE Our home was full of contrasts, contradictions and extravagant eccentricities . . .
BELOW The domestic staff. Independence put an end to this style of uniform.

circular arch, were paved with black and white tiles on which nomad desert rugs and carpets from my mother's Tunisian journeys were scattered. Above the fireplace, my mother sculptured a bas-relief of a naked lady sitting on a cloud drawn across the sky by a graceful, long-horned gazelle; she dropped stars through her fingers to the mortals below and had a distant Mona Lisa smile. "How can I go and sit with the lady on the cloud?" Dorian, then six years old, asked her one day. "In an aeroplane, I suppose," she replied, smiling down at him from the scaffold on which she perched, and there and then carved a little aeroplane on the plaster in the right-hand bottom corner, level with his eyes.

The furniture was made to order by Asian craftsmen in Nairobi. Large, heavy and simple, it was built to fit the scale of the vast rooms. An elaborate crystal chandelier from Murano hung above a large round wine-coloured Chinese lacquer dining table. On the walls beside my mother's African drawings, alcoves with hidden lights displayed a variety of *objets d'art*, collected during their travels across the world. On the wall opposite the fireplace they hung a thirty-foot rectangular mirror imported from Belgium, adding a third dimension to the already spacious interior. The house was full of contrasts, contradictions and extravagant eccentricities, but as a whole the effect was harmonious, pleasing and inviting.

Trees of all shapes and sizes were planted round the site and started their upward climb to the sky. Bougainvillaea, poinsettias and a variety of untamed African flowering shrubs and cacti intermingled in splashes of colour, with the acacias and wild olive, jacaranda and pepper trees. Two rows of cypresses imported from Italy marched down either side of the avenue leading to the lake edge.

I remember little of those early days. The faded snapshots in the albums showed me that Dorian, Oria and I were cared for by statuesque African women who resembled the people of my mother's drawings. We dressed in shabby, comfortable clothes, never wore shoes, and were surrounded by animals wild and domestic: there was a large Great Dane called Biribi, a monkey on a chain, a baby zebra, crested cranes on the lawn, pigs and horses and cows, and always smiling Africans. It was a fairy-tale existence; we knew of no other.

When we were old enough we were taught to ride the thorough-breds my father had imported from Ireland. A great lover of horses, he

Merry March, five times winner of the East African Derby: racing days were
exciting and tense, filled with expectations, victories and defeat.

could now at last indulge in his favourite sport. A trainer and jockey arrived from South Africa, and a race track was laid down along a three-mile stretch by the edge of the lake. Young, lightweight African boys were put into the saddle and with them we learned to handle the high-spirited horses before we could read or write.

My father was an exacting tutor. Every morning for an hour he put us through our paces in the ring, teaching us to grip with our knees, sit up straight, keep our heels down, look elegant, move in rhythm with our mounts. He was ruthless and demanding and turned a deaf ear to our tearful complaints of fatigue and aching muscles. "You must teach your horse to read and write before you can leave the ring," he would tell us when we pleaded with him.

As we grew older and stronger we took part in the early morning gallops. At dawn each day the yearlings raced down the track, stretching their fine-bred limbs like "feline" gazelles, and came to a halt at the end of the track, steaming, quivering and snorting. My father drove his horses to their limits as he did their riders, but the strenuous daily exercise paid off and his racing stable grew to be one of the most important in the country. Once we won five races at a single meeting in Nairobi.

Racing days were exciting and tense, filled with expectations, victories and defeats. We would be scrubbed clean of farm dust, our freshly shampooed hair tied up in big taffeta bows on the tops of our heads and our feet crammed into white socks and shoes. We would all dress up in our fine clothes, my father in a white linen suit and a panama hat and my mother in long slinky Gatsby dresses, wide-brimmed floppy hats and high-heeled shoes from Paris. Dorian looked like a little man in his grey flannel longs, his English blazer and his tie, a felt hat set cockily at an angle. Everyone knew everyone on the race track and we quickly became familiar with the horses, trainers and jockeys. We were part of the "smart racing set" and mingled with the elegant, idle and often outrageous members of Kenya's renowned Happy Valley.

We returned each year to Europe by steamer to spend the late spring and summer on the Riviera or visit our relatives in Paris and in Uncle Maurice's château in Orsay. We were known by our cousins as *les petites sauvages*, and in the photographs that survive of these holidays we look discontented and tearful and do not seem to have been enjoying the "civilised life". The elephant stories my parents brought back with them from their Congo safari gave birth to "Babar", the famous children's story-book character created by my mother's cousin Jean de Brunoff and later made internationally known by his son Laurent. *Babar sur l'Isle au Oiseau* was based on Naivasha.

In winter we returned to Naivasha where we shed our clothes and shoes and were let loose to regain our freedom with our African friends and animals. Naivasha was full of wild creatures that roamed fearless across the land. Herds of eland and buffalo and zebra, long-horned impala, tiny dikdik and clipspringers lived on the hills in the backland. At night, they came down to drink from the lake and graze on the lush green grass and young papyrus shoots that grew along its edge. The trees were filled with chattering, chirping birds and monkeys of all sorts; colobus, vervets and baboons swung through the trees and raided our crops at night. Thousands of bats lived beneath the straw roof of the house and poured out in great sheets at exactly 6.45 each evening to spend the night in the open. They would invariably find their way back into the house, where they hung from the ceiling and the curtains, and left bat droppings everywhere they went. I was always terrified of bats, more so than of any other wild animal, because one day, when I was six years old, one got caught in my hair and we had a terrible time getting it out. Finally we had to cut the hair in which it was entangled. I never forgot the experience.

Lake Naivasha was the home of every sort of African water bird. Geese, ducks, pelicans, flamingoes, crested cranes, cormorants, coots and lily trotters weaved their lives alongside one another, sticking to their territory, always in harmony, never interfering. The giant saddle-bill storks and long-necked Goliath herons stood motionless, camouflaged against the wall of papyrus, or strutted through the mud with long, gawky strides, picking at passing fish in the dark, shallow water. Mauve water-lilies sitting on flat dark green leaves opened at dawn and closed at dusk. They spread like a carpet for miles across the water while dragonflies with transparent wings flitted over the fragrant velvet blooms. Beneath them lay the domain of the tilapia and black bass that fed and thrived and multiplied on the mosquitoes and little insects hovering everywhere.

Lake Naivasha was a pulsating miracle of nature, renowned for the largest variety of birds on any lake in the world. The black and white fish eagles dominated the lake. They perched like monarchs on the tops of tall fever trees and gazed arrogantly across the water, calling to each other, their heads thrown back, their shrill, piercing cries echoing through the hills. When the sun rose and when it set the great birds took to the sky. They rode the wind and circled like kites round their feeding grounds. They plunged into the water with swift unbroken swoops and rose back into the sky with fish wriggling in their powerful claws. The pelicans came and went, gliding silently across the sky in perfect triangular formations, to and from their feeding and nesting grounds. Sometimes they flew so low we could hear the air swooshing through their great expanded wings, and sometimes, if they were flying out of the sun, their shadows preceded them on the ground – the only sign of their passage overhead.

We visited friends around the lake in fast speedboats, putting birds to flight like winged runners ahead of us. We weaved among the sleeping hippo until, exasperated, they woke and came for us, plunging through the water at astonishing speed. Tormenting the hippo became one of our favourite games. It was fast and dangerous and we were scared stiff. Hippo, like many wild animals, can become lethal when aroused. The light aluminium boat would have been easy prey for them. I still shiver at the thought of the engine stalling in those moments; but it never did. At night they came out of the lake and grazed on the lucerne fields. In a vain attempt to discourage this habit, our father sat up night after night with his gun on the edge of the mosquito-infested papyrus swamp and waited for them. But it was rare that he ever bagged one. Wary animals, they are highly sensitive to the slightest noise or scent and are well protected by precocious *askikari* birds who warn them of approaching danger. Hippo are among the most difficult beasts to hunt.

Dorian, Oria and I grew up on Lake Naivasha. We were part of it, we shared it with the animals and the birds. We cared nothing for the things that European children did. Our friends were black, our toys were made from bits of stick and string. We played with live animals instead of dolls and toys. We were looked after by a bevy of laughing black servants who were always there to care for us, amuse us, tell us stories, play with us and clean up after us. We grew up naturally like the trees and flowers that surrounded us. There was no discipline, no restriction in our lives. For our first few years we spoke only Swahili, and when later an Austrian nanny called Adelina joined us, we added German and then English to our vocabularies.

My mother needed to detach herself from the domestic demands of her family; she built herself a studio some distance from the house, where she could be alone in her private creative world and sculpt and draw the people who wandered through our lives; the people of Africa. For a few shillings they would sit for hours, sometimes days, on a high stool, patient and immobile, while she silently stole their beauty from them, transposing it onto thick sheets of paper sent from Paris, or clay from the Nairobi hills.

My father moulded the contours of his newly acquired land. He had a passion for trees, and lined the farm roads with long avenues of jacaranda and pepper trees. He bought a herd of native Boran cattle and, guided by his new friend Gilbert Colville, began experimenting in cross-breeding with European bulls.

Then the war came and took our father away from us. I was eight years old. It was almost as if my life started then; I began remembering. My father once told me that the best years of his life were his 1914–18 war years. I could never understand how he could say such a thing. I knew nothing about the war, but the little I had seen on the movie screens, read about in books and been told in stories conjured up visions of hell in my young mind. As I grew up I tried to put some meaning into his words, and realised that it was perhaps the daredevil excitement of war which had appealed so much to him. Time must have obliterated the horror and terror from his memory.

Anticipating the outbreak of war, he left for Italy in August 1938 with a friend in a two-seater Puss Moth. They followed the Nile from Juba to Khartoum and on to Cairo, Tripoli and Tunisia, and landed in Cannes at the beginning of September, covering the six-thousand-mile journey in just over one week. His return to Italy marked the end of a long exile. In Rome he presented himself to the Commander of the Third Dragoons, the regiment to which he had been attached in his youth, but was informed that it was unlikely that Italy would enter the war before 1942. He came back to Kenya to take stock of the situation. Shortly afterwards, a telegram arrived to tell my mother that her father was dying of cancer. She caught a train to Kisumu where she boarded the Imperial Airways hydroplane on Lake Victoria and left for Paris. Many years had gone by since she first looked upon the now familiar landscape. She had become a part of this Africa, here she had lived the best years of her life, and here her new roots had grown into the soil.

My mother sculpted and drew the people
who wandered through our lives,
the people of Africa . . .

RIGHT   One of my own photographs
30 years later.

They followed the Nile, which wound north like an abandoned ribbon across the vast gold expanse of the Sahara, to Cairo; flew over the Mediterranean to the island of Corfu, carpeted with spring blossoms, and so on to Naples and Lake Bracciano outside Rome. Hit by the *mistral* over Corsica, they bumped uncomfortably across Port Cros in the mist. All the landmarks of her youth welcomed her back. She disembarked in Marseilles and caught the train for Paris where, like apparitions from another world, her mother, her brother and his young wife Nicole awaited her on the platform of the cold, grey Gare de Lyon.

The next year turned into a nightmare. Philippe Bunau-Varilla's death was protracted and painful and the strain of watching him die brought back the migraines that had plagued my mother's adolescence. In an effort to find a cure she had her gall bladder removed and followed stringent diets, but to no avail. The pages of her diary were filled with distress:

"Still no relief from migraine. '*Il ne faut pas avoir peur*,' Father said to me as he closed his eyes and went into the last coma, his face grey and shrunken. The war is upon us, I must return to Kenya. What will happen to Mario and the children?

"Paris is full of departures. War is on everyone's lips," she wrote. She did not stay for her father's funeral. She could not risk being caught in Europe. She said goodbye to France and to her family, and was never again to see her mother, who died before the war ended.

The day after her return, my father tried to leave for Italy but was stopped at the airport at Nairobi without explanation or justification. Abyssinia to the north seemed to offer a way of escape, and with Michele Colonna, a friend who had settled there and come to Kenya, to buy cattle, he studied every possible route. But the roads had been tightly sealed. There was nothing they could do but await events.

They were not long in coming. "*Attenzione, attenzione, la dichiarazione di guerra e già partita!*" Mussolini bellowed three weeks later from the balcony of the Palazzo Venezia in Rome to the thousands of upturned faces below. The grim message came over loud and clear on the radio set between the two arched windows in the library in Naivasha. It was nine o'clock on the evening of 10th June, 1940.

Oria and I had been sent to bed early that night. We did not really understand what was going on; I can remember only the gestures of impatience with which we were dismissed. Never before had the nine

Mario in 1938. He tried to return to Italy before war was declared but was stopped at the airport in Nairobi.

o'clock news seemed so important, so fraught with nervous tension. We crept down the stairs in our pyjamas and peeped through the crack in the open door and saw my mother and father sitting tense and crumpled in the deep armchairs on either side of the wireless. My mother's hands were clasped tight in front of her; I could see her knuckles white in the light from the lamp beside her. My father's head was cupped in his hands, his elbows bore down on his knees. They both stared at the floor. An unfamiliar stillness hung around them, broken only by the clear, Italian voice that sprang from the simple brown box between them.

"I'm caught," I heard my father mutter in a broken voice as he lifted his head and looked at my mother. Tears streaked his face. I had never seen him cry before. She put out her hand to grab his clenched fist, and said nothing. A loud knock on the front door brought them back to their senses and sent us scuttling up the stairs. They switched off the wireless. A man in a policeman's uniform, accompanied by two African askaris, stood in the dark outside the glass-paned door.

"Hello, Mario," we heard him say, as my father opened the door and asked them in. "I'm sorry, old boy, I'm really sorry, I've come to collect you." The voice was embarrassed and hesitant. "Come in," we heard our father say. The welcome was strained. The man at the door was Pat Davies, Inspector of Police for the Naivasha district; the two uniformed Africans accompanying him remained outside. My father poured Davies a drink and then excused himself to collect his belongings. That night he was taken away.

CHAPTER 6

Then the War Came

The telephone rang in the American Embassy in Nairobi and awakened Mabs and Smithy Talbot Smith. It was still early. The sun had not yet risen.

Surprised and angered by his curt conversation with the headmaster of Kenton College, Smithy drove to the school and found Dorian, still only nine years old, sitting on the stone wall of the entrance. By the imposing wrought-iron gate, with its smart English public school insignia, lay a white bundle neatly tied at the four corners. It contained his belongings. There had been no time for packing. He had to be out of the dormitory before the other boys awoke. Though he himself was a British citizen, Britain and his father's country were at war. The bedsheets in which he had slept seemed the most appropriate suitcase with which to make his hasty exit.

That same night, we discovered later, the farm in Naivasha had been surrounded by troops and police, for fear that our father would escape. Ridiculous rumours of a planned airlift had spread around my father's daredevil personality, my father who was now considered "a dangerous Fascist".

Mother left the next day at dawn for Nairobi and when Oria and I awoke we found both our parents gone and only a tearful Adelina, our governess, still there to explain to us what had happened during the night.

When my mother arrived at the American Embassy she was surprised to find Dorian sitting at the breakfast table. Mabs Talbot Smith had prepared an American breakfast for him – waffles and maple syrup, toast and jam and peanut butter. A fire crackled cheerfully in the living-room, and the conversation at the breakfast table was full of war and British incivility.

Dorian remained with Mabs at the Embassy while my mother drove to the P.O.W. camp that had been hastily erected in Kabete a few miles outside Nairobi. The eight-foot-high barbed wire enclosure with sentry boxes at its four corners rose up through the leafy blue gum trees, and the long line of corrugated-iron-roofed barracks told their silent tale of men deprived of freedom. Behind this enclosure our father was held captive. Men known and unknown to us wandered about the compound.

Our father had been appointed captain of the internees and given private living quarters. His room was bare except for a wooden chair, a camp bed, and his still unopened suitcase. Bent forward, his head cupped in his hands, in his familiar stress position, he sat like a broken tree.

He rose to greet my mother. Together they tried to make coherent plans for the future but my father could talk of little but escape. He could not and would not face the prospect of internment.

All enemy alien property in Kenya was confiscated, but Naivasha was in my mother's name and she had kept her French nationality. The farm at least was safe.

My mother visited the internment camp in Kabete each week and for many of the prisoners she was their only link with the outside world. They crowded round her, listening to the news she brought; news of the Italian advance towards Moyale in the Northern Frontier District of Kenya, the British bombing of Assab and Diredawa in Abyssinia and of the Libyan ports. Each Italian victory carried fresh hopes of a speedy end to their captivity. She always left them momentarily elated and hopeful that the Italian army would soon invade Kenya and set them free. "I'll become governor of Kenya," my father said jokingly each time she kissed him goodbye, but two months after he was taken from us, a telegram arrived: "MARIO REMOVED FROM KABETE CAMP TO UNKNOWN DESTINATION." It was signed, "SMITHY".

My mother burst into tears. She covered the clay head she had been working on in her studio with a moist cloth and walked home in a daze. We trotted beside her, holding her hands, our feeble, anxious questions only half answered.

When we got back to the house we found one of the Maasai herders lying beneath the pepper tree covered with a blanket. Standing beside him on one leg, his companion told us without emotion that he had been gored in the groin by an angry bull. A large smear of blood had seeped through the grey blanket, and a green bottlefly buzzed over it. Fighting back her distress, my mother swabbed the deep ugly wound with cotton wool soaked in Dettol, dressed it with gauze, and had the man lifted onto the back seat of the station-wagon. We drove him to the hospital in Naivasha, twenty miles away, and from the post office my mother telephoned Talbot Smith in Nairobi.

He was not able to give her much information other than that our father had been taken that morning by boat to a still unknown destination. Three weeks went by before news of his whereabouts reached us. He had been shipped to Durban in South Africa, and from there to Koffifontein, an abandoned diamond mine on the edge of the Karoo desert. The Italian advance from Ethiopia and Somalia had made the British nervous, and there were too many Italians in Kenya, even behind barbed wire. So my father joined the ten thousand prisoners of war and two thousand Catholic priests in the Koffifontein camp. We heard of him only sporadically. We knew he was alive and in good health, but no more. News came now and then through the families of his fellow internees and the Red Cross, but when his letters arrived they were savagely defaced by the censors. There would be just the date and "Dear G"; the middle of the page would be cut out and on the bottom border of the hollow frame only "Love, Mario". We all wrote to him each week, but never knew if our letters ever reached him.

Because we were still so young, Dorian, Oria and I soon adapted to life without him. My mother kept his memory alive. To alleviate her distress and anxiety, she talked about him constantly, and as the months and years went by he became a sort of legendary figure. My mother's staunch Bunau-Varilla character forbade any outward manifestation of her turmoil. "*Il ne faut pas avoir peur*," her father's last words, helped her to face her loneliness. She made a point of never accepting any invitations or being seen alone in the company of men, in case rumours reached my father and added to his torture.

My parents' marriage seemed outwardly happy, even from time to time idyllic. But in reality it was a difficult partnership. My father had remained an essentially Latin male, torn between his necessity to dominate and his respect for my mother's independent character. Her self-assurance and determination had awed and attracted him, but being married to and living with her was quite a different matter. The strong, domineering characteristics she had inherited from her father were far removed from those of the docile, self-effacing females in my father's household in Naples. She remained deeply in love, and completely loyal and devoted to him all her life, and he let himself be loved. But the dilemma they faced as the war–clouds gathered had crucial repercussions for both of them.

They shared a fierce sense of family responsibility. Threatened with arrest and incarceration though he was, it was out of the question that my father, while our mother was still away, would abandon us children, even to the care of friends. She, on her side, felt allegiance to her dying father. Should she stay with him, as her instincts urged, or return to Naivasha, as her husband was pleading with her to do, so that he could leave Kenya for Italy while there was still time?

"What if I have really failed in the terrible ordeal?" my mother wrote despairingly in her diary. "There was in that one week enough to fill my entire life with remorse for I alone was responsible, if even then only a tool in the hands of fate."

My mother had become well acquainted with the anguish of captivity. This was the second time she had lost a husband to the enemy. The Germans had taken one in 1915 and now the British had taken another.

One day it was announced on the radio that four prisoners from the Koffifontein camp had escaped. One had been shot, one recaptured, and two had got away. No names had been given. Our father had talked so much of escape in the Kabete camp. That week my mother was particularly nervous. Snatches of her conversations with our neighbour betrayed her distress, but when we asked her she dismissed the subject with a smile and a hug. Two months later a heavily censored letter finally arrived and told us that our father was still behind the wire.

It was only when he came back that we learned of his part in the escape. They had taken five months to dig the tunnel which started beneath the floorboards of his own room and passed beneath the vegetable garden to a point a hundred yards beyond the barbed wire. They worked at night, digging like moles, depositing the earth on the vegetable beds that grew higher and longer and wider each day. But as the final preparations were being made, my father went down with a violent attack of malaria that had excluded him from the escape he had masterminded.

CHAPTER 7

Running Wild

With the outbreak of war all funds were frozen in the European banks and for the first time in her life my mother had to earn money to keep us alive, so she exchanged her artist's smock for the khaki drill trousers and shirt of the farmer. She bought some pigs. The Africans sold her the potatoes and cabbages, maize and beans grown in their meagre plots; the lucerne my father had planted for the racehorses was mown and chopped. Everything went to feed and fatten the pigs that were sold to the Uplands Bacon Factory thirty miles north of Naivasha.

Jack Hopcraft, her dearest friend and neighbour, paid her daily visits, advising and guiding her, and from him she learned the rudiments of farming. The racehorses were put out to grass and the jockey and trainer paid off. The race track soon disappeared beneath the fast-growing Kikuyu grass, and the cattle grazed where the horses had raced. What had once been a playground now became a farm.

We outgrew Adelina, and Miss Erica, a German–Swiss lady, joined our family as governess. Something had to be done about our education. Because our father was an enemy alien, the English schools would not accept us, so we had lessons at home. From eight to twelve and from two to four each day we sat on stools around a table and learned to read and write and spell. Miss Erica was a stern, competent teacher. She was kind, loving, short-sighted and ugly. There had been unhappiness in her life, but we never found out what it really was. We had vaguely heard that she had been abandoned by a man who had taken her to Venezuela and then run away with another woman. The British tried to put her behind barbed wire on the grounds that she was an alien, but with the help again of Talbot Smith, my mother was able to prove that she was Swiss and not German. They also tried to intern my mother, but she reminded them that despite her marriage she had kept her French nationality, and they left her alone.

We hated the discipline of our daily lessons, but Miss Erica was a clever teacher who quickly understood that her greatest rival was outside the classroom. We learned arithmetic with the carrots, potatoes and maize cobs we gathered each morning before class. We caught flies and bees and insects, and dissected rabbits and stillborn calves and lambs for our biology lessons; we picked flowers and leaves in the garden for our botany classes and Miss Erica illustrated our geography and history lessons with postcards and anecdotes from her own travels. We knew the capitals of every country in the world, the names of all the rivers, and the highest mountains. We learned about the Scriptures, the great works of art, the artists and musicians.

In the evenings my mother would take over. Her stories were vivid and she awoke, in me especially, a deep interest in the desert. Seating us round the fireplace, she would read to us from books carefully chosen to fit Miss Erica's lessons. Our home was full of books, in Italian, French and English; they were our only form of entertainment. We spoke French, English and German, Swahili, Kikuyu and Maasai. Our conversations flitted from one to another and were often incomprehensible to strangers. A lot of importance was given to correct articulation and pronunciation and in order to achieve this we were made to stand on the hillside opposite the classroom window and recite poetry to my mother sitting inside about fifty yards away. She had to understand every word we said before we were dismissed.

Our unorthodox education was extended to the farm. We learned to drive the cars, lorries, tractors and ox-wagons and to supervise the Africans at work. Despite our age, they obeyed us as though we were adults, and together we carried out the daily chores of the farm.

For a long time the pigs were our only source of income, and we brought their number almost to one thousand. Then, suddenly, disaster struck. One day a young Ndorobo warrior brought us a week-old baby warthog he had found in the bush. Delighted by the new arrival, we gave it to one of the sows to suckle. Three days later one of the piglets died and was followed in quick succession by the whole litter. Then the sow became ill. We took one of the dead piglets to the vet in Naivasha for a post mortem.

"It's swine fever," he told us sternly, peering over his horn-rimmed glasses. "The disease is lethal and spreads like wildfire." He asked us if we had any warthogs on the farm, and the horrible truth struck home.

Miss Erica, Oria, my mother, Dorian and I in 1939.
". . . Sometimes a marauding hippo fell to my father's gun . . ."

Each morning we inspected the stys and my mother would shoot the sick ones with her revolver. Within two months all our pigs had died.

To console us, she set up a little private farmyard for us beneath the pepper trees near the house. A signboard painted in black letters read *Oria and Mirella Farmland*. Each time my mother returned from one of her visits to Nairobi she brought us back a new pet. We had geese and chickens, rabbits, guinea-pigs and white mice, turkeys and diminutive multi-coloured bantam cocks with long, graceful, curving tails and pretty trousers. One day she returned with a pair of white turkeys that looked like snow peacocks on the emerald lawn. Maina, a young Kikuyu lad, was our friend and devoted "slave". He was always laughing, and did everything we did not like doing. One night a rat gnawed away the side of his foot. He had felt nothing until he woke the next morning, and he could not walk for a week.

Dorian was not interested in our playground. He was involved in more manly activities. He spent most of his time in the workshop fiddling around with the machinery and fixing the tractors with Kimani, the mechanic. At a very young age he had learned to handle a gun, and when he was fourteen my mother gave him one of my father's rifles.

Dorian's constant companion was Reson, a magnificent slim Ndorobo warrior with plaited hair that fell to the middle of his back. He was a wild and gentle youth who had wandered into our lives from nowhere in search of work. But there was no work for him, so we created it. He was assigned to my brother and became his tutor in the mysteries of Africa's wilderness.

Reson taught us the secrets of the bush. Together we learned how to move fast and silently with rhythmic steps to avoid fatigue, to watch the ground we trod, to keep on the right side of the wind and to walk bent in half when approaching wild creatures. Reson was an instinctive hunter. His tribe hunted for survival. He took Dorian into the hills to the salt licks behind the farm where the buffaloes, the eland and zebra gathered. In Kenya, where hunting was for men, a boy who could handle a gun and bag a good trophy acquired immediate status. Dorian's trophies were carefully salted and mounted on carved shields, and proudly hung on the walls in the house.

His hunting prowess kept Oria and me in awe of him. We longed to be part of his bush adventures, and spent hours on target practice to prove we were his equals. On rare occasions he would condescend to take us with him, but only as a special favour.

My mother was not happy about our dawn wanderings in the hills, and our forays had to be planned in secret. We would sleep with a long piece of sisal string tied to our wrists and dangling out of the window to the ground below. Reson would come before sunrise and pull on the string. Silently, we slipped out of our beds, into our clothes and out of the house and headed in single file towards the hills, shivering in the cold pre-dawn. Dorian and Reson were ruthless; they did not wait for us, we had to keep up with them, and if we broke the rules we were glared at fiercely and called *mwanamuke* (females).

Reson was soon joined by two of his brothers, Oriunga and Kwanini, and a cousin called Longonot. There was no work for them either, but we allowed them to hang around and share Reson's hut. They posed for my mother in her studio, and giggled shyly, covering their mouths with long slender hands when they saw the results on paper. They recognised one another by the beads and ornaments in the drawings, not from the facial traits, and were completely baffled by the clay sculptures. Posing for my mother was a much sought-after occupation, one which suited their indolent natures. It was an easy way to earn money without exerting themselves. Wives, daughters, children and relatives were brought shyly to her studio door in the hope that she could use them. These wild, beautiful people were our childhood friends.

With them we devised our favourite sport, "piggering", the Naivasha version of pig-sticking. Voss, our pure-bred Alsatian, and Flossey, our Rhodesian Ridgeback, produced several litters and over the years we bred a pack of thirteen hunting dogs. Led by Dorian and Reson, we would set off in single file across the flat open plains, the dogs firmly leashed with thongs. Oria and I, as *wanawake*, were invariably pushed to the back. Reson's hawk eyes scanned the land around us for the almost indiscernible animals hidden deep in the long grass. We watched him, waiting for his signal. He would stop in his tracks, his hand outstretched in front of him. He seemed to grow several inches as he arched his neck and back, peering like an eagle in the direction of his outstretched arm and middle finger. The grass had moved, a wiry up-turned tail protruded like an antenna from a dusty grey back. For a split second, animal and man stood motionless watching each other, sniffing the air. Suddenly the pig was off, sometimes with a string of little ones in its wake. They darted through the grass, heads held high, tails thrust upward. The dogs went wild, pulling frantically at their leashes, the muscles of their legs taut and quivering, their nostrils extended to catch the scent.

The instant they were unleashed they pelted, long and sinewy, after the terrified animals, yapping excitedly as they ran. Reson and his men followed in a red line, their ochre *shukas* wrapped tight and short around their loins, a *rungu* (knob kerrie) in one hand, a sharp slim spear in the other. The hunt was on. Dorian, Oria and I, breathless and barefoot, brought up the rear. As the distance between hunters and quarry lessened the pigs scattered in all directions searching for a burrow in which to hide.

The heated chase came to a halt at the mouth of the shelter. Panting, sweating and excited, the dogs pawed ferociously at the soft, powdery earth and crawled one at a time deep into the tunnel. When they backed out for air the pig would shoot out into the open in a last desperate attempt to get away. As he burst into the daylight the fangs and spearheads sank into his little grey body. He crashed to the ground, bleeding and covered in white dust.

A merciless outburst of triumphant laughter exploded over the shuddering, dying animal. Finally, his feet lashed together, he was carried home hanging upside down from a sturdy *leleshwa* pole, accompanied by a chorus of excited chatter.

My mother disapproved of piggering. Like Miss Erica she considered this kind of sport gruesome and unladylike. Yet I think she secretly relished the way her children were growing up in such contrast to her own painfully constricted upbringing.

With our simple, untamed lives, we knew nothing of the taboos of sophisticated societies. At a young age we learned from the people and animals on the farm about life and death, sex and reproduction. Living things were born, grew old and died. Flowers bloomed and fell. Old animals, people and machinery deteriorated and stopped. The people on the farm came to us for help when they were sick or wounded; blood was part of life, whether it came from a man or an animal. It did not make us cringe and nature herself was our teacher.

Twice we were plagued by locusts. They descended on us un-announced and unexpected. There had been rumours of swarms in the country but no one ever seemed to know where or when they would strike. Communications were bad, there were no telephone wires in the

Naivasha or other outlying districts, and news travelled by word of mouth, often slower than the advancing swarms.

A bright, sunny day would suddenly become dark. All heads would instinctively tilt skywards and eyes would momentarily freeze as the winged land-devastators, moving towards us with fierce determination in a cloud one mile square, made for any sign of green. Within minutes they would drop to the ground and the sun would re-appear. The trees dripped, the ground crawled, the leaves and blades of grass bent and rapidly changed shape in front of us as the voracious mandibles went to work, cutting, sawing and gnawing everything that grew. Like a victorious advancing army the locusts moved forward, leaving ruin in their wake, the land behind them totally denuded. Branches and stems of plants stuck out forlorn and hopelessly lacerated.

Every available pair of hands grabbed hold of something and charged at the invaders, banging on empty tins, beating the ground with branches, lighting smoke stacks. Any available vehicles – cars, tractors and ox-carts – were driven around as if in a drunken frenzy, squashing as many of the invaders as they could. We could hear the bodies crunch and squash beneath us and turn into a slippery jamlike paste, but somehow the more we squashed, the more locusts there seemed to be. To our disgust some of the African children and Jaluo men from the Lake Victoria region would thread them on twigs and roast them over the fire. Dorian tried them and said they tasted like roasted chestnuts. When there was nothing left to devour, the cloud rose from the ground, left the branches of the trees and took off into the sky in search of fresh pastures, leaving us cursing "bloody locusts" until they returned the following year.

The early formative years spent in Naivasha moulded our minds and bodies. On the one hand we became vigorously independent and self-assured, but on the other we were shy and undisciplined, and our knowledge and experience were limited to the confines of our little African kingdom. This was, however, to have a serious effect on us when we left. Our close, happy, daily contact with the Africans taught us the simple rudiments of survival, uncontaminated by the multitude of complications and necessities with which the white man is faced in the daily struggle for his livelihood. We were children of both worlds.

Mungu (God) reigned over our lives. The unquestioned spirit of fatalistic resignation was never questioned by the Africans, and gave them that inner serenity which helped them to cope with illness, pain, hunger, discomfort and sorrow. Everything was *shauri ya mungu* (God's affair). Calm, unruffled and always ready to laugh, but also proud and dignified, they had a wonderful, childlike simplicity. My mother captured this aspect of them vividly in her drawings. Although they were not easily upset, they were capable of extreme violence when angered and would stop at nothing. Then suddenly they would forgive and forget as if nothing had happened.

The Africans' diet of maize meal cooked in water, beans, potatoes, and wild green leaves was deadly monotonous and could have been the reason for their apparent apathy. The Maasai who drank milk and ate meat, roasted or cooked on an open fire, were more alive and spirited. Huts were perennially choked with smoke that lined the interiors with a fine sticky black soot and seeped through the thatched roofs, hovering in a wispy blue-grey opaque mist above them.

Their spartan way of life made them tough and taught them to be cunning, to lie and steal with outrageous dexterity. They learned to handle hunger, thirst and pain very young. Mothers gave birth to children on bare floors in smoky huts, or wherever they were when their time came. The children either survived or died. If they died, they died. It was *shauri ya mungu*. God decided their fate.

The arrival of the white man upset this way of life. To the white man, the people of Africa were like the country's flora and fauna – there to be admired and used or abused at discretion. Our white skins and our shillings put us, whether we liked it or not, in a position of superiority. The Africans observed us with wonder and respect, well aware that we represented a substantial source of material gain. Cecil Rhodes had once said, "Teach the African to want." And so they took what they could by whatever means whenever possible and in exchange, respectfully and obediently, carried out the chores we left for them; it was a deal which more or less satisfied both sides.

Where we went wrong was when we tried to help by persuading them to use amenities essential by our standards, for in so doing we humiliated them. We urged them to adopt soap, clothes, hospitals, transport and the multitude of unnecessary objects that clutter our lives, and when they did not live up to the white man's standard we conveniently dismissed them as inferiors. "What can you expect from a black man?" was a question I grew up with. Then one day I read a remark by the French writer André Gide: "*Plus le noir lui semble bête, moins le blanc est intelligent* (The more the white man looks on the black as stupid, the stupider he is himself)" and began to question my own outlook. But from a very early age Dorian, Oria and I had accepted an attitude based on friendly contempt: we knew no other and it seemed to work. Our view was confirmed by our mother, for whom the human race was sharply divided between whites and blacks (or yellows), Jews and non-Jews, upper classes and lower classes. We were white non-Jews and were thus cut off from the rest by an invisible barrier which we never questioned.

Even as children, our friendship with Africans went so far but no further. Africans, other than servants, were not permitted in our home, and those who did enter had to take their shoes off before crossing the threshold. They stood to attention when spoken to and addressed us as *memsahib* and *bwana kidogo* (little master). Our names were always prefixed by these titles. We were born in the colonial era, we grew up in it, we were part of it, and the resulting intonations of command never wore off.

*

In the summer of 1944 our mother heard of an American mission school in Kijabe about forty-five miles away, set high on the Eastern Rift Valley escarpment and appropriately called the Rift Valley Academy. It catered for the children of the American missionaries in Kenya and we were gladly accepted among them. So in July 1944 we finally went to school. I was thirteen years old.

We arrived in the pouring rain after an exciting and rather scary trip through the massive bamboo forest, where we skidded along the wet and slippery dirt-track road. My mother several times lost control of the car and we finally skidded into a deep ditch full of water. We slushed barefoot and ankle deep in the soft, gluey, red mud that squished like putty through our toes. After a lot of pushing and pulling and digging the car was hauled out an hour later by a large truck that suddenly appeared like an eerie monster through the mist. The sodden forest, shrouded in rain vapour, rose around us. Diffused rays of light played on the tall, green and yellow striped bamboo, igniting the curtain of rain drops hanging from the ends of long slim leaves; the giant cedar and pine trees stood out massive and dark among them. Back safely on the road we followed the lorry to the turn-off leading to the school. The wide mud tyres with their heavy chains cut a trail for us which helped keep the wheels of our rickety old car on a steady course. We climbed out of the car bedraggled, wet and caked in mud, slightly apprehensive of what lay ahead.

Ken and Dorothy Downing, the headmaster and his wife, appeared almost immediately on the front wooden porch that ran the whole length of the quaint rectangular school building, welcoming us with cheery round faces lit by their American smile. We looked at them darkly, not quite understanding what lay behind this jovial couple, who were so unlike anything we had imagined would be connected with school.

We spent two happy years at the Rift Valley Academy. The easy-going American way of life coupled with our African environment made the transition painless. There were only thirty-six children in the school, mostly Americans and a few Greeks. Our "foster parents" were young and loving, straightforward missionaries united by their faith in Jesus Christ, their Lord and Master.

On arrival we were presented with a black-bound Holy Bible which we opened and shut several times a day. The verses within were drummed into our heads many times throughout the day. We crossed the threshold as sinners or lost souls and left "saved" from the waywardness of the world outside. Alcohol, cigarettes, movies, jazz music, dancing, make-up, provocative clothes, and swearing were, of course, prohibited and regarded as tools of the devil. We soon found out, to our dismay, that our mother was a sinner. On her weekly visits, which caused us great embarrassment, she appeared wearing slacks, lipstick and eyebrow pencil, and smoked cigarettes openly. We tried to ignore the insinuating glances and muffled whispers of disapproval on the part of our friends, but when we knew she was coming, we would run down the road to meet her and make her extinguish her cigarette and wipe the make-up off her face. We begged her not to wear slacks and transparent blouses and she agreed at once.

The Rift Valley Academy was set halfway up on the side of the steep escarpment that rose from the bed of the Rift Valley to the top of the Kinangop plateau. Kijabe, which means "wind" in Maasai, was a small station on the railway running from Nairobi to Kisumu on Lake Victoria. It was very cold at night in Kijabe and we all had the healthy, pink-cheeked look of mountain people. Cedar wood fires were lit in the cold mornings and evenings in the heavy old-fashioned fireplaces and were kept stoked throughout the day. We slept two and three to a room on iron hospital beds with thin mattresses and lots of blankets.

There was no running water in the building. We used enamel basins and jugs for washing and the "long-drop" lavatories were outside. When we visited them at night it was not unusual to be stopped in our tracks as something scuttled away into the trees or surrounding bushes. I once bumped into a skittish elephant who would not give me right of way and had to call some friends to help me shoo him off with sticks and stones.

New arrivals had to go through a period of initiation. Star-gazing was a particularly unpleasant trial. We had to sit on a stool on the darkened verandah and look up at the stars through a large cone-shaped funnel. As we gazed up bewildered into the dark sky a bucket of cold, muddy water was emptied down the funnel and everyone roared with laughter. But we did not think it funny at all.

When we misbehaved, we were beaten on our buttocks on Saturday evenings in front of the whole school. It was a terrifying experience. One night, with tears in my eyes, I watched poor Dorian being caned, but I did not know he had wisely put blotting paper and sheets of thin cardboard inside his pants to soften the sting. Boys and girls were kept apart except for games and classes. We played tennis and baseball, and every Saturday the whole school would go hiking through the forest. We cooked trout caught in the rivers and climbed steep embankments to find breathtaking views stretching to the horizon, or dark forests alive with black and white colobus monkeys, green and orange parrots, butterflies and wild flowers of every colour. We swam in the rivers and dams with our clothes on and slung mud at the boys. The young teachers who accompanied us never tried to stop our exuberance, and sometimes even took part in our crazy games.

One day a lion cub was brought to us by a Maasai and became the school mascot. It lived with us for a long time and became tame and friendly, wandering into the classroom and sprawling under the desk to sleep, making it very difficult for us to concentrate on our lessons.

The older boys would go down each week to the bottom of the Rift Valley and hunt eland and impala for our weekly meat ration. We ate only wild meat. One day a leopard took two of our dogs in one week. We found their remains at the bottom of a ravine where it had its lair. Some of the older boys sat up for several nights with the headmaster. One night it crept across the length of the roof of the main school building and as it crouched to jump down, they fired and dropped it.

My mother would drive over at the end of term to pick us up and we often returned home with a bunch of friends piled in the back of the farm van with us. We always stopped to collect the mail at the Naivasha post office and one evening among the letters was a pink cable from Talbot Smith: "MARIO LANDED IN MOMBASA YESTERDAY STOP WILL KEEP IN TOUCH." My mother's voice quivered as she read it out to us in the light of the car's headlamps. As we all spilled out onto the road, cheering and hugging each other, I noticed my mother's eyes were full of tears.

CHAPTER 8

There He Was . . .

Our "Papi" returned to the camp in Kabete in June 1944. We went to visit him there the day after his arrival and found a broken man. He had no teeth, his hair was white, his face drawn and deeply furrowed. We did not recognise him. Had he changed that much or had we forgotten him? All that remained of the image we had of him was the twinkle in his laughing brown eyes as he gazed and gazed at us, for we too had changed. We sat around his feet and looked at him. But we would never know or understand the ordeal he had been through, or the irreparable damage that had been done to him.

One night, two months later, he arrived back in Naivasha unexpected and unannounced. A knock on the front door and there he was in the dark, holding his suitcase, with the same Pat Davies who had taken him away. My mother screamed when she saw him. They wept in each other's arms. The phantom figure we had learned to live without was suddenly with us again.

He took a little getting used to. Four years are a long time in a child's life, and we were still only on the edge of adolescence. We remembered him vaguely, as tall and dark-haired, bursting with life and energy. Now his gaiety was forced. He was tired and nervous and quick to anger. Small things irritated him, especially noise. He was vulnerable to everything and everyone. When his old friends came to the house to welcome him back he left the room and retired upstairs on the approach of their cars, and for years afterwards refused even to see his faithful neighbours the Hopcrafts and Colvilles. His hatred for the British lasted the rest of his life. He never forgave them, and he had no qualms about letting them know it.

Before the prisoners of war were released, they were each put in the dock of the Nairobi law courts and questioned about their ideas and intentions. When my father's turn came he was icily polite, but he called into question their honour, upbraiding them for having stopped him from leaving the country before Italy's declaration of war. He calmly told the officers of the court that they were savages and that, but for the Romans, the British would still be on the same level as those whose lands they had come to colonise. As a result he was the last man to leave the camp and his attitude in the courtroom led to a further year's internment on the farm. He could not leave its boundaries without special police permission, which he was too proud to request. Sore and angry, he locked himself away from the world and picked up the running of the farm my mother had created.

After the first rush of stories, he rarely talked about himself and did not seem able to share with anyone the inner burden he was now carrying. He knew no one would understand it. We were too young and he was too proud to tell our mother. But by keeping silent he slowly shut himself off from any form of release, and it was not until many years later, when I was with him in Paris and a friend of mine remarked, "Your father is a broken man, what happened to him?" that I realised how unaware and unthinking we had been. As he grew older his silences grew longer and in the last ten years of his life he hardly spoke at all.

My mother told me many years later that she had become pregnant again soon after my father returned, but had lost the child. She was now too old for maternity. Only then did I begin to realise the effect that long separation had on their marriage.

He had never got used to living behind barbed wire and at such close quarters with others. He disliked most of his fellow internees, especially the priests. Unlike him, most of the inmates of the camp were Fascists, and those who were not became so out of boredom or rebelliousness. Even the priests became Fascists, he told us indignantly. He longed for news from home, but the censored letters, when they arrived, heightened his frustration and infuriated him. Radios and newspapers were prohibited. Clandestine wirelesses were manufactured with the help of the bribed wardens, but when the sets were discovered, the owners were put into solitary confinement.

The mental stress of captivity began to affect my father's body. He developed pyorrhoea, a painful condition of the gums, and on Christmas Day, in 1942, had eight teeth extracted without anaesthetic by a priest with a pair of pliers.

During the four years of his confinement, my father learned about horticulture, an activity much encouraged in the camp as it provided excellent and fruitful outdoor physical occupation for the frustrated captive men. He applied his new knowledge to the farm, and set to work with renewed vigour and determination to enlarge and develop it once again. He broke new land and planted new crops and divided the cattle, which had multiplied during his absence, into milk and beef herds, crossing them with imported European bulls to produce hardier, larger, more productive animals. He grafted imported Washington Naval shoots to the indigenous wild lemon trees and laid down the first major citrus plantation in the country. The work provided him, maybe for the first time in his life, with a concrete goal. The Bunau-Varilla fortune had now largely evaporated, and the necessity to provide for his family made his work all the more worth while. He became a farmer.

Between silences, in the first years after his return, he told us many tales about his prison camp days. He described how he had kept his sanity by giving lessons in mathematics and navigation to the less educated men, and set exams which many passed brilliantly. An eighty-piece orchestra was formed in which he was the leading violinist and every Sunday afternoon they gave concerts of classical music for their fellow internees and the warders. Books and sheet music were provided by the Red Cross. The P.O.W.s built swimming pools and tennis courts and held tournaments with silver cup prizes. He spoke lovingly of the flowers and vegetables he grew and of the prizes he won at the horticultural shows in nearby Bloemfontein, but despite the humour and bravado his stories were often tinged with suppressed anger and bitterness.

Ironically enough, while my father was interned in Koffifontein a prison camp was built at Naivasha. It spread for miles across the flat plains just outside the little township, scarring the countryside, and was occupied by Italian soldiers captured in Abyssinia and Somalia. With nothing better to do, the bored Italians volunteered for the strenuous unpaid job of building the main road from Naivasha to Nairobi.

Each week when we went to the little town of Naivasha to deliver our farm produce, we passed the long row of sunbaked, sweaty men in their rough white and navy shorts. We would greet them in Italian from the car shouting, "*Eviva l'Italia.*" They quickly learned to recognise our van and would line up along the road waving their caps to the astonishment of the wide-eyed African askari who remained convinced that we were "Very Important People".

One day soon after my father's return, three of the internees from the Naivasha camp obtained permission to visit us. We were the only Italian family around the lake and thus the only family who had not been permitted to employ prisoners to help on the farm. The three men came on foot for twenty miles along the dusty road. Hot and flushed and sweating, their boots covered in dust, they arrived at our front door. One of them was dressed in the grey-green uniform of a military chaplain.

"*Buon giorno, Rocco,*" he said in his clipped Milanese accent, as my father stepped out to meet them. "Are you the Rocco who served in the 9th Lancers in Milano in the 1914 war?"

"I certainly am," my father answered. The old twinkling smile reappeared in his eyes.

"I'm Monsignor Trossi, do you remember me?"

"*Buon Dio, non è possibile!*" my father cried, throwing his arms round his shoulders. "Of course I remember you. I taught you how to ride!"

Trossi came back alone to visit us again a few days later. He spent many hours with my father, reminiscing, rediscovering, and was well and truly shocked to find that we were still unbaptised and being educated in a Protestant mission school. He convinced my father (I don't know how) that this was unthinkable in a Catholic home. We were not really a Catholic home, we were nothing. Until we went to school, religion had been merely a collection of beautiful fairy stories, told to us by our mother in the evening around the fire.

Thirty musicians arrived one day with their home-made instruments and filled our house with Bach and Beethoven and Mozart. The beautiful grave sounds echoed through the vast house and hung from the trees in the garden. We had never seen a real orchestra before, and we sat in front of the musicians on the floor and listened wide-eyed and entranced. For the first time, serious music came into our lives. We ate pasta and tomato sauce and drank Italian wine beneath the trees in the garden, and on that day my father laughed again, for the second time since he came home.

A few weeks later an enormous box arrived in the back of a truck. Inside was a fountain beautifully carved from the porous grey Naivasha stone in the camp: it represented a bambino holding a dolphin, like the fountains in Italian piazzas. Trossi told us that, ever since they discovered our existence, we had become the object of great curiosity in the camp and the subject of many conversations and dreams. The fountain, which is still at Naivasha today, was the focus of their pent up longings and frustrated creative energies. My father, who recognised all that the gift implied, was profoundly moved. He wept when he saw it standing in his African garden.

Monsignor Trossi finally persuaded my father to have us baptised. Dorian had already been baptised in the Protestant faith, so Oria and I were subsequently put through an intensive course on Roman Catholicism by the *monsignor*. We complied with our parents' wishes, without ever understanding why it was suddenly so important. We had never talked about it before, and were rather confused at what this soft-spoken man was saying to us. His teaching was so different from all that we had been taught at the Protestant Rift Valley Academy.

The date for our baptism was set. My mother had long white dresses and mosquito net veils made for us by the Indian tailor in Naivasha. They were our first long dresses. We were subsequently baptised and received our first Holy Communion on the same day, in front of a simple altar made from a wooden table covered with an antique Florentine embroidered tablecloth. We tried to remember the *Ave Maria* and *Pater Noster*, so hard to memorise in Latin, as we listened anxiously to the chickens and ducks and dogs from our little farmland calling to us from outside. We drank the wine and swallowed the Host while my mother and father and Dorian sat behind us, mumbling their responses. It was a very solemn occasion, but Oria and I were bored to tears and couldn't wait to return to our animals.

A year later, on our annual visit to Europe, we were confirmed in Rome. We only had one real lace veil for the ceremony, so one of us had to be content with a mosquito net one. This led to a wild free-for-all in the *pensione* bedroom, witnessed by a horrified Aunt Lisa and a furious mother who tried to separate us. Oria and I fought like wild cats; neither of us would let go of the veil until it was torn to shreds. In the end, we both had to wear mosquito net veils.

PART III

Winds of Change

CHAPTER 9

Outside Africa

I was now fifteen, and this Roman holiday made a real impression on me. Our mother and Aunt Lisa traipsed us through the Vatican and showed us the Sistine Chapel and the beautiful Michelangelo sculptures, and we visited all the famous historic sites. We were constantly followed by sassy young Italian males who tried to pick us up and sometimes even pinched our bottoms. When they became too persistent, my mother chased them off with her umbrella.

Oria and I were more interested in this aspect of our visit than in what our mother was showing us. We consumed huge plates of pasta, risotto and ravioli and drank fizzy Frascati wine. We had never seen fruit like Italian fruit and sank our teeth into fat peaches and juicy grapes and dark-red blood oranges – Kenya had many things but nothing like this European fruit. We were always surrounded by lascivious men who made preposterous propositions, which displeased my mother but amused Oria and me.

One day when we were on a train travelling to Naples, one of these young men was sitting opposite us in the compartment. Oria and I hid behind the newspaper we were reading, and tried to ignore him until he set our newspaper alight with his cigarette lighter and caused a great commotion in the compartment. The trick paid off. When we arrived at the station he was so apologetic to my mother that our hearts melted. He carried our bags to the taxi and next day sent us a bunch of carnations. When we met him in the street a few days later we invited him to tea and before long we had our first boyfriend and the two families became closely acquainted.

Oria and I fell so much in love with Italy that we were reluctant to return to Kenya, but we still had some more schooling ahead of us before we could explore the world further.

Now that we were Roman Catholics it was no longer proper for us to attend a Protestant mission school, so Oria and I left the Rift Valley Academy and joined the Loreto Convent in Nairobi, while Dorian, no longer an outcast in society, was admitted to the Prince of Wales School, two miles from the Convent. The two schools were known as the Heifer Boma and the Cabbage Patch, and the heifers and cabbages often played matches against each other and had romantic dates among the trees in the forests that separated our schools.

We adapted effortlessly to our new and very different surroundings and to the kindly white-robed Irish nuns who looked so like penguins, we thought. Like true Shepherds of Christ, peaceful and serene, they herded us around the severe stone buildings, their rosaries and crucifixes breathing silent prayers to each other. We went through the mechanics of prayer and confession without any religious feelings whatever, while chugging through our classes was like walking through the sticky mud of the bamboo forest. I found it hard to concentrate and it was only fear of my father that got me through the final stages of my scholastic life at the age of nineteen.

Naivasha had always been home to us. Kenya was our homeland and we were never quite able to sympathise with our parents and those of their generation who referred to Europe as "home". Two generations ago colonial children would go "home" for all their schooling. Then the children of the last generation went "home" just for their university education. Now in the third generation they seldom go "home" at all, for the concept of the mother country has all but died out.

When Dorian, Oria and I left our schools in Kenya we were faced with a choice: to join the clan of Kenya "cowboys" and their sisters who were strong in the arm but weak in the head, or pull up stakes and face the gruelling continental curriculum.

My parents had remained essentially European and were well aware of the consequences the free and easy life we had been leading in Kenya would have for our future. Dorian was their chief preoccupation. Because he was their only son, they had ambitious plans for him. My father wanted him to follow in his grandfather's footsteps and become an engineer, but no career could have been less suited to Dorian's capabilities. Because of our father's festering hatred for anything British it was decided that Dorian should join the *Politechnico di Torino*, the toughest university in Italy, but he soon found out that the Italian system was completely different from the British colonial one and that it required a mental discipline and preparation he did not possess.

As for Oria and myself, my parents differed as to the direction we should follow. My father felt we should be prepared simply to become good wives, mothers and homemakers, but my mother thought we should have what she called serious hobbies which would not only occupy our spare time but also be something to fall back on in case our eventual marriages were not successful. She never convinced my father about this, but he maintained that decisions relating to daughters should be taken by the mother and for sons by the father, so he gave in to her. We did not care one way or the other, though we did not much relish my father's suggestion that we join the smart but severe *Poggio Imperiale* convent for young ladies in Florence. How could we possibly adjust to navy-blue serge skirts caps and black stockings? We were only just getting used to our shoes.

I was an intensely physical adolescent. I was quite content to use other people's brains and had no particular urge to awaken my own.

When I was nineteen my parents sent me to be 'finished off" at the House of Citizenship in England, a smart school for young ladies in the village of Ashridge in Hertfordshire. There about eighty girls were assembled under the expert tutelage of Miss Dorothy Neville-Rolfe, a middle-aged spinster whose father had been an admiral. Dressed in angora and shetland twin sets and tweed skirts that hung to mid-calf, with a wave of hair held by a kirby grip half covering her furrowed brow, this intelligent, well read, nervous and frustrated lady looked a bit like our friend Gilbert Colville, I thought: she could have been his sister. She was much liked and feared by all the girls, and used her sharp wit and cutting tongue to keep us in line. Later she gave me a most influential reference.

I spent eighteen painful months at the House of Citizenship, and grew fat and ugly. I was cold and miserable and lonely, and could not relate to most of the girls, who were so different from me. I only made one friend. Her name was Uni and she was Norwegian.

When I had been there for almost a year my father came to visit me. It was the middle of winter and the fog was so thick he couldn't get back to London that night. Miss Neville-Rolfe invited him to spend the weekend with us. That evening he sat down at the grand piano beside the fireplace and played us his repertoire of Neapolitan songs. A great singsong broke out as the barriers of embarrassed English self-control slowly collapsed, and for one unforgettable evening, Naples came to Ashridge. It was as if a lamp had suddenly been lit on the cold grey flagstones of our grim English castle. Next morning at breakfast there was a rush for my table.

When he flew home to Kenya, my father left his new car for me to ship back to him, but ten days later I packed my belongings, left a note on my bed and drove it to Dover myself.

My father's threats, which had got me through my exams, had had less effect on Oria, and her results were not too brilliant. She was, however, already showing signs of having inherited some of my mother's artistic talent, so she went to Rome to join the fabric design studio of an Austrian countess called Friedline. She remained with her for a year and contributed imaginative designs, strongly influenced by Africa. But, like my father, Oria is a sprinter and not a stayer, and she soon found the work monotonous. A year later she left and joined my mother, who was on one of her visits to Paris.

I joined them there and told them of my misery at Ashridge. My mother was very understanding and did not seem too upset. I was twenty-one. My sleepy brain slowly began to awake, and in Paris I really opened my eyes for the first time.

Several members of my mother's exciting family were still around. An uncle was the head of *Vogue*, another owned *Le Jardin des Modes*, and another *Les Arts Décoratifs*. I was happy to be suddenly a part of this creative family. When my mother suggested that I take up photography I leapt at the idea, and became an apprentice in the studio of Harry Meerson, where I embarked on the first exciting years of my adult life.

Harry Meerson was an unconventional bohemian photographer with an acute sense of beauty. His stunning, graphic pictures reflected his love for beautiful women. He was photographing the summer collections for *Vogue* when I walked into his studio for an appointment made by my uncle, Lucien Vogel, and stepped into his world of light and action. Several smartly dressed ladies stood around amid a pile of long, open cartons. Sheets of delicate white tissue paper floated over the floor and mingled with the wild collection of dresses draped all over the room. Cigarette smoke filled the air and hung around the strong lamp bulbs. It curled down the shafts of light and drifted towards me in the adjoining, darker room.

An amazing-looking creature in a gossamer dress hovered against a high wooden stool covered in thick white paper. Behind her a muslin backdrop filtered the light and made her look as if she were floating. She was tall and thin with incredibly long legs and silver fingernails. Her face, with its high cheekbones and hollow cheeks, large blue eyes and cloud of brown hair, seemed unreal. A fan on the floor made her dress and hair move softly as in a summer breeze. Her name was Ivy.

Meerson, in a black turtle-neck cashmere sweater and elegant slacks, moved casually through this chaotic scene, adjusting a lamp, arranging a fold in the dress, pinning a piece of tissue over a reflector with a clothes peg. He wove his way among the mass of electric wires coiled like serpents on the floor, cajoling and joking with Ivy, giving her directions in hushed tones, making her feel like a queen.

I stood in awe at the open door. I had never seen anything like this before. Then he turned and saw me. I was terrified – what was I doing here? I felt like an intruder in a dream.

"Oh, hello. You're Mirella, aren't you?" he said, turning on his magician's smile.

Everyone looked round and welcomed me. I clutched my handbag and nodded back. With this brief introduction, I entered Harry Meerson's world.

Two weeks after I entered his studio, his assistant walked out on him. Meerson was furious. "Well, Mirella," he said, "we've no choice but to go on. I'm in the middle of the collections. Will you help me out?"

"But I don't know anything," I stammered.

"I'll teach you," he said.

Meerson was immensely patient, tolerant and understanding. He also realised I was bewitched by him and his work. Nothing else existed for me, and he loved me for it. I worked with him eighteen hours a day, not bothering about time, sleep or food. I became his slave, and adored it. My knowledge of photography was not even elementary. I had taken only a few photographs with a Rolleiflex my mother had bought me, so I followed Meerson's every move in the studio and in the darkroom. A week later, at the end of an intensive session, he gave me two handfuls of film and said, "Develop them." I had never been in the darkroom on my own before, and I was filled with anxiety as I tried to imitate each of the moves I had watched him make so many times. I unravelled the films, and lowered all twenty-five of them together into the developer. I slipped my fingers over the clips to agitate them, and discovered to my horror that on contact with the water they had all stuck together. I should have immersed them one by one. Panic rushed through me, sweat broke out on my forehead. I heard my heart beat in my head. I slipped my hand into the tank, the glutinous, wet gelatine confirmed my fears. A sharp knock on the darkroom door made me jump.

"How are you doing?" Meerson's cheery voice echoed through the dark. My mouth went dry, I caught my breath.

"Okay, except for one thing."

"What?"

"I'm in trouble," I said feebly.

"What do you mean, you're in trouble?"

"All the films have stuck together in the tank, and I can't get them unstuck."

"*Merde*," I heard him say as he paced up and down outside the door. He tried to give me instructions from outside, but by now I was losing control of the situation. I pulled the soaking, sticky mass of film out of the developing tank, plunged it into the hypo, and slipped out of the darkroom to face him. He knew immediately that the mistake had been his, not mine. He should never have put me into the darkroom alone so soon.

Hot, trembling and flushed, I watched his anger subside and he smiled at me. "We'll have to reshoot," he said, gritting his teeth and shrugging his shoulders bravely. He put his arm around my shoulders. "Let's go and have some food. You can only learn by your mistakes, you know." I could have hugged him.

Little by little, I mastered photography, learning by my mistakes. I'm still making them today, but I found out that photography can be like a drug: it distorts your vision, your attitude and your emotions. You respect and fear it; it becomes an outlet for your feelings. Once I knew that, for better or worse, my eyes became my life.

After two exhilarating years in Meerson's studio my father broke his back in a riding accident. I took a leave of absence to return home to Naivasha, promising I would come back. But I never did.

One day, as I was flipping through a photography annual, I came across an advertisement for the New York School of Photography. I showed it to my father. A month later, I was on a plane out of Africa once more. I stopped in Paris and went to tell Meerson of my change of plan.

He realised that my mind was made up, and did not try to stop me.

I spent two long, lonely years in New York, completely out of my depth. I could not cope with the pace, the size, or the people of the city. I went to live with three American girls in a house on East 75th Street and knew nobody else. I had been given some letters of introduction by my uncles in Paris, but they were to people so high up in the hierarchy that I felt as distant from them as from the tops of the towering skyscrapers.

I enrolled at the School of Photography and handed over $1,000, half the money I had. A week later, I called on Irwin Blomenfeld, the famous fashion photographer, to whom I had been given an introduction. He received me with friendly warmth, and asked me to tell him about myself. When I finished my tale, he quietly informed me that I had made my first mistake.

"Photographers are born. Only assistants go to school," he told me. "You're wasting time and money. You have learned enough already from Meerson. You must take your own pictures; it is the only way you'll learn. Photography is knowing how to see, the rest you can learn on your own, through trial and error. You must leave the school."

I looked at this kindly little man, with his big, hooked nose and strong central European accent, surrounded by the pictures of the beautiful women he worked with. He had just shattered my plans. What was I going to do now, and where was I going to start? And what of the thousand dollars I had just put down? My eyes wandered over the spacious studio with the great window along one wall overlooking Central Park. The hum of New York seeped through the walls like the distant echo of a giant's drum. I felt trapped and confused.

"Come back and see me whenever you want," he told me comfortingly as I left the studio. "If there's anything I can do to help, let me know." I felt like asking him to take me into his world, as Meerson had done; I waited for him to suggest it, but he never did.

Every day for a month I still attended the School of Photography, but Blomenfeld's words kept marching through my head. I took his advice and left. With half of my allowance gone, I moved out of the house on 75th Street, and rented a room in the apartment of a Russian princess on 99th Street on the edge of Harlem.

I got a part-time job as secretary to the head of the East African Tourist Bureau and worked there in the mornings. In the afternoons I took my pictures. Then I met Joe de Casseres, a struggling young fashion photographer who suggested we share a studio together. We found an abandoned, derelict warehouse on West 22nd Street which we scrubbed and swept and painted for a week and with a few hundred dollars turned into a functional studio with a darkroom and a telephone. We set up his strobe lights, hung rolls of background paper, erected the enlarger and were in business.

Joe was a soft-spoken, kind-hearted New Yorker. He knew a great deal about the technicalities of photography, and I learned the hard way, as Meerson and Blomenfeld had told me to, by making mistakes. I sank my secretarial earnings into the studio and used the remaining money my father had given me to pay for my room. Each week I went to see Blomenfeld who became a close, dear friend. He looked at my pictures, dissected them and patiently gave me his criticisms.

Then at a dinner party one night I met Jean-Paul Marx. I was twenty-two. He fell in love with me and asked me to marry him. Jean-Paul was ten years older than I and had a good job in a shipping firm. I half moved into his comfortable, bachelor apartment on the river, and lost my virginity. I wrote to my parents to tell them that I wanted to get married. A week later my mother arrived in New York to take me back to Naivasha: Jean-Paul Marx was a Jew. I was not really in love, and followed her back without protesting too much.

CHAPTER 10

Emergency

Soon after my return from New York, in 1952, Dorian also arrived back in Naivasha from Europe. After three years in the *Politechnico di Torino* the mental stress of trying to keep abreast of the tough university curriculum, coupled with the frustrating student city life, gave him a bleeding stomach ulcer. He returned to Kenya to reconsider his situation with the family and reached Mombasa three days after the new Governor, Sir Evelyn Baring, had declared a State of Emergency. It was the beginning of the Mau Mau troubles, which were to last for the next four years. The Kenya government announced a general call-up for every white male between the ages of eighteen and forty.

For all practical purposes the Mau Mau rebellion was confined to the Kikuyu tribe, at that time the key to African politics in Kenya. The Kikuyu had a passion for secret societies and a great respect for the power of oath. Tens of thousands of traditionally peaceful men and women swore to kill and burn whenever necessary, in support of the Mau Mau cause. The oath-takings were accompanied by the chewing of human brains and intercourse with dead goats, the intestines and gouged eyes of which decorated the oathing chapels. But the ceremonies themselves borrowed, in a striking way, the actions and rhythmic language of the Christian service of Holy Communion:

This is blood, and whether it be of man or beast, make it a cup of love and drink you all from it. Drink knowing that this cup is for trouble and restraint, sorrow and tears. But we who drink from it are united together in hope for the joyous day which, when it comes, will always be remembered. This is your remembrance, whether you are in difficulties or in pleasure.

In theory Mau Mau was anti-white but in practice the terrorists killed nearly one hundred times as many Africans as Europeans. All who resisted were cut to bits, strangled or buried alive, and brother butchered brother.

Two days after the state of emergency had been declared, eleven Europeans were murdered on their farms in outlying districts. Within hours a battalion of the Lancashire Fusiliers were flown in from the Canal Zone in Egypt and this deployment of British troops precipitated further violent resistance. The colonial answer to the growth of extremism was to meet it with force; no attempt was made to introduce social and political measures likely to remove the causes of the rebellion itself. The black man made for the forests and the white man reached for his gun; the Kikuyu went to war with the Wasungu (the white).

So a few days after his return home from Europe, Dorian registered at the Naivasha police station and was immediately called up. He joined the Kenya Police Reserve which was being hastily expanded to support the existing police force. He asked for a two-month period of leave to recover from his ulcer, and then left for Narok in the Maasai Reserve with a company of G.S.U. (General Services Unit) men from the Kamba, Nandi, Turkana, Boran and Samburu tribes, all known for their warlike inclinations, their tracking ability and their stamina.

In Narok Dorian was handed a file by the local police containing the names of fifteen men who had taken the Mau Mau oath. He arrested them the next day and under relentless interrogation they gave the names of a further thirty. Before long, he had put one and a half thousand men in jail and collected a file full of information.

As Dorian's investigation proceeded he came across an old Kikuyu called Kasatwa who lived in a large compound he had built himself in Norosora in the middle of the Maasai reserve. He was a crafty, rich and intelligent man who had made his money trading with the Maasai. He owned several *dukas* (shops) and a number of lorries. He had twenty or thirty Maasai and Kikuyu wives and over a hundred children, many of whom were active in the Mau Mau ranks. Kasatwa was well respected and so powerful that no one dared to inform on him or on the members of his large family. As Dorian's unit combed the district he picked up word of more oath-giving activities. This ritual was always carried out with the assistance of a young girl who carried a bottle of fat. The most binding part of the Mau Mau oath-taking rite consisted of seven small incisions on the left forearm over which a coat of fat was applied when blood was drawn, to form scars which remained as proof of allegiance.

Dorian was informed that one of the girls was Kasatwa's daughter. For a week he tracked her down, and finally found her asleep in a hut in Kasatwa's settlement. He took her back to the police station in Narok, interrogated her throughout the night and acquired a sixty-page declaration of all her activities, the places she had visited and the names of the people she had been with. She also confessed that the fat in the bottle was human fat, extracted from the bodies of the people they had murdered for refusing to take the oath. Finally she divulged the names of all the leaders and oath administrators. Within five hours she tied up all the loose ends that had eluded Dorian and his team for the past five months. One of the leaders, Paolo Gachanga, was arrested and later hanged on Dorian's evidence for multiple murder and oath-administering.

The trickle of active Kikuyu Mau Mau supporters who had taken to the Aberdare Forest and Mount Kenya before the emergency was declared became a flood of thousands after it. The forest bands consisted mainly of young warriors, some mere boys, though the oldest known supporters was nearly seventy, and there were also many women. The terrorists' routes were as obscure as their objectives. They rarely moved or operated in the open, and hardly ever attacked any soldier or civilian who could protect himself. By day all was peaceful but by night groups of rebels swept through the reserves and settled areas stealing food and money and if necessary taking life.

At first, existence for the terrorists in the forest was not too unpleasant. Some arrived with their most treasured possessions; other brought only knives, spoons, plates and cups. Some carried mattresses, blankets and sheets. Supplies of stolen food arrived regularly from the reserves, while supporters in the towns sent cigarettes, matches, penicillin and other medical supplies as well as ammunition and oil for cleaning guns. In the first months of the emergency, Mau Mau discipline was so strong that a terrorist who gave his money to a courier in the forest could be almost certain of getting anything he wanted from any shop in Nairobi. The Mau Mau were always short of precision weapons, but showed a remarkable facility for improvisation, making guns from odd scraps of iron plumbing, door bolts, rubber bands and bits of wire, though these guns tended to injure the marksman rather

Dorian as an officer in the Kenya
Police Reserve. "The black man made
for the forests and the white man
reached for his gun."

Mau Mau freedom fighter.

than his prey. The bushcraft of the Mau Mau regulars had reached a superlative standard: they moved at staggering speed when frightened, and some gangs had been known to travel seventy miles on their toes or on their heels or on the sides of their feet so as not to leave recognisable trails.

Dorian now set aside any notion of becoming a civil engineer. His dealings with Mau Mau gangs and the experience he had gained in Masailand had given him a clearer insight into the African mind and character. He had learned much about the Africans' methods of survival, their fear and the ease with which they are swayed by fast talkers, big promises, guns and threats, and also that no oath was sufficient protection against the more immediate prospect of death at the hands of the security forces. Very few adherents of Mau Mau were sufficiently dedicated to sacrifice themselves, and Dorian began to realise that in order to break the Mau Mau movement the Kikuyu had to be persuaded that they were fighting a lost cause.

He exchanged his khaki police uniform for the plain clothes of a civilian intelligence officer and set to work in the Rift Valley area. With him were four other young white Kenyans. They worked in close liaison with Mary Bunny, a young Englishwoman who headed the Kenya Intelligence Service in the Naivasha area and was the wife of a local Naivasha doctor.

In order to infiltrate the Mau Mau terrorists living in the forests the "pseudo gangs" were formed. These were groups of four or five men dressed in tattered clothes and headed by a white man with burned cork and stove polish smeared on his face, hands and feet, who went into the forest to track down, capture, and if necessary shoot the outlaws.

Dorian and his men joined one of these dangerous, exacting missions, and with Reson, the faithful Ndorobo tutor of his childhood, went into the forest to hunt men as they had once hunted wild game. But Dorian's feelings were mixed. His allegiance to the white interest and his desire to protect his own kind were at variance with the affinity he had felt for the Africans since his childhood. His green eyes were a major problem in his "pseudo gang" set-up, for they contrasted vividly with the dark brown eyes of the Africans. In consequence he had to keep them constantly lowered and wear a wide-brimmed hat. The Kenya Regiment, the police and the loyal members of the Kikuyu tribe recruited into the Home Guard were also learning to operate effectively within the forest.

On one of Dorian's "pseudo" patrols he and his men came upon a hideout deep in the Kinangop bamboo forest. It was two o'clock in the morning, cold and raining. A sentry squatted against a clump of tall dripping bamboo poles. Six men were hunched around a heap of smoking coals in a small shelter nearby made of leaves and branches. They spoke in low voices, their hands stretched over the hot coals trying to keep warm. A thick mist hung everywhere. Dorian and his men crouched in the thickets behind the sentry and listened. One of them pulled out the thin piano wire with its wooden handles from his dark green waterproof jungle jacket. The others watched from beneath the dripping rims of their felt army hats. They knew what was going to happen; they had practised it many times.

At a signal, they released the safety catches on their rifles. The man with the wire lunged forward and slipped the noose over the head of the unsuspecting sentry, pulling it tight across his neck. He slumped without a sound. The pseudos dived into the hideout. The hunched figures inside crashed through the leafy walls of their jungle shelter and plunged into the forest. Three of them were shot dead, one was captured, and two got away. It was an ugly game.

In April 1954, operation "Anvil" destroyed much of the passive organisation in Nairobi, and cut off the best supply line. Security forces sealed off the city and made over thirty thousand arrests. Those arrested, most of them Kikuyu, were taken to special camps and in a map-screening operation over sixteen thousand were detained as active Mau Mau supporters. As a result of all this the life of the hard-core guerillas deteriorated swiftly, and they were thrown back on the resources of the forest. Every edible plant was noted and animals were trapped with snares made out of salvaged wire from crashed RAF spotter planes. Sometimes they would eat raw monkey or meat so maggot-ridden that even the hyenas would not touch it, and wild honey was devoured with the combs still containing bees. They wore animal skins which they would not take off for a year at a time. Some wore caps which they pulled over their faces to protect themselves from the rain when they slept, and one gang was known to have slept without blankets on the ice near the peaks of Mount Kenya. Their recuperative powers from disease and bullets were phenomenal.

Determined though they were to keep alive, the incessant battle slowly sapped the dedication of many Mau Mau members. As the months went by more and more deserted and joined the pseudo gangs and after two years of the emergency there were more Mau Mau working for the gangs than against them.

During this time a famous witchdoctor had a dream – he dreamt that he and the thirty-five men who shared a cave with him should give themselves up. Next morning two "pseudos" happened to be passing. Startled and scared by the group in the cave, they were about to turn and run when the witchdoctor stopped them. "Come in, my children," he said. "Take us to your C.O. We want to join you." The two astonished men escorted them back in single file to camp, and instantly their gang of thirty-five "pseudos" was doubled in strength.

It was not only in the forests and hills that the Mau Mau movement bred and multiplied; it spilled over into the European-owned farms.

To try to control the Kikuyu on the farms every African was to be issued with an identity card with a photograph and a number to be tied round his neck. In reply, the Mau Mau warned that the number on the white card would be branded on the chest of any man who agreed to be photographed. In consequence, when the official government photographer arrived on a farm, half the labour force would have fled in the night, never to return.

Ours was among the more fortunate families during the emergency. Several of our friends were hacked to death; farm houses and implements were tampered with or destroyed, crops were set on fire, horses and livestock were killed or maimed so badly they had to be shot.

Dorian was called in to identify some of the captured terrorists connected with these savage murders. Among the six dishevelled, dirty men standing in the police courtyard on one occasion he recognised Maina, the young Kikuyu youth who had worked for us during the war and had been the smiling friend and "slave" of Oria and myself on our little farmland. When he had been refused a rise in salary, he had left us. For ten years, he slipped from farm to farm and from job to job in an attempt to overcome his nagging feeling of exploitation. He returned to us discontented and badly in need of work and stability. My father took him back, raised his salary by a few shillings and promised him a further rise if he worked well. But a few months later he left us without explanation after collecting his meagre salary. We never heard of him again until he was picked up in the Aberdares after having hacked to death his last white employer and the man's wife and three children.

Maina was sentenced to hang and Dorian went to see him in the Kamiti prison after the court case. During a tragic hour-long conversation Maina told him the bitter story which had started when, one night in his hut on our farm, an "enlightened" friend told him about the white man's exploitation of the Africans – a discussion that led this gentle youth to murder and the gallows.

I shall never forget the night a gang of fifty terrorists were flushed out of the papyrus swamp about six miles from Naivasha. Dorian had been tipped off by Paolo, the tractor driver on the neighbouring farm, who informed him that some men were hiding in the swamp between the two farms. He brought us one of them and triumphantly announced that he had pulled him out of the papyrus. The man led Dorian and his gang to the hideout; they found it humming with mosquitoes and littered with orange peel from our orchard, but the man's comrades had flown.

My father undertook the interrogation of the miserable, shivering captive. The prisoner had been in the mosquito-infested swamp, living only on oranges, for a week, under a continuous drizzling rain. But he would not speak and kept his eyes lowered and his lips tightly closed.

When my father realised that he was making no headway, he marched the man out of the house into the night and down the garden path to the swimming pool, and told him that he would drown him if he did not speak. The man remained dumb. In he went and disappeared from sight for a few seconds. He came up gasping and spluttering, but gave my father no more satisfaction than before. Oria and I, overcome by curiosity, watched aghast as this horrible game continued. Still refusing to speak, the man was then dragged to the car park where he was pushed down in front of the headlights and the interrogation continued. Still he made no reply.

An hour later my father finally put out his hand to him and lifted him to his feet. "Okay," he said, "you've won." He led him back into the kitchen, sat him down beside the fire and gave him a mug of steaming tea. "Take him to the police station," he told the guard. "This isn't my job." My father retreated to his room and remained on his bed for three days, staring at the ceiling. He could neither speak nor eat, so badly did he feel about what he had done.

But there were those for whom hunting Mau Mau terrorists turned into a sport. Rumours and bizarre stories of their feats were rife. One crack shot, it was said, had killed four men with one bullet, having waited to fire until the fleeing men were suitably aligned. Another prominent young terrorist-hunter collected twelve pairs of hands which he pulled out of his camouflaged jungle jacket and flung, all tied together, on the desk of his superior, when his story was questioned.

Dedan Kimathi was the great resistance hero of the Mau Mau rebellion. When he was eleven years old his dying grandmother sent for him and gave him her blessing according to Kikuyu custom; she laid her hand on his cheek and with her last words chose him to be the leader of the family; then asked that she be turned so that she could die facing him. She dipped her fingers in a goat's horn of blood and sprinkled it on his head.

Dedan believed that Ngai, the traditional god of the Kikuyu tribe, had guided his grandmother's hand and had chosen him to lead his tribe. He began to dream. He dreamed of lands where the cows were brown, of places in the sky where rows of people sat on wooden benches, of death being like a gate which opened and shut, of rivers running uphill, of people standing before him in white clothes with arms outstretched, and of Ngai speaking to him in his sleep. He believed everything he dreamed and his descriptions of these dreams made old men and women turn their heads away, for such things frightened them.

The rebellion dragged on. One by one the Mau Mau were hounded out of the forest. Only Kimathi and his gang of a hundred and fifty diehards remained in the Aberdares to the end. Surrounding them were five thousand men, many of them deserters from his own cause. Then Kimathi fell out with Gati, one of his lieutenants, who gave himself up to a young Kenyan called Ian Henderson.

Gati became the first deserter from Kimathi's inner circle. He sent a message to Henderson informing him that he wanted to talk and that, if he agreed, he should leave a message for him in a bottle at a designated place in the forest. For five days the bottle remained uncollected, and then one night it was gone. Five further messages were exchanged in this way. Finally Henderson himself sat on the track alone, unarmed, and waited. Gati and another man came towards him from out of the thick undergrowth. Clothed in skins that they had not removed for several years, with long beards and matted, caked hair that hung in lumps around their faces and necks, they looked like animals. Their drawn, strained faces and hollow, frightened eyes betrayed their terrible, five-year ordeal.

Gati's surrender was a major breakthrough for Henderson. It was the first time any direct contact had been made with Kimathi's gang. Gradually, as the net closed in on them, Kimathi's remaining men deserted him and joined Henderson, providing him daily with more and more information. Kimathi became nervous and murdered one of his henchman who had disappeared for a week and then came back. At last only his woman remained, and then she too was caught.

Kimathi was now alone in the forest. The bamboo piping that supplied water to the rebels' hideouts, the food and the ammunition stores scattered over the areas in which Kimathi and his original army of nine thousand men had manoeuvred, were slowly uncovered.

Like a hunted animal with a pack of dogs behind him, Kimathi crawled deeper into the forest, abandoning his lairs, never turning back. Henderson's men went in after him and followed his trail for many days under dire conditions. Then the trial stopped abruptly. He was somewhere in their net but they could not find him. Finally a soldier heard a noise in the bushes and shot. Kimathi was hit in the leg. They pulled him out and hauled him, handcuffed and tied, back to Henderson's camp. He was taken to the Nyeri hospital where he lay until his trial in the Supreme Court began. He was hanged in the Kamiti prison at sunrise on 24th November, 1957, after six years in the Aberdare Forest, convicted of 182 murders. That day, in the forest, the great *mugumo* tree with its huge trunk and heavy hanging branches reclining almost to the ground, under which Kimathi and his gang prayed to Ngai, fell to the ground.

The story of Kimathi's life in the forest, his resistance and his end placed him in the ranks of the tragic heroes of history. He had fought and died for ideals which, in the end, he alone believed in. Ian Henderson, decorated with the George Medal, also became part of the history of the Mau Mau rebellion.

A Cloud of Red Hair

Despite the upheaval of the Mau Mau emergency, life on the farm now seemed dull and monotonous, especially after New York. The few friends we had lived in Nairobi or on farms scattered all over the country and we saw little of each other. I became very restless and accepted an offer to join John Seago, a game trapper, on a two-month safari in Uganda, where he was catching white rhino for the Hamburg zoo. Seago was an intense, solitary man of about fifty with the tough, suntanned, sinewy look of those who spend long periods in the African bush.

Together with June and Peter Green, animal catchers from Whipsnade Zoo in England, a BBC cameraman to film the adventure, and a dozen sturdy Africans, we drove two Land-Rovers and two trucks in convoy for three days to Lira, an outpost on the Nile in northern Uganda. We picked out a camp site a few miles from the bank of the river to escape the mosquitoes. A fire was soon lit, the ritual tea was set out on a table beneath a tree, and the vehicles unloaded. By nightfall the camp was set up.

The rains had been very heavy that year and the grass had grown very tall. For miles around us the golden country undulated in the warm breeze. There was no sign of animal life, and I wondered why we had travelled so far to this beautiful, but seemingly barren place. I found out that evening as we sat and relaxed around the camp fire. The sounds of Africa rose into the night. The place was teeming with game, and we were able to pick out the nocturnal calls of the invisible wildlife around us.

"Tomorrow we shall set fire to the grass," Seago said, "and then you'll understand why we came here. Everything we are looking for is hiding in that grass, and in order to catch them, we have to burn it down."

We set off after breakfast, bumping across the hard ground and diving into the grass as we would have driven into the sea, flattening it in our wake. It was already very hot and still. I took a last look at the golden protective cloak as a match was held to a crumpled newspaper beneath one of the tufts. A thin spiral of white smoke rose. The paper disintegrated immediately into a heap of black ashes as the little flames grew and spread to the brittle stalks. We stepped back and watched the fire take hold. Great waves of heat rushed at us, the smoke stung our eyes. We jumped into the Land-Rover and reversed in our tracks as the flames lashed out in front of us. The silent world, so suddenly disturbed, was now filled with the crackling, popping sounds of destruction. The hidden life rose in panic. Animals of all shapes and sizes crashed through the long menacing stalks which, until then, had harboured and protected them.

I watched, stunned by the ghastly spectacle. White egrets headed like ghosts through the misty smoke curtain for the clear sky above. Waterbuck and gazelle, like panicked dancers, leaped and crashed through the burning grass, and tiny insects and beetles lit up momentarily, then joined the falling sparks. I saw a giant hornbill on fire dive to earth, flames licking at its enormous black wings.

I looked at my companions. Their expressions mirrored my own. No one said a word. We watched in silence as the curtain of death receded from us. Two hours later. the land lay black and smouldering and the cloud of smoke mingled with the soft transparency of the cloudless sky. In the distance the heavy curtain moved towards the horizon.

Early next morning, we travelled across the barren, blackened land again for an hour before we caught sight of our first rhino. It stood with its calf beside it, like debris after a storm. We approached them cautiously and planned the attack. John Seago drove the Land-Rover with the strong wooden crate and the medicine box, and Peter Green the catching truck with eight tough African catchers headed by Juma, their leader, in the back. The yards of two-inch sisal rope lay carefully coiled on the floor in the open back, a thick log about six feet long attached to one end. The lorry with the cage followed a short distance behind. The three vehicles charged at full speed directly at the two rhino. The mother lifted her head and stood for a moment silhouetted against the sky. She turned, sniffed the air and was off in the opposite direction, followed hard in her tracks by her calf.

We travelled fast across the pot-holed terrain, clinging to the metal bars. The vehicles rose from the ground with each hole and mound we hit, and landed with a crashing thump. Why they did not disintegrate each time, I'll never know. Gradually we caught up with the rhino and her calf until we were travelling neck and neck with the mother. Seago slowly inserted his vehicle between the two animals and veered the mother off to the left. The catching truck followed close behind, chasing the terrified calf. Juma leaned over the side, gripping the long pole with the noose attached to one end, and thrust it in front of the animal's head. As the vehicle closed in, he slipped the noose over the baby horn and protruding ears onto the neck. The men behind him heaved the log over the side and the coiled rope unravelled. Green took his foot off the accelerator and the truck slowed down. The calf galloped on, dragging the log for another hundred yards before it jammed in the roots of a tree and pulled the rope tight. Then Green slammed on the brakes. Exhausted and terrified, the calf was yanked to its knees, panting and snorting into the dust, defeated. We drove up to it, and the men jumped out and wrapped the rope around its front and back legs. A sharp pull threw it on its side and the ropes were knotted. The wooden crate was unloaded and the helpless animal manoeuvred into it and loaded onto the waiting lorry.

We caught four young white rhino in this way during two months by the Nile. The Greens cared lovingly and patiently for them, gently habituating them to their life in captivity. Within a week they were feeding from a bottle and munching fresh leaves and grass from our hands.

We had been in Uganda about six weeks when a visitor from Nairobi brought a letter from my mother with the news that Dorian was getting married. Surprisingly, I was shocked by this unexpected news. I had had enough of the safari and decided to return home. So I boarded the Nile paddle-steamer at Lira for the two-day journey to Kisumu on Lake Victoria. The muddy Nile drifted gently by and on either side of the river the banks were flanked with thick papyrus swamps. Goliath herons and white egrets disturbed by our passage rose into the sky, and hippo and crocodile slithered into the water. I watched this timeless, peaceful scene go by and thought of my hectic life in New York. John Seago had given me a baby Uganda cob as a parting gift. The soft warm creature lay unperturbed at my feet, its tiny black velvety nose and dainty hooves tucked snugly in its golden fur.

When I arrived on the farm Dorian told me about his plans. He pulled out a snapshot from his wallet and asked me what I thought of Francine. She had a pretty face with lots of freckles and a cloud of thick red hair. She was twenty-one, lived in Versailles with her mother and sister, and worked as an accountant for Thomas Cook in the boulevard de la Madeleine in Paris. Her father was dead and the family had very little money. He then went on to tell me of their chance encounter on a train, on his way to the ski slopes during a well-earned holiday in Europe. He had dazzled her with his stories of Africa and his Mau Mau adventures and a week later had asked her to marry him. I scrutinised her photograph and wondered how she would fit into Naivasha. My parents had invited her to stay before she took the final plunge.

Another bad drought had hit Kenya during the Mau Mau years. The lake had receded a long way, uncovering many more acres to cultivate. The hippo and water birds had follwed the lake and now lived on the other side of the papyrus belt almost a mile from the house. My father bought new tractors and ploughs, doubled the labour force and built a new village to house the people. Five hundred acres of fresh land were broken, turned and planted. A European export market for fresh out-of-season vegetables from Kenya opened up and large fields of green peppers, green beans, courgettes and asparagus were carefully laid out in long straight lines. Submersible pumps and boreholes were set up to irrigate the parched land and beat the drought.

Dorian, who had now joined my father in a serious attempt at farming, was thus able to put into practice the technical knowledge he had acquired in Turin. He built a large shed and designed a simple, but effective, apparatus with a conveyor belt for sorting and packing the fresh vegetables which were air-freighted the same day and sold the next at Covent Garden in London. But the vigorous growth of indigenous weeds and grasses became a major handicap. The women on the farm spent long hours bent double, carefully picking them out from amongst the rows of vegetables. It was a tough, unending race against nature: the cutworms went to work on the roots, the leaf borers and green caterpillars attacked the leaves and stems; wild boar, antelope and porcupines came at night to feed on the young plants, and the hippo trudged through the cultivated land on their way to and from their nightly grazing in the lucerne fields, trampling over everything and leaving trails like ditches behind them.

Dorian joined forces with Van Someren, a friend of his from the Mau Mau days, and began experimenting with insecticides, fungicides and weed-killers, then still in their infancy, carefully mixing the chemicals so they would affect only the harmful weeds and grasses. Within days of spraying, the long, straight green lines of young shoots stood out against the dark earth, clear of their suffocating enemies. Night-watchmen with shotguns and torches patrolled the fields on lonely, mosquito-infested beats to keep out marauding nocturnal visitors and sometimes provided the labour lines with much-sought-after meat rations.

When he returned to the farm after the Emergency in 1956, Dorian had brought with him a small Kikuyu boy called Joseph Kamau. Joseph's father had been killed by Dorian's men when they raided the hideout in the Aberdare Forest. Joseph was ten years old and an exceptionally bright little boy. Before long he had learned to manipulate the spanners and drive the cars and tractors, and in his free time was teaching himself English. As Dorian and I rode our horses across the farm, he told me of his concern for Joseph and the responsibility he was shouldering, and proudly showed me the work they had done together, almost as if he was talking of his own son.

"I'll get five thousand bags of potatoes off the land near the lake," Dorian explained as we galloped along the rough farm roads dividing the fields. He told me of his battle with the weeds, the insects and the game, and how he had beaten them. I was very impressed. A glow of satisfaction crossed his face as we gazed together over the lush green oasis, and at the water from the irrigation jets rising like fountains in long straight lines down the fields, spraying the thirsty plants. Peace and prosperity seemed to have descended upon our little kingdom again.

Then, suddenly, the long, two-year period of drought ended. Heavy storm clouds rolled across the sky, and the days were cold and dark. The tall trees swayed and groaned as great gusts of wind lashed the withered, thirsty leaves from the branches. The dust that lay inches deep over the parched hills rose hundreds of feet into the hot air in spiralling dust-devils and hung like smoke all over the farm. Everywhere fires broke out and ravaged the dry, brittle countryside, but thunder drums in the distance grew louder as the storms approached.

The water on the lake, which had lain flat and still for so long, now moved with white-capped waves towards the undulating mass of papyrus floating along its shore.

Each afternoon we watched the misty curtain of rain approach over the tops of the hills, obliterating every contour in its course and filling the air with its scent. A sudden hush of expectancy hung about. The wind rushed on, pushing and pulling clouds with it. A tiny line of dust a few inches high led the advancing rain, and then the large fat drops hit the ground. For a split second, we could almost count them before the heavens opened and great sheets of water descended on the world. It rained for two months, day and night. The land quickly changed colour. Water drained down the gullies on the hills, poured into the dry river beds and gushed into the lake. Swollen watercourses crept up their banks, uprooting trees and bushes and dragging them into the lake. With every storm the level of the lake rose as it seeped beneath the black, sticky soil and inch by inch crawled towards our fields.

The potato crop was three weeks from harvesting. Five thousand bags' worth lay ripening beneath the soil – and the lake kept rising. Each morning and evening Dorian and I went to inspect its advance. Pa waited at home for our report, seated stoically at his desk. He watched the sky and, as the rain-filled days went by, he smiled sardonically and shrugged his shoulders. "If it does not stop raining we'll lose the crop," he finally announced, echoing our own fears.

One morning, we found two rows of potatoes an inch deep in water. The next day ten rows stood reflected in the lake. Dorian plunged his hand into the sticky, soaking mud and groped below. He tugged at the plant and it came away effortlessly, unearthing a large number of sturdy, hard, pale brown potatoes. They were still intact and although very wet had not yet begun to rot.

Dorian looked at me. "I'm going to harvest now, immediately – tomorrow. The crop is lost anyway, we might as well try." The grim look left his face and was replaced by a demoniacal glint of determination.

"We'll pull the whole bloody lot up before the lake gets them," he almost shouted at me. "Come on, let's go and get it organised. It'll be a hell of a business because we can't get the tractors in. We'll have to do it by hand."

We ran home to announce our decision to Pa. Next day, every pair of hands on the farm was put to work. Dorian and Pa directed operations, one at each end of the field. They stood defiantly in the mud in their knee-high galoshes, guiding and watching the long lines of men, women and children bent in half, digging in the soft gooey earth, extracting the

. . . Dorian and Francine were married in the tiny church built by the Italian P.O.W.s.

mud-caked potatoes with their hands and stuffing them into the hessian bags behind them. A fine drizzle kept falling, announcing yet another heavy storm. For a week they fought on, tirelessly, with fierce determination, but the rain never stopped. After ten days they gave up; 250 bags were salvaged, and 4,750 went under.

Two weeks later the fields were part of the lake. The rotting potatoes floated on the surface. Mauve water-lilies began to grow and water birds returned. Maize stalks rose out from two feet of water and slowly bent and fell as their roots rotted. It had been a bad year; we had gambled with nature and we had lost. The lake rose fifteen feet that year, and we retreated to the backlands to start again.

With the abundant rain, the hills and backlands were once more covered with long, lush green grass. The cattle that had been reduced to walking skeletons by the terrible drought grew fat and shiny, and their calves sucked at swollen udders.

Francine arrived from Paris and Dorian went to meet her at the airport at seven o'clock in the morning. All the family had gathered in Nairobi to welcome her; we were all curious to know what she really looked like. We had arranged a pretty room for her in our Nairobi house and had cooked brunch and put flowers in all the vases. The African house servants in their white uniforms and red fezes peered through the kitchen window as she stepped out of the car.

She was tall and slim with carrot-coloured hair that fell to her waist, and was dressed in a smart Parisian costume. She had wide green eyes and lots of freckles on her pale European face. Dorian introduced her solemnly to us, one at a time. She looked tired and rather nervous as she smilingly bent to kiss each of us.

Over our cups of coffee and freshly baked brioches the polite conventional questions were asked. Our eyes flicked from her to Dorian, sitting proudly beside her.

'Well, what do you think?" he asked us later. "Do you like her?" "She's got thin lips," I ventured bitchily. "But if *you* like her, that's what's important." Was I resenting a female intruder in my brother's life?

Next day we took her to Naivasha. Dorian had organised a royal welcome for her. All the people on the farm lined the driveway to the house, carrying flowers and leaves and beating drums. They cheered and waved as we drove grandly past.

Oria and I helped her to unpack her bags and looked enviously at her pretty clothes. She pulled out her long white wedding dress carefully packed in tissue paper in a cardboard box, and showed us the little crown of synthetic orange blossoms. We placed it on her head and told her how pretty she was.

Dorian showed her around the farm and they went for long walks, hand in hand. They talked and laughed and seemed happy. She was excited by the new world she had entered, the new family she was about to join, and everyone soon forgot that she had really only come to have a look. Her enthusiasm was so contagious.

Dorian and Francine were married a few months later in the tiny church the Italian prisoners of war had erected at the bottom of the escarpment when they were building the road that linked Nairobi to Naivasha. The thickly forested cliffs of the escarpment formed a dark jungle backdrop, and the flat burned bed of the Rift Valley, over which my father had flown when he first landed in Naivasha, spread hot and hazy to the skyline in the distance.

The church was so small that only the family and bridesmaids could squeeze into it. The guests drove down the escarpment from Nairobi and stood outside under the pepper trees while the vows were exchanged. There were two little bridesmaids, Polish princesses, wearing red taffeta dresses, with flowers and ribbons in their hair, and two tiny page boys – one black and one white – dressed in satin shorts and long-sleeved shirts. Dorian looked very handsome in his dark blue suit. It was the first time I had ever seen him wear a suit, and Francine was a pretty bride, swathed in a cloud of white.

Pa was nervous and emotional. When the rings were exchanged I noticed his shoulders heave slightly and he began to cry. Sitting next to me was Lorenzo, a young Italian I had met a few days before, and had brought with me to the wedding.

CHAPTER 12

Lorenzo

I was twenty-six when Lorenzo entered my life. He landed in Nairobi one day, part of an Italian unit preparing a film called *Dio Nero – Diavolo Bianco*. He had seen some of my photographs in the Equator night club in Nairobi and rang me to ask for an appointment. I was forty-five minutes late for our first rendezvous, and wondered how we would recognise each other, but there was no mistaking him. He was leaning against a cement pillar, tall and thin with a blond afro halo around his small head. He wore casual Italian clothes and Jesus sandals with natural elegance. His blue eyes protruded abnormally from his pale thin triangular face. He looked like a Giotto painting. "What a strange, ugly face," I thought, "it can't be easy to catch the girls when you look like that" – but there was something wild and challenging about him. He bent to kiss my hand.

I brought him home next day for lunch to show him to the family. When he left, everyone agreed that he was unusual and my mother instantly labelled him *un parti dangereux*. We had never had anyone like him around before. He borrowed my MG and came back half an hour later with the roof down and the back filled with flowers: only Lorenzo in the driver's seat and the front of the car were visible. He had emptied all the stalls in the flower market for me.

Three days after we met, he asked me to marry him. We were sitting in my MG after a romantic dinner, it was midnight and pouring with rain that trickled on us through the canvas roof.

"Why do men always have to speak of marriage?" I laughed at him. "We don't have to get married to see each other."

A pained expression crossed his face as he said good night and climbed out of the soaking car. He stared at me through the window. His hair hung in bedraggled ringlets over his forehead, and a drop of rain trickled down his nose.

. . . Lorenzo was a gypsy, a vagabond, a man without purpose or direction.

I drove home and ran upstairs to tell my mother. "These Italians," she scoffed, "they're all the same."

Stung by my rejection, Lorenzo tried every trick he knew. He totally ignored me and began courting my sister, which drove me wild, of course.

I was nevertheless hired by his film crew as photographer/interpreter and guide, and agreed to go with them to Uganda to look for locations. During our trip, he told me about his extraordinary life. How he had lived in Tahiti, married a local girl called Terai Taupua, with Tahitian rites, and made a documentary film in the Carribean called *A Trip to Paradise*. He had been to Bali and Sumatra, hitch-hiked across Australia, almost died of hunger in India where he survived a crossing of the Rajastan desert on a bottle of Eno's fruit salts, and was at present crawling out of an impossible and passionate love affair with a beautiful Indian lady who had 365 saris, one for each day of the year, and was ten years his senior. He spoke in English, so that the others in his crew could not understand.

Lorenzo was a gypsy, a vagabond, a man without purpose or direction. My mother was right – *un parti dangereux*. I had never met anyone like him before, and I began to like him. We spent our first night together at the Mountain of the Moon Hotel at the foot of the Ruwenzori range and next day deep inside the Queen Elizabeth National Park we were caught in a heavy rain storm. Our truck bogged down hopelessly in the mud. It was four in the afternoon; we were several miles from the gate and the little resthouse. When the rain finally stopped a cold, clammy drizzle took its place. I knew it was prohibited and unwise to be in the park at night, and suggested we go to look for help while there was still some light.

It was a memorable walk. We met many wild creatures: elephant, buffalo, hippo, baboons, all came out on the road as soon as darkness fell. I knew that wild animals were not dangerous unless disturbed, but Lorenzo, who had never been in Africa before, had no such experience, and I wondered how he felt. He betrayed nothing of his thoughts.

Soaked and bedraggled, we reached the resthouse after a tramp of more than six hours. The warden was English and held strong views about the behaviour of "Italian tourists". Furious and unsympathetic, he told us in no uncertain terms how stupid we were to have put ourselves in such a dangerous situation, at risk from the animals and out

of reach of help. Surprisingly, Lorenzo waited patiently and calm for him to run dry before asking him for a cottage in which we could spend the night and a vehicle to retrieve our friends. The warden had no choice: he had to help us. And from the bathroom behind the little room into which we were grudgingly ushered, a shining white tub and a gas water heater beckoned invitingly.

"You have a bath and go to bed," Lorenzo said, putting his arms around me. "I'll go and relieve the others. Will you marry me?"

My father had always told us that we should take the man we wished to marry on safari in order to find out what he was really like. Lorenzo had passed *that* test.

I had to return to Naivasha ten days later, and left the film crew to continue their location hunting without me. Shortly after I left, the director, who was then in Bukavu in the Congo, told Lorenzo he had to return to Nairobi to look into some financial matters. "You drive the car back and I'll meet you in Nairobi in four days' time," he said. But Lorenzo read his real intentions.

As soon as he had left, Lorenzo started off and drove all day and night, stopping only for fuel. The director in the meantime had called me from Nairobi, asking me to come and meet him there for further location-planning, as he put it. On my way, I picked up a cable at the post office in Naivasha.

"DON'T MOVE UNTIL YOU HAVE SEEN ME. ARRIVING THIS EVENING. TOP SECRET. LOVE. LORENZO." I turned back home and Lorenzo arrived that evening, having covered the thousand kilometres in just over twenty-four hours. "Not bad," I thought, as he raced up the winding stairway towards me.

Next day I stood on the balcony, listening to Lorenzo speak to my father.

"Mirella and I would like to try and get married," I heard him say.

"What do you mean, 'try'? Either you do or you don't. Marriage is a serious matter, it's not a game," my father answered, attempting to sound indignant.

Lorenzo had not much to offer other than his charm. My father remained unconvinced and withheld his consent. "Stay away from her. You are too much of an adventurer to get married." My father recognised himself in this impetuous young man; they were so alike, it was comic.

Lorenzo in Tahiti . . . he married Terai
Taupau (right) with Tahitian rites.

Dismayed but not really surprised, Lorenzo talked to me for hours and the more he talked the deeper I fell in love with him. He finally cabled his father and asked him to come to Kenya to meet my parents and help him out.

In the meantime, my father had written to his bank and his friends in Italy for information on Lorenzo and his family. When the replies came he handed them to us and said laughingly that if he had only these references to go by he ought to drive Lorenzo out of the farm at gunpoint. "He is an adventurer with no fixed source of income who travels to distant countries like Hong Kong, India, Tahiti and Bali and is often seen driving fast cars in the company of exotic women," was their general line. But the reports on his father were excellent.

When Giulio Cesare, his father, known as Cesarino, arrived in Kenya, he was surprised to see that I was not black. Tall, handsome and well dressed, with a firm head of white hair, he was an older version of Lorenzo. The essence of the Italian aristocrat, he in his turn quickly charmed my family. He spoke beautiful French and English and, like Lorenzo, played the guitar and the harmonica. In the evenings the two of them would sit with my father, conducting improvised jam sessions and harmonising what my mother referred to as their "naughty old lines", while she and I gazed lovingly at these three rogues from different generations putting on their act for us. Each day for a week Lorenzo and I watched our fathers walking around the garden arm in arm talking and laughing, about us I suppose, and looking like a pair of Roman senators.

Lorenzo and I did not want to get married in a church. It was too binding. Our parents objected. "What will people think?" my father asked. "That you are pregnant or that he is a Jew." But Lorenzo and I did not care what people thought.

On 2nd March, 1957, two months after we met, we were married in Naivasha in a simple civil ceremony surrounded by a mass of family, friends and laughing Africans. I did wear a white dress with orange blossom in my hair but no veil.

Lorenzo hired a morning suit and top hat. When he appeared I did not recognise him and thought he was one of the guests. A black jazz band played a syncopated wedding march as my mother fought back her emotions. There was a three-tiered wedding cake crowned with a sugar movie camera sent by the French patissier of the Norfolk Hotel, and

Mirella in 1957 on Lorenzo's first safari.
"I need a girl like you around."

everyone, black and white, got drunk. We went to Zanzibar and Mafia Island for our honeymoon, which turned out to be more of a fishing-moon. The film was never made and the crew returned to Italy without Lorenzo. Two months later we ourselves migrated back to Europe. This first severing of my umbilical cord with Africa was very painful and I wept all the way to Addis Ababa.

We went to live in Rome, where I quickly began to taste the bitter-sweet agony of life with Lorenzo.

I was young, unaware of the world, and ignorant of people and their behaviour. I married Lorenzo as easily as I had switched lovers. It was probably the most foolish, irresponsible, exciting thing I have ever done. Years later, I came to the conclusion that most of the men I had met fell into three categories – those prompted by their heads, those by their heart and those by their sex. Some – not many – were a combination of all three. Lorenzo belonged to the last category – these I have found are the most attractive – they are sexy, amusing, fun-loving, careless, irresponsible and lazy – they dress well and have a lot of style. Most people like them. They are excellent lovers and lousy husbands. Women usually find them irresistible or are terrified by them. Men either envy or despise them. No one can remain indifferent to them.

Love and life together came as a shock to both of us. We were quite unprepared for what lay ahead. We grabbed each other by the hand and jumped in at the deep end. We sank slowly downwards, coming up only now and again for air. The sea bed was a long way down. On our descent we met many strange and varied fish, some still unknown to us.

Dorian had once told me that the three most important decisions in life – one's career, one's mate and one's religion – are usually taken at an age when most people don't know what they are doing. I was soon to learn the truth of this remark.

"Lorenzo's mother died when he was seven," Cesarino told me one day. "You will have to be more of a mother than a wife to him; do you realise this?" Then he laughed. "The only pleasure he ever gave me was nine months before he was born." But when his father died sixteen years later, Lorenzo's grief was immeasurable and I began then to understand the meaning of these words.

For six years we lived on the top floor of an ancient house overlooking the Trevi Fountain. We gutted the crumbling attic and decorated it with our dreams. During this time we travelled to the East – to Japan, Hong

Kong, Thailand and India – to make a film on oriental love. Marina, our first child, was conceived in Katmandu. I instinctively returned to Kenya for the momentous event. On 25th July, 1960, I became a mother. Marina was born at the Aga Khan Hospital in Nairobi, while Lorenzo was away filming with a friend in Stockholm the story of three Sicilians selling ladies' underwear in Sweden.

Everything I had experienced till that moment, including my marriage, paled in comparison with Marina's birth. I had given the impending event little thought, and not much fuss had been made over it in the family, and I approached the birth rather more like an animal than a thinking woman about to undergo an experience which could never be rivalled in its emotional intensity. And I went into it without Lorenzo. I realised later that this was to have serious repercussions on my attitude towards him, but he was as unprepared for parenthood as I was. I did not know then that I should never have had children, that I was not an instinctive mother, despite my Neapolitan blood and having so naturally become one at the age of twenty-nine. But I was still too immature to make the most of this incredible event.

Two months after Marina was born we left for the Caribbean where Lorenzo directed his first feature film, *Venere Creola*, the story of a black cock fighter and his many affairs. I left my little Marina in the arms of a huge Italian wet nurse and the tender care of Lorenzo's father. For one month the physical tug of separation was almost too much to bear. Then I began to forget her. When I returned she had changed so much that I felt completely estranged. This too was to have a serious effect upon us both, and I was bitterly to regret and to pay for my unawareness. How much I would now give to relive these events. That week in the hospital with Marina, surrounded by flowers, family and friends, would never repeat itself and remains a uniquely tender memory.

Lorenzo and I soon realized we were drowning. Our Roman nest never became our home. It was a showplace where curious people came to invade our privacy and to stare. We did meet a great many of them, but only a very few were worth while. One of these was Michelangelo Antonioni, who was preparing *The Eclipse* when he wandered in one evening. He was interested in us, took me out to dinner and made me tell him of my life in Africa. A few days later he called me to say that he had written me into his script and wanted me to play the part. Very surprised and after much hesitation I accepted, but I did not enjoy the experience or like my performance. I am not an actress.

I had had a brief flirtation with the movies once before. Soon after I married Lorenzo, I went to America on a publicity trip for a film I had worked on in Kenya called *Beyond Mombasa*, and ended up in Hollywood where I was approached by Columbia Pictures. They offered me a screen test and the famous seven-year contract, but they also told me I would have to forget about Lorenzo. So I walked away and flew back to Rome. When I told Lorenzo he was furious with me for throwing away such an opportunity to leave Italy and work in America. He told me he did not care if I succeeded, what angered him was that I hadn't even given it a try, or asked his advice. We nearly divorced. We were not yet aware then that we were afflicted by the same personality clash as had plagued my parents' lives.

Six years after I married him, I left Lorenzo for the first time. I went to live in Paris with my three-year-old Marina in a small studio apartment on the Left Bank belonging to my sister, and joined the sad and lonely ranks of separated women.

When I married Lorenzo I had created an image of a giant in whose shadow I would live. I clung stoically to my belief in our union and waited patiently for ten years for him to cast his shadow, but he never did. At first beside him, and then from afar, I watched him struggle with himself and the ruthless movie world in Rome. He strayed so far from the path of his dreams that he got completely lost. Bewildered and frightened, we did not know how to handle our relationship and made all the classic mistakes. My father had of course been right: Lorenzo was too much of an adventurer to stick to one woman. His father had once told me: "We all have a cross to carry through life, and Lorenzo will be yours."

CHAPTER 13

Uhuru

The Mau Mau emergency came to an end in 1956. Jomo Kenyatta, Kenya's first leader, had been sent into confinement by the British. His return in 1961, after eight years, eight months and two days of exile and detention, was without doubt the most significant event in the country's history.

Day after day Africans trekked to the house at Gatundu hoping to be the first to greet the man they now regarded as their Prophet and Deliverer. The women agreed that the first to see him would begin to ululate, and their cries would be heard by people far away, thus passing the message from ridge to ridge, from hut to hut, until it reached all the districts of Kenya.

They began arriving in the area on foot, on bicycles, in lorries, buses and cars, blocking all the roads, trailing goats, sheep and chickens behind them. Gifts poured in from all over the country and, on that same day, a polythene bag containing the entrails of a goat was left on the doorstep of the Colonial Secretary's flat in London. Pinned to the door of the flat was a notice which read: "Sacrificial goat for Mau Mau oathing release protest."

Next day, thousands more Kikuyu traipsed to Kenyatta's house and cheered as he shouted, "*Uhuru na Umoja, Uhuru na Mapenzi, Uhuru na Imani* (Freedom and Unity, Freedom and Love, Freedom and Peace)." Scarcely twelve months before, he had been labelled by the Governor "a leader to darkness and death".

When Kenyatta went to Nairobi several days later, the staid and solemn atmosphere surrounding Kenya's Parliament buildings was shattered. A wildly excited crowd swept aside police barriers to welcome their leader as he walked out of the building to greet them.

On 11th December, 1963, a radio message was sent from Nairobi

telling the world of Kenya's independence. The Duke of Edinburgh arrived from Zanzibar to preside over the end of sixty-eight years of British colonial rule. People of all races poured into the capital to celebrate independence. Two hundred and fifty thousand of them gathered in the Uhuru Stadium, their eyes cast skywards as they watched the rain clouds gather. The heavens opened and the rain poured down mercilessly as the ladies in their evening gowns, the heads of state, prime ministers and guests in full dress stepped out of their Rolls-Royces and Daimlers, hopelessly stuck in the red Nairobi mud, and picked their way to the tarmac.

As the Union Jack was lowered for the last time and the new black, red, green and white flag of Kenya was hoisted, the Duke of Edinburgh bent slightly towards the new President, Jomo Kenyatta, standing at attention by his side, and whispered, "Are you sure you don't want to change your mind?" as the strains of "God Save the Queen" blared out.

The last four hours of the Kenya Colony and Protectorate were filled with pageantry as 1,200 African dancers from Kenya's main tribes, in their colourful costumes, skins, feathers, rings and bangles arrived in the arena and staged a brilliant display of tribal dancing – in a dazzling array of shields, spears, skins, masks and ornaments. Then the old rhythms of Africa gave place to the pomp and ceremony of modern military music as the 300 men of the massed bands marched into the arena. After the Royal Salute to the Duke of Edinburgh, the guards faced each other in front of the Royal Box and the colours were handed over from the King's African Rifles to the Kenya Rifles. The old maroon fez with the royal cypher and crown was replaced by a black peaked forage cap, with the Kenyan coat of arms on badges of rank and uniform buttons.

"When you go back to England," Kenyatta said to the Duke, "take our greetings to the Queen and tell her we are still friends. It will be a friendship from the heart, more than what was there before."

The focus of attention at one point was on a group of former Mau Mau generals wearing smart new khaki uniforms with peaked caps and red tabs on their lapels. Some still had their long matted hair hanging to their shoulders under their caps. One of them arrived in his jungle skins, his simi and bows and arrows in his hand. Kenyatta walked over to them and examined the knives strapped to their chests. They told him they had come from the Aberdares and Mount Kenya. Kenyatta crossed to the dais and asked the Duke of Edinburgh and Mr MacDonald if they

Jomo Kenyatta . . . "Are you sure you don't want to change your mind?" the Duke of Edinburgh asked him on Independence Day.
(*Photo: Marion Kaplan, Camera Press Ltd*)

would like to meet the generals, but they both shook their heads in polite refusal.

Six months later many of these men were in gaol, having found it impossible to adapt to a peaceful way of life.

In June 1963, six months before independence, Kenyatta told the Director of Settlements that regardless of the cost in money, in lost production, in sorrow and in time, thirty thousand African families were to be settled on the white man's land before independence "Otherwise," he said, "we'll have a rebellion on our hands which will cost infinitely more." From Wanjohi, once the famous "Happy Valley", to Ol Kalau and the Kinangop, two hundred white families were removed from thirty thousand acres of land in six months and the British government paid £27,000,000 in compensation.

Bulldozers and tractors ripped and flattened the white man's country and made room for the wave of land-hungry, oppressed black people. Chickens, goats and mongrel dogs made their homes on mantelpieces, beneath bow windows without panes, or in niches where once antiques had stood. The roses, no longer cropped and pruned, went wild and grew through the cracked walls. Their delicate blooms peered unashamed through broken windows, and hung like living pictures on the crumbling walls. Charcoal fires, beneath sooty pots, burned in grandiose fireplaces where crackling flames once shone from polished English brass. Snotty African children in dirty cotton shirts played on flaking floors where the *musungu* had once danced in polished shoes.

Anticipating trouble, Dorian remained in Naivasha on Uhuru day. In a small celebration of their own, he waited with the farm labourers for midnight, beside the same old radio that had announced the outbreak of war to our parents. As the Kenyan National Anthem was played, there was an outburst of cheers and everyone ran out into the night and sang Kenyatta songs, hailing Jomo as their leader. Dorian and Reson looked at each other and winked. Reson spat on the ground – an old Ndorobo habit showing disapproval or distaste, got up, shook his head, and walked off to his hut, his gun slung over his shoulder.

PART IV

Not White Man's Country

CHAPTER 14

Dominio di Doriano

But the indelible stamp of British colonial rule had survived in Kenya and in Government House. Only the pigment changed: the pomp and ceremony remained essentially British. In the law courts, white wigs now framed black faces, but the high court judges continued to be English. In the field the stiff starched uniforms, knee-length socks and pith helmets held their own. With apparent ease and confidence the black senior government officials endorsed the habits of their white oppressors. The African slipped into the white man's role and a new type of colonialism was born when the Kikuyu replaced the British and the natives were referred to as Africans instead of "wogs".

Somehow Naivasha and the family fold had remained unaffected by these unsettling events. Time and the seasons had gently mellowed the great pink house and moulded the wandering garden that spread around it. The trees grew higher and thicker, the bougainvillaea and the rambling, flowering bushes spread, as my mother, with her indomitable energy, pushed the boundaries of her creation further up the hill and down towards the lake, and turned it into the sort of unkempt garden which the English are specialists in creating. She kept the house immaculate and filled it with exotic arrangements of flowers; she nagged her house servants so much they became the slickest in the country. She spent many hours each day teasing and prodding and encouraging her flowers to grow and her pathetic ragged gardeners to work. Eventually the garden grew so big she could no longer control it, and it turned into a wild hodge-podge of overgrown bushes, cacti, giant weeds and long African grasses.

My father persisted with his experiments on the farm. In his endless quest for a superior breed of cattle, he ended up with an interesting, if motley, herd of cattle of all sizes and colours, but without any identifiable species. He planted Italian poplars by the lake to prove that they could grow in Africa, and then lost interest in them. For the same reason, he produced outsize carnations and tomatoes from seeds and cuttings a friend had brought him from the Italian Riviera. They grew so large that he propped them up with twigs from his poplar trees, but within a few days these too had sprouted; so he watched them grow side by side until the poplars smothered the carnations. Both my parents were artists and what mattered to them was the act of creation, after which they grew bored, lost interest and turned to something new. For both of them, however, life on the farm provided the necessary occupational therapy they needed to keep their minds and bodies alive and well.

In July 1964 Oria met Giunio, a young Italian engineer on a reconnaissance trip in Kenya for the Santa Rita satellite base. Oria and I were introduced to him at a dinner party while we were holidaying together at the coast. He scarcely noticed me; his eyes shot past me to Oria and their contact was immediate and unquestioning. In her white dress with frangipani blossom in her hair she looked very much the sultry maiden of the tropics. That night she did not return home with me.

Oria and Giunio's romance was short and fiery. Within a month of their meeting they were married at our home in Naivasha. My father, Lorenzo and I were away in Europe at the time and were unable to attend the simple civil marriage ceremony in our home by the lake.

"We have launched our last ship," my father wrote laconically in his diary, as if he were ticking off the dates in his own life.

Outwardly, nothing much seemed to change in Naivasha. The Africans on the farm remained unaltered; a little older, perhaps a shade more battered and worn, but always cheerful, optimistic and eternally resigned. Each time Oria or I returned from abroad they would greet us with a new child and assure us that all was well.

But between Dorian and my father and Francine and my mother, and then later, maybe as a consequence, between Dorian and Francine, an unsettling rift began to appear. The rift seemed to grow each time I returned, and Dorian fell silent and sad. Always respectful and submissive, he struggled without joy through his days, and at night withdrew in suffocated frustration. A personality clash, reminiscent of my father's with his own father, was repeating itself. Each time Dorian gave an order or prepared a plan, my father would find a reason to countermand or change it. One day I talked to him, and urged him to move away. After much soul-searching and hesitation he left for Tanzania with a friend to start a new venture of his own.

In three years they broke two thousand acres of virgin land in the Tanzania plains and planted them with beans. It was a delicate, high-risk venture, like trying to make a living playing roulette, for its success depended on the rains. Intrigued by his crazy but challenging new scheme Lorenzo and I drove to Arusha to visit him. A little rain had fallen, all the beans had germinated, the young shoots had sprouted and lay like a fine pale green carpet in the vast brown untouched Africa around it. Dorian was living in a small wooden house with a corrugated-iron roof which he and three Africans had built on the top of a small hill from where he could watch his tractors and men at work around the clock. "This is where I live now," he said proudly. "It's not much yet, but it's all I need, and it's MINE."

With Dorian no longer on the farm my father now had to run it on his own, but his health began failing and he seemed suddenly to be ageing. Like a piece of worn machinery his body seemed to be breaking down. He had violent attacks of gout which crippled him for days, his endless cigarette chain-smoking had given him asthma and he had often to resort to an oxygen cylinder for relief. He was in and out of hospital the whole time and I got more and more involved in helping him on the farm. Either single-handed or with the help of Oria and Dorian, when they were around, I moved in and kept the farm going until he was well enough to take over again.

I had always got on very well with the Africans and enjoyed their company, but commanding the people on the farm, many of whom had watched us grow up, was different. With the added experience of my safaris behind me, I had begun to understand the code of "birth, copulation and death" by which they lived. Black people are natural, they possess the secret of joy, which is why they can survive the suffering and humiliation inflicted upon them. They are alive physically and emotionally which makes them easy to live with. What I had not yet learned to deal with was their cunning and their natural instinct for self-preservation. I set out a plan which, given a bit of luck, would turn the farm into a productive and profitable enterprise that would support us all.

The foundations on which we were to work had been established long ago by Dorian and my father and a skeleton force of old hands who had worked with them, were there to help us. John Mugo, the *karani* (headman), kept the books and supervised the labour; John Gatibaro, the mechanic, looked after the workshop and the machinery; and Reson, the old Ndorobo from our childhood days, cared for the cattle and the herders.

They had all been with us for many years, and formed the administrative structure of the farm, creating a link between us and the labour force, but they themselves also needed to be constantly watched and checked. The African does not measure time and has difficulty in understanding the importance the white man gives to it. The consequent disparity in productivity, the incomprehension and the constant, futile comparisons with the white man are among the main reasons for the intolerance and exasperation that often exists between the two races.

My parents never really adjusted to this situation and Dorian, Oria and I were still often caught off guard. However, remembering what André Gide had said about the blacks and whites I began accepting the Africans for what they were and stopped expecting them to be what they were not. With their smiling faces, their constant good humour and their ability to turn most situations into a joke, they somehow always managed to undermine our impatience and to endear themselves to us.

We held meetings in the farm office, or sat beneath the trees and on the fields with them and together we devised a plan of action. We enlisted the workers' help and tried to make them feel involved; we explained that we all had to pull together if our little venture was to succeed. If they stepped out of line, we warned them, they would feel the consequences. We were of course always in agreement and a general good-humoured togetherness was quickly established.

With the help of Roger, a meticulous and well-organised friend and neighbour, an ex-Public Works engineer and RAF pilot, we mapped out the land and divided it into plots. It all suddenly looked very professional.

Oria and I would rise each morning at six and work through the day planting the vegetables for the English export markets, branding and sorting cattle, and breaking new land. A deep sense of achievement welled up in me each time I rode my thoroughbred mare, Cassia, across the neatly planted acres of lake frontage, or inspected the herds with their fat, shiny calves. Our African teams worked beside us with renewed vigour and enthusiasm; their wit and good humour spurred us on.

With Roger's help and Dorian's advice we finally laid a pipeline from the lake front up the side of the hill behind the farm to provide water for the cattle nearer to their grazing grounds, a project we had talked about for almost fifteen years, but never executed. For two months a team of tough men hacked the pipe bed out of the hillside. The bush was thick and the ground hard and stony. For eight hours each day they worked under intense heat, and very slowly inched up the mountain, singing, laughing and chatting as they wiped the sweat from their faces and pulled thorns from their hands and feet. We celebrated the completion of the pipeline at the top of the hill with a large bonfire and bottles of beer and mutton roasted on an open fire.

As the crops matured and became ready for harvesting, the honeymoon period ended abruptly. We had to impose a curfew to curtail the stealing; armed guards patrolled the fields and were instructed to shoot at anything moving around the closed area after dark. "We don't want any of you to come and complain you have buckshot in your arse," we warned. The rows of silent faces looked on amused and we wondered what they were thinking. The old master/servant relationship replaced the initial feeling of togetherness and the eternal division between the haves and have-nots reasserted itself.

One day, a beautiful young Samburu warrior came to ask for work. His name was Nessa. "I am a *syce* (groom)," he told me when I asked him what he could do. I hired him, mainly because of his appearance, his gentle manner and the intelligent way he talked, and put him in charge of the stables. I gave him a hut and a week's advance on his salary to buy food.

A few days later a friend came to visit me. "I hear Nessa is working for you," he said. "I know him well, he used to work for me on my ranch. He is an excellent shot, but trigger-happy. He had to leave my ranch because he shot too many people while on guard duty."

"That's interesting. Perhaps he should guard the potatoes instead of the horses," I replied. Next day, Nessa went on night duty. We did not enjoy patrolling at night and I badly needed someone to keep watch.

My years in Africa had taught me never to take what I was told at face value. Explanations, interpretations and often downright denials turned situations into riddles. Making use of tribal discord, we put people from different tribes on the same job and, devoid of any feelings of disloyalty, they quite unabashedly reported each other's alleged misdeeds, sometimes with and sometimes without justification. In the latter case the practice was known as *fitina*. This is a form of personal vengeance, which can be used to secure jobs or wives, or to repay a grudge and dealing with it was one of the most difficult and intricate problems we had to face. But theft was rampant everywhere and some sort of watch was essential. The crops, the cattle, the milk, the tools – everything the Africans wanted and did not possess – were in constant jeopardy. The farm could not function without labour and the farmer was always vulnerable.

Nessa tenderly fondled the gun I gave him, delighted at this elevation in his rank. I handed him also an army greatcoat, and a hat, and briefed him well, assuring him that any information he divulged would remain confidential.

"You must not wander around during the day. When the night shift is over, bring the gun and coat back to me and go to bed and sleep," I told him. "You must be awake at night. There are a lot of crops in the fields, and it is your job to protect them from thieves." Nessa assured me he had understood.

Several days later, as I was riding my horse, I saw him walking around the neighbouring labour lines in broad daylight. "What are you doing here at this time of day? You are meant to be asleep," I called down.

He looked at me with his velvet eyes and smiled mischievously. "I'm following clues," he said, in a half-whisper. "I'll come and see you at nightfall and tell you."

At seven o'clock he appeared, fully dressed and armed for the night. "They are stealing the potatoes," he said triumphantly, and told me how each night the bags were being loaded onto a waiting lorry which stopped under the *mukuyu* tree on the main road. Was this *fitina*? "Come with me and you'll see for yourself, if you don't believe me," he said. "The night-watchmen are the organisers and are splitting the proceeds with the gang from Roger's farm."

I put on my jungle jacket and a pair of boots, grabbed a gun and told my parents I would be late for supper.

"They will meet about two hundred yards down the road," Nessa said, as we walked through the silent night. "You wait here in the maize.

Don't move. I'll go and meet them; they think I am with them. When I shoot, you come out and help me."

I ducked in among the tall maize stalks and watched his torch zigzag away from me. Lights flickered on and off in the direction he was walking and, after a while, figures carrying empty sacks began approaching. They passed in front of my hiding place, stopped by the pile of potatoes, and cheerfully started shovelling them in while Nessa watched.

The potato guard kept sweeping his torch beam around him. I ducked each time it passed over my head. Several times, it scanned the areas I was hiding in and moved towards me as if wanting to make sure all was well. Then the guard saw me. "*Musungu* (white man)," he shouted into the night. As if struck by lightning, the men dropped their bags and fled.

Nessa fired into the air and streaked after them, crossing the roughly ploughed field in his Japanese flip-flops. Alarmed by the shots, one of the men flung himself on the ground. I followed in hot pursuit and caught up with Nessa astride the prostrate thief. With one hand he gripped him firmly by the back of the neck, and rubbed his face into the ploughed soil. He pulled the trembling man to his feet and hit him across the head. "You bastard, you bloody thief," he yelled, his voice quivering. He was showing off to me now. "Get up, you bastard." He kicked him to his feet. "Show us the potatoes you have been stealing." He marched him back to the pile of potatoes.

"*Apana piga mimi* (Don't hit me please)," the man whimpered. '*Mi na kubali, na kubali* (I admit it, I admit it), please don't hit me any more." I felt suddenly sorry for the miserable fellow.

When we got to the potato pile the guard was standing over it looking very imposing, his rifle under his arm. "Thieves," he said to me, in a challenging voice, "we caught them."

I looked at Nessa who was trembling slightly. He dropped his gun, swung round and caught the guard by the back of the neck. His eyes flashed at me in the dark. "Get down on your knees too, you thief, you think you're so clever. Shovel the potatoes in with your friend."

"Me, what do you mean, me?" The guard looked up, imploring. "I'm not a thief. I'm the night guard."

I shone the torch into his face and said, "Go on, do as you're told, or I'll shoot your head off." I wasn't really angry yet, just helping Nessa out.

The guard dropped to his knees under the pressure of Nessa's hand. "Go on, shovel them in," Nessa shouted, and kicked him in the rear. We stood over the man with our guns. I didn't really fit the role. The guard kept turning to me imploringly, trying to explain that he had not had anything to do with it.

"Shut up," Nessa told him quietly. "Keep shovelling." Then he pulled him to his feet. He tied the two potato thieves together by the wrists with his belt, and marched them off in the direction of our house.

When we arrived at the front door, they stopped outside while I went in. Pa and Ma were finishing their evening meal. They looked up at me surprised and alarmed at my absence, my appearance, and the gun in my hand.

"Where have you been?" my father asked.

"Catching potato thieves," I replied.

"You're mad," my mother added. "Why do you have to do these things. I really can't understand you." She was obviously annoyed.

"Come," I said. "They're standing outside."

My parents got up and followed me. The three men outside were joined by two cattle guards who had heard the shots. In their army overcoats and hats, their shotguns slung over one shoulder, they flanked the culprits with the tell-tale bag of potatoes at their feet. The little group, silhouetted against the starry sky, formed a silent picture of hunters and hunted.

"What is the meaning of all this?" my father said in a stern croaky voice.

"*Bwana*, please, I have nothing to do with it, I can explain," the night guard pleaded, and looked up at him beseechingly.

"You bloody liar," I found myself shouting at him. A sudden rage pushed the words out of me; my exasperation had got the better of me, and I hit him across the mouth with a cane I had picked up on the entrance table. I had never hit anyone like this before and was surprised at the violence of my reaction to his persistent denial. It would have been so much better if he had just kept quiet.

"Don't hit me, *memsahib*," he sobbed, as he covered his face with his arm and spat a mouthful of blood to the ground. Full of remorse for having hit the poor fellow, I felt like dismissing the whole session, but I could not retreat now.

"Give me your gun and your torch and take off your coat," my father told him, and then turned to me and said, "Take them to the police."

The man obeyed without further resistance. What else could he do? His wrists were untied and I watched him unbutton his greatcoat. As it slipped off his body, the impressive protector of the farm turned into a shabby, snivelling, common thief, dressed in rags. As he handed us his coat, he shrank in size, his thin arms and bow legs protruded from his dirty short-sleeved shirt and shorts and put him on a par with any other small-time criminal.

Everyone piled into the car and we drove to the South Lake police station. It was ten o'clock at night. When we arrived, the place was empty except for a corporal, sitting behind a wooden table with an old-fashioned black telephone. He looked up sleepily as I marched in.

"Yes, ma'am, what can I do for you?"

"Where is the Inspector?"

"He is in his home."

"I want to see him, please," I said firmly. "We caught some thieves stealing our potatoes."

"Where are they" he asked.

I turned to Nessa and told him to unload our cargo. He marched them in, carrying the bag of stolen potatoes. It was essential that we produce evidence to back up our accusation.

"Did you steal these potatoes?" the corporal asked the two men.

"No we did not," they answered without hesitation.

Nessa now calmed down and, beginning to get bored with the whole thing, laughed and told them to stop lying. Triumph and disgust crossed the gentle contours of his face. The men were led into a small, dark, damp-smelling cement cell. The heavy door slammed behind them and the key turned. I had had enough for the night and longed to get home and go to bed.

"The Inspector is not in," the man who had been sent to call him returned to tell us. Nessa and I made a statement of the evening's events to the corporal on duty, who slowly and painstakingly tapped out the report with one finger on a heavy old typewriter.

When we got home, I made Nessa a cup of tea and slipped a hundred shillings in his hand.

"Each time you catch someone I'll give you a hundred bob. Don't worry, I'll stand behind you. We must try and clear up this place." But as I heard myself speak, I knew I was fighting a losing battle.

My feelings about the whole African scene were very mixed. I intensely disliked doing what I had done that night. There would no doubt be many repetitions and I did not like the prospect though it was part of the farmer's lot.

Next day, everyone was talking about the night's event. Nessa had earned himself the reputation of a *kali*, guy, spying for the *memsahib*, and people began to fear and avoid him. He quickly became very unpopular on the farm and wandered about alone. I was his only ally. But when the case came up in the little African court in Naivasha several months later, it was dismissed for lack of sufficient evidence because I was absent, and the two men came back to the farm to ask for work, as if nothing had happened.

A few months later Oria told me that Nessa was stealing the onions and the oranges. Deeply dismayed, I confronted him and asked for an explanation. He denied all accusations, and said he was a victim of *fitina*. I watched Nessa closely for a week, without saying anything. Each time I went to look for him he was not on duty. He had taken up with Nalutesha, a tall, young, good-looking Maasai woman working for Oria. We had been told that together they delivered the stolen bags of onions and oranges to the milk lorry on the main road. I talked it over with Oria and we made a plan to catch them out.

One night Oria called at their hut. When the door was opened Nessa and Nalutesha stood facing her both stark naked. Several nets of onions and oranges were stacked in a corner of the hut awaiting delivery. They just stood there unashamedly like Adam and Eve and said nothing.

"Give me your gun, Nessa," Oria said to him, trying to keep her voice calm. "You had better not let my sister see you around tomorrow." Nessa smiled sheepishly, shrugged his shoulders and handed her the gun.

He was dismissed and we never saw him again. We heard several months later that he had got caught up in a drunken brawl in Nairobi and had had his throat slit.

Nessa was replaced by another young warrior who claimed he was Reson's son, but he did not last either and was replaced by yet another, and another and still another. Reson had been with us almost twenty years; he had watched us grow up and we had watched him grow old. One day he told us he had always hated working and wanted to return to the reserve. He was a *mzee* (elder) now and it was time to sit back and let his wife and children look after him. He had grown thin and lost many teeth and was often on sick leave. My father had tried for years to cure him of the chronic syphilis from which he had suffered since he was a warrior, but to no avail. He had pains in his body and his back, his knees were stiff and he now spent many hours each day huddled over a fire in his hut wrapped in a worn, dirty blanket, chewing tobacco and spitting on the ground. Yet we were sorry to see him go.

A pleasant, intelligent-looking man of about fifty presented himself for the job. Dika was a Boran from the Northern Frontier District of Kenya. He seemed knowledgeable enough and answered the questions I put to him with prompt replies in good Swahili, He extracted some excellent letters of recommendation from a plastic wallet he carried in the back of his pocket: tattered letters, dated ten and fifteen years back and held together with Scotch tape. I hired him after the interview and gave him a week's advance on his salary and a few days' leave to go and collect his family. He returned with a bunch of pretty, slender girls with brown satin skin, and some tough-looking, lean men with wild fiery eyes and loud, guttural voices. They were his daughters and his sisters, his wife, his cousins and his in-laws – all tall, handsome people with the straight noses and soft, elongated eyes, long, thin hands and delicate wrists and ankles typical of their tribe.

We had never employed any Boran before and I liked the idea of having this group of decorative people working for me, so I hired the lot. They formed a little settlement of their own within the compound, and kept much to themselves. They were Muslims, and considered themselves superior to the common labourers on the farm.

Dika and his group quickly became my favourites. He himself knew a great deal about cattle, and I was impressed by the interest and goodwill he put into his work. We became good friends and his family held a special place in my heart. Their little group was known as "Mirella's Borans".

Dika explained to me that the Boran, like the Maasai, were milk-drinking people, and asked that I allow them to milk a few cows to avoid milk being stolen. This seemed reasonable enough and I acquiesced on condition that the calves did not suffer. "When the milk drops, change the cow. Don't let me find your family growing fat and my calves growing thin," I warned him. "Don't worry, *memsahib*," he answered.

One day he came rushing up to me, alarmed and out of breath. "*Memsahib*, there are eight head of cattle missing. All the best Charolais

heifers in calf." He spat out the words with rage. "Call the police quick. I will go up into the hills with my men and look for them. If I see any Maasai I will shoot them."

His blood was up, but I knew that the chances that he would catch up with the thieves were slim. The Maasai are adept cattle thieves and menaced herders with spears and *rungus* and will kill if necessary.

The inspector from the South Lake police station promised me he would send out a foot patrol immediately to cut off the thieves before they reached the border of the Maasai reserve. Dika and his men returned twelve hours later, tired, footsore, empty-handed and very angry. They had followed the tracks for several hours but had lost them in the thick undergrowth.

Next day they went back into the hills and returned at dusk with one of their men wounded in the leg. They had chased the thieves all day and had got into a fight with them. One of Dika's men had been slashed as his naked quarry slipped away from him into the bushes. They had shot one thief and thrown his body into a ravine for the hyenas.

"It is better that way," Dika explained. "The police would start asking questions instead of looking for our cattle." They continued their search for a week after that, and left each day at dawn but returned empty-handed at night.

A week later I had to go into hospital in Nairobi for a small operation. From my hospital bed I called the police station each day to ask for news of the cattle. They eventually informed me that eight heifers in calf had been retrieved outside the Ngong meat market in the vicinity of Nairobi, and gave me a brief description; they were ours all right. Delighted at the successful outcome of our chase, I made arrangements immediately for the heifers to be returned to the farm. But the Veterinary Department told me that they had to remain in quarantine for two weeks. During the next ten days, four of the heifers gave birth to their calves and then one by one they all died of rinderpest, before the quarantine period was up. They had all contracted the disease on their journey from Naivasha to Ngong.

Dika seemed as upset as I was, and tightened the security in a rage. But despite all his show of solidarity, two years later he too was caught illicitly selling the milk from the dairy to the other labourers and had to be dismissed.

Frustrated and angry at having been hoodwinked again by someone I

. . . the Boran girls had long slinky bodies, brown skin and the delicate hands and wrists typical of their tribe.

thought I could trust, I watched my group of beautiful Borans walk away from me with their arrogant stride and haughty expression. Heads held high, their belongings perched on their heads, their flowing robes billowed behind them gracefully, as they walked out of my life back into Africa.

Most of our time on the farm was spent chasing up the people who worked on it. People who were stealing or shirking work, sleeping under the trees, beneath tarpaulins and under cars or tractors, or sitting around gossiping. They would always, persistently and convincingly, deny all allegations even when they were caught red-handed. The Africans are the most refined, cool-headed liars I have ever come across. They taught me a few things about keeping calm under duress. I ultimately came to the conclusion that the African intensely dislikes working for anyone other than himself, and when necessity forces him to do so he retaliates by offering a minimum of exertion for a maximum of gain; his apparent laziness and lack of initiative are his only means of revenge for being, as he considers, exploited, and he depends for his survival on his ability to lie.

The lack of initiative is usually justified by a claim that they are awaiting orders. They can stand by and watch things slowly grind to a halt; weeds grow, flowers die, roofs cave in, water tanks leak and collapse, dust and cobwebs spread, and then, when questioned, they answer with a disarming smile: "But I was waiting for you to return" – and proceed to put things right with immaculate precision. Yet I have sometimes visited the homes of friends, absent for a long period, and found the place looking spotless; the servants on duty dressed in starched white uniforms inviting me in for tea or drinks as if the mistress of the house was just around the corner.

It is therefore impossible and unfair to make generalisations about "African" behaviour. So much has to do with their attitude to life, their resentment of exploitation, their fatalism and their belief in *shauri ya mungu*, the will of God.

Life on an African farm has its ups and downs, with the downs often more frequent than the ups. It is an unrelenting battle in which the farmer has to deal not only with the people but also with the temperamental weather, and the abundant wildlife which can undo all his sweat and hard work in a moment. Once, in despair, I christened Naivasha "Heartbreak Farm".

None the less, from Naivasha I drew the necessary courage and strength to live my life without Lorenzo. He visited me frequently on the farm, for he too was having difficulty adapting to life on his own. In Africa at least there were rarely any problems between us, and we lived intense, happy moments together, on safari in the bush, by the sea, or on the farm, and Amina was conceived on Lake Rudolph.

A year after we first left each other we went back again to Lake Rudolph and returned to a world we had almost forgotten. We camped on the shores of the huge African lake and shared the blistering days with the wild birds and the Turkana people. Lorenzo fished for Nile perch and I took some new photographs. We were so remote from our own complicated "civilised" world that we lost our protective shells, and for a delicious giddy period we found each other again.

At the end of the safari we had dinner in Nairobi with Jack Block, a long-standing friend of mine. I showed him my pictures of Lake Rudolph and spoke to him of my idea of making a record of Africa's last vanishing tribes before they disappeared for ever. He seemed intrigued and was most encouraging. Without telling me, he wrote next day to a friend in London recommending me and my project. The man was Sir William (Billy) Collins of the well-known publishing house.

I returned alone to Paris with my pictures, pregnant again, and Lorenzo returned to his new Mediterranean lady. Amina, my second daughter, was born in Genoa by caesarian section, two months prematurely. Lorenzo was not there. She weighed just one pound and lived in an incubator for two months. When she was ready to emerge into the world I took her back to Paris in a wicker basket.

I was so enmeshed in my emotional problems that I did not bother to open a letter which had arrived from London and let it lie on my desk for several weeks. Then I opened it. It was from Billy Collins inviting me to come to London and meet him.

It was a turning point in my life. I was able to break the curse of obsession and possession. I emerged from my despair and anguish and turned my back on them. I was able at last to live without the malady of doubt. There were silences in my head. Periods of peace and enjoyment. It was as if the cancer in me had ceased gnawing, but it was the result of struggle, of many years of passionate living. I embarked on the greatest, most satisfying adventure of my life. *Vanishing Africa* was born.

CHAPTER 15

Vanishing Africa

I arrived in London unannounced and found that Billy Collins had left for Australia the day before and would not be back for three months. I was received instead by Adrian House, one of his senior editors, a charming, grey-haired, very English gentleman, who said he could give me a quarter of hour at the end of the day.

I showed him my pictures and told him of my project. "I want to record the tribal life and customs of the African people before they change for ever," I said, and we talked about my life in Africa and the new independent government. The fifteen-minute interview spilled into several hours, at the end of which he suggested I send my photographs to Billy Collins in Australia, with an accompanying letter from him.

I returned to Paris. Forty-eight hours later the phone rang in my apartment. "Mirella, listen to this," Adrian said excitedly. He read me a cable he had just received: "'MARVELLOUS PHOTOGRAPHS STOP PUT HER UNDER CONTRACT STOP GET WORLD EXCLUSIVITY GIVE HER FIVE THOUSAND POUNDS AND TELL HER TO GO STOP BILLY'. You had better come back to London to discuss plans." Next day I was back in Adrian's office.

Three weeks later I landed in Nairobi, having packed my bags, let my flat in Paris and called Lorenzo in St Tropez to say goodbye. My new life had begun. It had all happened so quickly I had not stopped to think what I had let myself in for.

It was only when I was back on the farm that the full extent of my project became apparent to me. I had no idea how to begin. Billy Collins had given me *carte blanche*. I was free to do what I liked and it was now up to me to deliver. I felt like a painter in front of an empty canvas and I still had no idea where to put the first brush stroke. And what of my children and the condition of my soul?

It took me three months to get organised. I discussed my plans with Dorian and Oria who, fortunately, were in Kenya at the time, and with the help of my ever-supportive parents, I sorted out my life. I bought a second-hand Toyota Landcruiser on which the farm mechanic built a sturdy roofrack and two jerrycan holders, procured a tent and camping equipment from a friend leaving the country; stole Kimuyu, the family cook, from the house, and then turned to Oria and said, "Come with me, I can't do it on my own."

Oria and Giunio had now been married for several years. But Giunio was often away; his work sent him to distant countries, most of which did not welcome women. He lived on oil rigs, platforms and rough drilling boats in the Persian Gulf, the North Sea or in the Pacific and Indian Oceans, with his divers, mechanics and engineers. It was a tough, nomadic life full of storms and waves and blistering sun.

Oria once tried to follow him to a rig near Bahrain in the Persian Gulf. She entered the prohibited area dressed as one of Giunio's men, in oilskins and rubber boots, her long hair tucked beneath a seaman's cap. She got through the security checkpoint with false identity papers and lived for a week on the steel barge with Giunio and his divers before she was discovered. She was instantly removed and Giunio nearly lost his job.

She then set up a home for them in Milan, but he was seldom there to share it with her, and she quickly became bored with her new life. Her energy found no outlet in the asphalt city she had exchanged for her free-wheeling African world.

Milan and Naivasha had nothing in common, nor did Giunio's life and hers. Giunio knew that if he did not change his life he would lose her, and while she waited for him, she found the company she needed and could not get from him in the pounding city. They left each other. Oria walked out of their house and returned to Naivasha, wounded, relieved and a bit surprised at his sudden show of strength and determination. A year later they were divorced, but they remained close friends.

Oria and I had drifted apart after we left school and went to Europe – our marriages separated us even further and I for my part was so involved in my own survival I almost forgot her. But in Naivasha, after she had left Giunio, we found each other again. On the morning of 23rd November, 1967, we set off on the first leg of my big African adventure.

OVERLEAF   Samburu Warrior. . . . I wanted to record
the tribal life and customs of the African people.

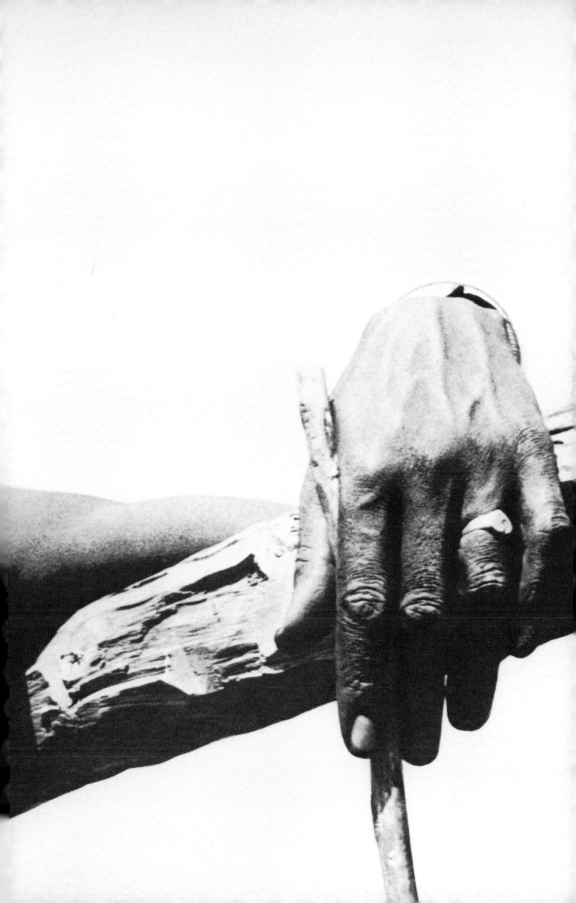

My parents, Dorian, the children, the house servants, the dogs, cats and a handful of farm labourers stood around watching our final preparations, helping to load the car, fasten the canvasses, tie the ropes and pose for a commemorative photograph. My parents, arm in arm, looked on proud and perhaps a little apprehensive; everybody clapped and cheered as we drove off in a cloud of dust, the Landcruiser packed tight and top heavy, and began the slow, hot drive to Maralal and the Samburu tribe.

Oria left me after the first safari, and I adapted slowly to my new nomadic life. While I explored Kenya with my camera, I met many kinds of people in the outlying districts. The tribes I visited differed greatly from each other, but they all shared one similarity, which I discovered later was very important to the survival of the human race. They had adapted to their environment and did not crave for things beyond their immediate needs. They seemed primitive by our standards, but their simple code of life was built on the basic laws of survival: eating, sleeping and reproducing. They solved their problems in their own ways, and law and order were kept by the elders of the clan. Women never questioned their positions as perpetuators of the tribe and the children grew up naturally, according to the teachings of the elders for generations back.

After each safari I returned to the farm in Naivasha to service and repair my vehicle, stock up with provisions, develop my film and look at my contact sheets. In my quest for the still uncontaminated tribes of Kenya I had to enter troubled areas in the reserve where few if any outsiders were admitted. Those who entered had to provide legitimate reasons and be granted special permission which was often difficult to obtain, and the officials in Nairobi could not understand why I was so interested in photographing "backward" tribal life, rather than the modern Africa which had emerged since independence.

In the two years I spent on my eight safaris, collecting my photographs, I travelled thirty-five thousand miles criss-crossing Kenya and worked in areas so varied that it was sometimes difficult to believe that I was still in the same country.

The night I arrived in Watamu, a tiny village beside the Indian Ocean, I retired early and was soon sleeping heavily after a long, hot drive from Nairobi. I had left the large arched window of my bedroom wide open so I could listen to the wind in the palm trees and feel the cool breeze on my tired body. The moon was full and it was very light outside. Several hours later I awoke suddenly to see a figure shuffling about not far from my pillow. His arms hung long and slightly bent on either side of his stocky body. He looked like a large ape. Startled, but surprisingly cold-headed, I shot up stark naked onto my bed and shouted at him to get out. He just stood there staring at me in the dark, and then moved very slowly to the foot of the bed and stopped. I grabbed my pillow, the only thing I had within reach, and clobbered him over the head with it, trying hard to hide my fear. He flew at me, and hit me across the face. He then slithered towards the window leaving me transfixed and terrified, still clasping my stupid, useless pillow. He quietly bent down to pick up my radio, jumped out through the open window into the night and disappeared down the path onto the beach. I woke the servants and sent them after him, but the beach was quite deserted, his footsteps lost in the thick seaweed lying on the sand. Half-heartedly, I went to notify the village chief and the police and was very surprised when the intruder was picked up the next day just as the sun was rising, standing by the bus stop wearing two suits of clothes. In his basket they found my radio and a large wad of money, all part of the night's loot. He had visited four homes before mine. The following day a small boy came up the path to my house and handed me a letter.

Plot 10, Watamu

Dear Madam,

I am writing this letter with the utmost integrity towards everything in general. I fully sympathies with you for the unfortunate night you had your radio stollen and the rough time the intruder gave you. I relize what a shock it had been to you asspecially a lonely lady in an isolated are like the one house you are occopying. I fully sumpathies with you beyond any reasonable doubt.

I have a feeling I must share with you. The first time I met you I fell hard in love with you and realizing very well the fact you are married. I have invainly fought this feeling back to control my emotions but fell back on the point that I must let you know that I am deeply in love with you. You might be aware there are moments were a man could not controll himself against them.

Please do not be hard on me in case you are not pleased in the manner I have present myself to you as far it is, I have played square and

there are cards for you to take your turn.
Excuse all the stuff if you do not fit in the picture and lete me know of
the proceedings.

Yours afficionuley,
Sub Chief,
Watamu.

While I was searching for the shy black-veiled Bajun women of the
coast, I set up my headquarters in a small house on the beach and
disregarded the unfortunate incident of the thief. Every day at noon
when the light was too strong for pictures, the tide was low, and the coral
reef lay only inches below the surface of the water, I would spend long
hours lying in the sun or bathing in the warm sea. One day I noticed two
black specks in the distance standing out against the pale midday sky.
They grew larger as they approached, until two men dressed only in
diminutive striped *kikois* knotted around their hips stopped a few feet
from me. Their tattered straw hats were pulled low over their eyes, a
worn coconut basket at the end of a stick hung over the shoulder of one
of them. I greeted them in Kiswahili and asked them what they had in
their basket. They squatted on their heels beside me.

"Shells," they said, "Do you want some?" and laid them around me.

"Where do you come from?"

"From the village over there," one of them said, and looked up at me
from beneath his hat. I saw the most beautiful black face I had ever set
eyes upon.

"What is your name?" I asked him.

"Shaibu," he answered. "What is yours?"

He invited me to tea at his house that evening to meet his family.

The coastal people of Kenya are a mixture of Arab and Bantu, and are
not renowned for their height or beauty, but Shaibu was an exception.
He was long and sinewy, and when he turned his head he arched his neck
in a way which made him seem aloof and inaccessible. The skin of his
face was smooth and silky and light brown. It rippled in the sunlight – I
wanted to touch it. His long fine straight nose, delicate nostrils and soft,
slightly slanted brown eyes were not typical of the tribe.

I spent six weeks at the coast and saw Shaibu every day. I went fishing
and diving with him, and later sailed with him and his brothers in their
dhow to the Arab town of Lamu and to the Bajun Islands.

... "What is your name?" I asked him, "Shaibu," he answered ...
I looked on Shaibu not as a black man but simply as a man ...

OVERLEAF   When I left for the Bajun islands with Shaibu (top left) and his
brothers on their dhow, I immediately trespassed onto his territory.

Shaibu had never left his village. He spoke no English and he could not read or write. But he and Kimuyu became a tightly knit team, without whom I would never have been able to get through my project as I did. They relieved my solitude and the deep depressions I fell into. Their gaiety and sense of adventure, their unquestioning and total loyalty under any circumstances, helped to turn my two years into an unforgettable adventure.

Once in the Northern Frontier District I met an old man leading his camel along a dry river bed, looking for water. It was midday, and the sun bit into my back. The light was intense and around me Africa lay parched and silent, like a solid brown sea. The old man came up and squatted beside me while his camel sucked thirstily at the muddy water in the hollow at our feet. Dressed in a tattered pair of khaki shorts, an old sweat-soaked raincoat, and the relics of a felt hat, he told me he had been a soldier in the King's African Rifles for many years, had fought with the British in Burma, and had returned to his tribe when he was demobilised.

"What are you doing here?" he asked me in his croaky voice. I told him I was taking pictures and explained about my work.

"What do you think of all these changes that are taking place in our country?"

"What do you think?" I asked in return, more interested in his answer than in my own.

"I don't know," he said. "I find it very difficult to follow this new government."

"Do you think you were better off when the *musungu* were running the country?" I asked hesitantly.

"Oh, yes, *memsahib*, it was better then. The people in the government today seem more interested in power and in their own ambitions than in helping us who live far away. We never see or feel any of the things these people come to talk to us about."

I did not answer and we sat in silence for a while.

"Can you go back to Nairobi and tell them that we are not pleased?" he asked me.

"Yes, I can," I answered. "But I don't think anyone would listen to me."

The camel had sucked up all the water in the hole, and towered above us waiting for us to be done. The old man got up.

"*Haya Kwaheri* (goodbye), I must go home. The sun is very hot and I am tired. I have walked since daybreak, maybe I will see you again in the village."

I watched them winding away down the dry river bed: tiny wisps of dust jumped from their feet. I sat for a while listening to the silence, and in my mind saw a confused picture, all out of focus; the only thing that seemed really real was the fierce Africa that surrounded me.

Oria was with me again. Together we travelled to Kapedo, north of Lake Baringo, where we spent several days at a Catholic mission. Kapedo was at the end of nowhere. We had been told that there was a beautiful waterfall in a deep ravine. The road was almost non-existent, there was no sign of life. Great boulders and deep gullies, fallen trees and lacerated roots lay across the land like the left-overs of some giants' battle. Night was falling when we pulled up in front of a small grey stone building.

Three smiling nuns with strong Irish accents came out to meet us. They asked us in, gave us orange squash, and invited us for dinner. The next day was Sunday, and they asked us if we would like to attend mass.

We woke early the following morning, and found our tent encircled by hundreds of Turkana squatting at a safe distance. They had come from all around for Sunday mass and had set up watch around our tents to see what would emerge from them. Many had ostrich feathers in their earth-caked hair; the women and girls, their necks stiff with beads, were greased with fat and red ochre, and glistened in the early morning sun.

When we stepped out of the tent a murmur broke from the crowd. Little by little our inquisitive audience inched towards us until our tents were surrounded and we were greeted with a lot of guttural sounds, hand-shaking and spitting. Kimuyu and Shaibu were amused by these wild people, but they soon became annoyed by their persistence, and managed, we never found out how, to persuade them to move on so that they could go to the lake to fish.

Father O'Reagan, who came from a mission a hundred miles away, arrived in his Land-Rover at eleven o'clock. The Turkana, with their feathers and beads and acrid-smelling grease, moved from our tent to the stone schoolhouse. They trooped in from the sun and sat on the wooden benches in the cool interior. An altar with a clean white cloth, a crucifix and two silver candle-holders had been set up at one end. Father O'Reagan slipped on his robes. Two black assistants swung incense

OVERLEAF   Rendille elders at the District Commissioners *barrazza* in the Northern Frontier District. "... Can you go back to Nairobi and tell them we are not pleased?" they asked me.

burners, and a mission boy read the sermon in Turkana before the Latin mass began. My sister and I were an obvious distraction. We tried to remain as unobtrusive as possible, but I could not resist raising my camera to take a picture. The congregation stirred and covered their heads with their cow skins and cloths. I put my camera down and the mass continued. At the elevations someone farted loudly and a wave of muffled giggles broke out. Oria and I looked at each other from beneath lowered eyes and bit our lips. The priest and nuns frowned and pretended they had heard nothing. At that very moment Kimuyu and Shaibu appeared outside the door with the largest perch I have ever seen slung on the end of a pole.

The Turkana rose to their feet and clattered out of the church into the sunlight and rushed like demented animals after them. Within seconds the fish was torn from the pole and slashed to pieces with their sharp wrist knives, and an unbelievable free-for-all ensued. Shaibu and Kimuyu, shaken by this unexpected onslaught, scrambled out from beneath them and watched their fish disintegrate and be carried off by the fortunate few who had got in first.

When the mass was over I apologised to Father O'Reagan for the interference. He just looked at me with kind laughing eyes and shrugged. "It is quite natural," he said. "These people come to the mission driven by hunger and sickness. The masses and religious teachings are only a pretext for our presence in their midst; the daily contact is what matters. If we have one real convert in a thousand we are lucky." We left the next day carrying with us a pile of letters from the nuns for their relatives in Ireland. They had not been home for over five years and had been to Nairobi only three times since they settled in Kapedo.

On Lake Rudolph, we came across a white man who was building a tourist lodge on a spit of sand in Ferguson's Gulf. I crossed the bay with Shaibu in one of the long slender canoes provided by the government to encourage the Turkana fishermen to catch more fish, and scrambled up the sandy embankment on the other side. A great silence hung around us and the place seemed quite deserted until we heard hammering in a nearby hut. A sunbaked European stood on a stool, banging a nail into a window frame. He turned when I greeted him. He had wild, pale blue eyes, hard and piercing, but when he saw me his expression softened to a surprised smile. He was obviously not used to visitors, especially females. We introduced ourselves. Shaibu standing beside me greeted him in Swahili. The man did not answer and seemed not to have noticed him. Shaibu repeated his greeting louder and the man threw him a mumbled, off-hand acknowledgement.

Inside the hut it was dark and cool and all around were stacked cases of beer and sodas and Coca Cola; a collection of unmatched glasses stood on an enormous white enamel fridge. The man poured me an ice-cold gin and tonic and dropped in a slice of lemon. Shy of Europeans he did not know, Shaibu remained outside. I asked my new acquaintance if I might give him something to drink. The man looked at me surprised and, after an initial moment of hesitation, acquiesced. He was about to pour some iced water into a glass when he looked up at Shaibu. He put down the glass and bottle of cold water, picked up a tin mug, filled it from the tap and handed it to him. Shaibu swallowed the lukewarm water, put the mug back on the window sill, and walked away from us. I followed him with my eyes and then turned and glared at the white man beside me, suddenly furious at the preposterous situation. Here we were, three human beings in one of the remotest corners of the earth, unable to drink a glass of cold water together in the shade because we were of different pigmentation. Then I remembered how many times I myself had done the same sort of thing in the past, when whites and blacks did not drink from the same glass, and how on the other hand I had always been hospitably received by Shaibu's people. The European asked me to stay to lunch, but I could not accept. I felt that my place was now beside Shaibu; I thanked him and bade him farewell and slid down the shady embankment with Shaibu.

We left Ferguson's Gulf a month later, the fleeting images of the lake now captured on my film – its misty colours, its shining fishermen, the arrogant-faced women with their urgent stride, leather skirts flapping behind them in the wind, fat, polished children with silver fish on their heads, long, skinny girls with pounds of coloured beads around their necks, and old men with hands like claws. A beautiful, primitive people and their magic lake.

I always tried to make my returns to the farm coincide with the children's holidays. They loved to listen to the stories of my adventures and followed my life through the pictures I brought home.

Amina, once, when only a tiny child, burst out as the lights came on: "Oh, Mama, I'm so proud of you!" My parents too were avid listeners and never missed a slide projection.

The first serious signs of old age were beginning to manifest themselves in my father, now well past seventy. He had been suffering from gout for many years and we often had to sit with him through the night holding ice packs against the painful, swollen joints.

One morning a few days after my return from Lake Rudolph, he suddenly left the breakfast table. When my mother went to look for him she found him sitting on his bed bent double, holding his head in has hands and complaining of severe pains in his stomach. We drove him to Nairobi. A few hours later he was in the operating theatre. Over the years the doctors had given him Cortisone to relieve the pain of his gout and the side effects of this drug had eventually perforated his stomach. The wound would not heal. Three days later, the internal suture began to bleed again. The doctors said another operation would be fatal, and he weakened steadily as the bleeding increased. One afternoon, just a week after he had entered the hospital, he feebly dictated his will to Oria standing by his bed. In it he told us to look after our mother and asked to be cremated beneath the cypress trees in the garden. Dorian was to light the bier.

We called Dorian, far away in Tanzania, on the radio and sent a plane to collect him, but when it arrived it could not land for the rains had been so heavy that the strip was inundated. The pilot flung him a message in an empty cartridge case and flew home. Dorian arrived in Nairobi in his mudcaked Land-Rover at three o'clock the following morning.

We entered the hospital room together. Our father, breathing faintly, lay in the soft white folds of his bed, staring at the crucifix on the opposite wall and did not seem to notice or recognise us. "Go home and get some sleep," I told Dorian. "Oria and I will spend the night in a room beside him."

When I entered his room again he turned his eyes towards me. A faint light streaked the sky outside his window. The moon had set, the stars had gone, a crested crane flew by. A new day was breaking. He had survived the night. I held his hand and we looked at each other. He smiled at me, and seemed surprised to be still alive. When the sister came in and asked him how he was, he murmured, "Okay," and then feebly added, "Thank you, sister, thank you for this new day, thank you for life." I knew now he was going to make it. Slowly the bleeding stopped, the tubes were extracted and a month later he left the hospital like a shadow, weak and thin, but alive. His body had shrunk and he suddenly looked a hundred years old. His great vigour and zest for life had hidden the slow corrosion of the years and we had been quite unaware of the change that was slowly taking place. He shuffled around, bent and tired, with hollow cheeks and sunken, ancient eyes. He was so frail that it was difficult now to imagine the man I had grown up with.

He returned to the farm where he was greeted by flower-waving Africans and all work stopped for the day as they lined the road leading to the house. An ox was slaughtered and the meat distributed between them as was the custom for the celebration of a special occasion. *Mzee* Rocco had come back to them – but he was going to have to start letting go of the reins.

When my father was strong enough again, we handed the farm back to him, and I returned to my book and the bush, heading north again with Shaibu and Kimuyu to Marsabit and the Boran tribe. But this journey was the end of my *Vanishing Africa* project. Two years had passed since I had landed in Nairobi. September was gone. The rains were due again, and I knew I had to get out of the area before they broke. Every day new signs told me how little time I had left. The wind pulled at my tent, keeping it in constant motion, flapping and groaning. It grew very cold and dark, far away great claps of thunder rolled through the sky, and then the heavens opened. It poured for hours, and the red soil around the tents turned into sticky clay and slipped away in rivulets. We did not wait for morning, but broke camp, packed the soaking tents, and left at six o'clock that evening. The return journey was disastrous. Every half-mile we had to stop and dig ourselves out of the mud. It took us three days and three nights to cover the hundred miles back to Nairobi. The same trip had taken us nine hours in the dry weather only three weeks before. I had had enough of life on safari, and decided to close down. My romance with Africa was over.

Vanishing Africa was published two years later, in September 1971, and became a bestseller. Princess Anne opened the exhibition of my photographs in the Time-Life building in Bond Street in London, and Lorenzo's father flew from Italy for the occasion. Oria and Lorenzo and their friends worked with me into the early hours of the morning hanging the outsize pictures. When we had finished, two years of my life looked down at me with the wild eyes of Africa.

OVERLEAF Wilderness children in Marsabit.

CHAPTER 16

Storm Clouds

For three successive years the rains failed in Tanzania and Dorian lost all his bean crops. He was forced to close down and sell off his tractors and ploughs to pay his debts. He dismissed his men and left Tanzania, beaten again.

He was now over thirty, and returned to Naivasha to try yet again to run the farm with his father. Naivasha had increasingly magnetic powers for all of us, for it represented a haven of peace towards which we instinctively turned when all else failed. Our parents were always there to receive and welcome us; they kept the place together and were always ready to listen to our stories and offer help or advice.

But Dorian was in trouble. His marriage was not working out and he had failed in his third attempt at self-assertion. Francine had been unable to pierce the thick protective shell of our family. She found Oria and me overbearing and resented my relationship with Dorian, although neither of us was aware of this feeling at the time. The growing tension between her and myself exploded one day at the breakfast table in front of all the family when, after a stupid argument about some fried eggs, she and I flew at each other and I struck her in the face. Within seconds we were locked in combat. As she rose to strike me back I grabbed hold of her long soft carrot hair and pulled her head down at right angles. She caught hold of my shirt and like two fiery dragons, we breathed heavily down each other's necks. Neither could move. Dorian at the head of the table sprang to his feet, shouting, "Let go of her," and socked me in the jaw, more surprised than infuriated. Attracted by the scuffle, the house servants came rushing from the kitchen. With Oria and Dorian on one side they tugged at us until they separated us. Tight-lipped and shaking, Francine and I glared at one another. With a handful of red hair in my fist I stomped out of the room pulling my bewildered children behind me. I saddled my horse, and disappeared into the hills for the rest of the day.

My mother always said that Dorian had been born under an unlucky star. Yet he is an eternal optimist, a survivor who refuses to let life get on top of him. A strange mixture of contradictions, he is initially the victim and ultimately the victor of his circumstances. He is a dreamer and his dreams keep him afloat. Like most over-loved people, he was badly loved and had been unwittingly smothered by the women in the family. We somehow always expected something more from him, but kept telling him what to do and say and think. For the sake of peace he held his tongue, always agreed with everyone. As stubborn as the rest of us, he took little notice of what was said to him and went his own way.

He found the companionship he failed to get in the family among the Africans on the farm. The African has a particular gift for communication and will rarely turn his back on anyone seeking his company. He is an avid listener and an inexhaustible conversationalist which probably accounts for the fact that one seldom feels alone or lonely in Africa. My parents remained unaware of this but as they grew old the faithful natives were always there, unquestioning and attentive, to care and to listen to them, indulging them without anger or bitterness when they gave vent to the frustrations or obsessions of old age. I once listened to my mother telling her ragged gardener about her father and the Panama Canal. He listened attentively nodding his head, not understanding a word. A friend of mine on Mount Kenya once told me that when he came down from the mountain he avoided seeing a white man for the first twenty-four hours; white men made him nervous, he said, and he felt more comfortable in the company of the Africans.

I watched Dorian struggle in suppressed frustration through his days. I knew deep down that the solution to his life was not working on the farm beside my father. He must either do it on his own or not at all. So after almost a year I urged him once again to leave the farm, to walk away from the family and his filial duties and think of himself. When a business opportunity came up in Nairobi, I encouraged him to accept. He left the farm once more, taking Joseph Kamau with him. The move proved a turning point in both their lives.

In Nairobi Dorian went to live with Francine and his two girls in a small town flat, but their troubled marriage did not survive and collapsed shortly afterwards. Her departure hit him very badly and, like a pair of matriarchal elephants, Oria and I moved in at once on either side of him to try and fill the gap she left. We redecorated and furnished his new bachelor apartment, took him around with us and our friends and played hostess to his when he felt like entertaining them. We cared for and mothered his daughters, who were sent to boarding school with mine. And time slowly healed his battered soul.

Two years later he joined a Greek entrepreneur who appointed him managing director of his chemicals firm. Dorian's quick intelligence, his profound knowledge of the country and its people, coupled with his two years of business experience in the city, now put him in a position where, if he kept on his toes, he could rise rapidly in the fast developing country.

Although I often found life on the farm frustrating, the challenge was stimulating and provided the freedom and satisfaction few other occupations offer. There was also something very seductive about being the *musungu* with all the answers, the one whom others instinctively turn to for help and advice of any kind.

We were entertaining some guests from Europe to lunch one day when James, the old houseboy, slithered up to my father who was carving the roast, bent down and whispered to him that a woman giving birth on the next-door farm was in trouble and had sent for help. "Will you go and see what is the matter?" my father said to me. I stuffed down the last mouthful on my plate, got up from the table, collected the messenger waiting in the kitchen and drove to the infirmary for the dresser. "I am very busy now, ma'am" he said to me, but promised he would come on his bicycle as soon as he had finished.

I entered the woman's dark, smoke-filled hut and waited for my eyes to adjust. I was greeted with relieved smiles from her family as if all would now be well, just because I was there. She lay on a roughly hewn, wooden bed breathing heavily. Three older women and her husband stood around her bed and several small children played on the hard-beaten, soil floor. A black, soot-encrusted pot simmered over some raw embers glowing in between three stones beside them.

I put my hand on the woman's forehead; she moaned, turned her head and placed her hand on her belly. Her knees were drawn up and her legs were apart. "The baby is caught, it can't come out," she said feebly. The child hung out of her, limp and grey. It had been like that since morning, she told me, and it was now two in the afternoon. I tried to slip the four fingers of my right hand into her body to ease out the child's head but quickly gave up. It was a painful complicated business and I was no expert. I tried to feel the baby's heartbeat but I knew it could not possibly still be alive.

The dresser appeared in the doorway. He put down his box of instruments, slipped on his rubber gloves and examined the mother. "We must cut, madam, the head is caught."

"Do you know how to do that?" I asked him.

"Yes of course I do," he laughed.

He extracted a small pair of scissors and slipped them up into her vagina beneath the baby's chin. Gently but firmly he pressed down on the scissors. I held the woman's hand and gave her a piece of cloth to bite on. The scissors were slightly blunt and the dresser was having difficulty in cutting through the thick outer membrane. The woman squeezed her eyes tight and held her breath each time he pressed down on the scissors but she did not utter a sound.

He repeated this three times before the one-inch incision was made and the baby's head was freed. I picked it up by its legs and tried to resuscitate it. The wrinkled body hung cold and lifeless and pathetic like a skinned chicken from my arm. I poured hot and cold water on it and patted it on the buttocks but it was too late. I placed it on a folded blanket and left the hut. "*Kasa Roho Mama, ne Shauri ya Mungu* (Tighten your heart, it is the will of God,)" I said to her by way of consolation as I left.

Next day I passed her hut on my horse and stopped to ask how she was. I found her sitting outside washing her clothes. She told me she was fine and pointed to a mound of fresh earth beneath a tree when I asked her where she had buried the baby. She was pregnant again for the ninth time when I saw her again a few weeks later.

Life on an African farm is an intensely physical and emotional experience. It keeps bringing one back to the basics of survival and few people remain unaffected by it.

The turbulent day is shut out when you return home each evening. With muscles aching, skin burned by long hours in the sun, hair and face caked in dust, and hands that throb with broken finger-nails, you sink into an armchair or hot bath and unwind with a long drink or a strong cup of tea, sifting the events of the day through your brain and planning the next. It is difficult to keep the farm and the Africans out of the conversation.

My mother tried hard to steer our talk onto other topics. She kept in touch with the outside world through a little radio that rarely left her side and the many papers in several languages that choked our post box. She spoke to us of world politics, hijackings, wars and speeches of heads of state, but like a jealous lover the farm and its affairs always crept back.

Our conversations in Naivasha were echoed on the remaining white farms across the country. The Hopcraft family like ours was part of Naivasha. They owned the farm next door, and had been our first friends around the lake. They had watched us grow up, and we had watched them get married and have babies. They spoke with the same fervour as ourselves about the challenge of the new Africa. Three generations of Hopcrafts had each found their counterparts in our family.

When they arrived in 1906, the land on which we were now both farming still belonged to the government, and was roamed by nomadic Maasai. Grandpa Hopcraft, then a young man of twenty-two who had come from South Africa after the Boer War, had walked across the lake, which was then almost completely dry. Guided by an old Maasai and a Somali, he was advised to buy land on the north side of the lake where the grazing was better and the land free of cattle disease. Heavy rains fell shortly before the final deeds were signed, and the surveyor was forced to swim across the nearby Malewa river in full flood to reach the farm. But when he was in midstream, a python took him and he disappeared from sight with all the papers for the farm. These were later retrieved, clinging limply to the roots of a thorn tree, which had been swept up by the torrent, but the surveyor's body was never found.

Hopcraft returned to England and married his nineteen-year-old sweetheart, who followed him to Naivasha. They lived in canvas tents for eighteen months while the house, which the family still occupy, was built by two African stonemasons, with stone hacked from the farm and sand scooped from the lake bed. Once a week, a full day's ox-wagon trip took them to the diminutive Naivasha village, a few miles away, for their weekly provisions. Here on the farm at Naivasha their four children were born and here Grandpa and Grandma Hopcraft now lay buried beneath a *mukuyu* tree facing the lake they had once crossed on foot. They knew of no other life and there was never any question of giving up.

Many of the farms around the lake had already been Africanised;

gentle, unsettling persuasion had forced their owners to sell up and leave, but like us the Hopcrafts with a handful of neighbouring farmers refused even to discuss the possibility of pulling out, and Naivasha remained one of the last white strongholds in the country.

From our sun-drenched homes, as the years went by, we watched the approaching cloud of expropriation advance and wondered when our turn would come and how we would react when it did. While we waited, we listened to the stories and watched the others leave. Refusing to accept the inevitable we endeavoured to come to terms with the new nation's growing pains.

Three of our children, Fiametta, Valeria and Marina had already left the country and were at school in England. Only Amina, now almost thirteen, remained in Kenya. At her farm school she lived a carefree existence unharassed by the problems of growing up. Set on a ridge at the bottom of the Rift Valley, forty miles north of Naivasha, Greensteds School was surrounded by rolling grasslands that stretched to misty blue horizons – Amina's horizons, vast and still unfenced.

Her school had been built in 1932 to provide primary education for the children of European settlers in the outlying districts. With Kenya's independence, it had become integrated and, although it remained predominantly white, Amina lived in an atmosphere free of racial discrimination and had a healthy relationship with her coloured school companions – a relationship born from close daily contact in an atmosphere where staff and teachers did not differentiate. Yet Amina's friends, I noticed, were always white.

When I asked her about this, she just shrugged her shoulders and answered, "I don't know what it is, the Africans are different, they stick together as if they were shy of us. In class they are keener than we are and are good at sports like running and jumping. It seems to come naturally to them and they always beat us, but they don't like water and are afraid of the swimming pool." She did eventually make one African friend, a lovely girl with ebony silk skin and large dark eyes. Her name was Illuminata, and she was the daughter of a minister. Amina brought her to the farm one half term. She was the first African friend to share our home.

When I went to pick them up at school, I would leave early and on the way visit my friends the Coles, who owned a ninety-thousand-acre ranch in Elementeita, about thirty miles away. The vast estate lay at the foot of the Eburu range, between our farm and Nakuru, and was an excellent short cut for my visits to Amina. It also provided an excuse to break my journey and visit my three "soul-mates", Richard, Hugh and Berkeley Cole.

Their mother had been a childhood acquaintance of mine and her parents were friends of my parents in the 1930s. The three Cole boys were good friends of mine. Berkeley was alone on the farm that day. He hugged me in his usual effusive manner and led me into the drawing-room of the rambling old colonial farmhouse. He rang the bell for his houseboy to bring us tea. We flopped into the large divan and let ourselves sink into the deep cushions. The room was cool and simple; polished fire irons hung against the dark wood frame of the open fireplace; a pile of logs stacked neatly beside it waited for the crisp, cold evening.

Berkeley was twenty-seven years old. He was the grandson of an Irish peer, but he was different from his ancestors. An open-necked T-shirt draped his thin body; his white jeans were sawn off below the knees; he wore no shoes. "Have a joint," he said, and he turned and smiled at me, while I kicked off my dusty sandals.

"Thanks, but let's have a drink first," I answered, and together we began to unwind after another hot day on the farm.

As we talked the stark bright light outside melted into long shadows. Night crept gently into the house and over the vast expanse of Africa around it. The houseboy came in to light the fire and bring in the ice for drinks. He had changed from his brown day uniform into the white starched one he wore at night and for serving meals.

Over drinks and dinner, and later by the fire, sipping Irish coffee with thick farm cream, Berkeley told me how he and his family were preparing to leave the country for good. Three generations of Coles had lived on that farm, and in that house, just as we had in ours.

"My parents are going back to live in England," he told me. "My father is in his late fifties now, and the pioneering spirit has left him. All this land was virtually uninhabited when my grandfather first came to Kenya in 1906. He bought it from the government and built this house. He suffered from acute arthritis which in his day was incurable. His condition grew steadily worse until, when he was forty-five, it completely paralysed him and he could not stand living any longer. He shot himself. He had talked it over with my granny. She was very understanding, and did not try to stop him. He is buried on that rise, overlooking the lake, under the monolith over there; we built it because three times his grave was raided by Africans looking for his watch.

"My father imported some Santa Gertruda cattle from the King Ranch in Texas and slowly, over the years, built up our present herd. I myself have laid down many miles of fencing, piped the water, built the cattle troughs and water tanks."

I watched Berkeley talk, lying back in the heavy white chair, his legs straight out in front of him, his feet bare. Pictures of him at work on his enormous dusty sun-scorched domain flashed through my mind. I understood so well what he was saying and how he felt. He had been hooked by Africa as I was.

"There are people on this farm who have been here since before I was born. I always got on very well with them. We have a good understanding and I will be really sorry to say goodbye to them. I think they too will be sorry to see us leave."

"What is going to happen to them when you go?" I asked him.

"Oh, they've all been looked after by my parents. Each one will receive a sum of money and my parents bought plots of land for some of them in the settlement schemes. They do not want to stay on the farm with the new owners, or go and work for someone else. Most of them are old now and want to retire."

"Why did you suddenly decide to sell out and leave?" I asked.

"Farming is no longer what it was when my parents were young. There have been a series of nasty little incidents and there will be more. The police are useless and corrupt, I can't stand the petty African bureaucrats we now have to deal with, and I'm sick of trying to make the Africans do things they don't want to do. Then my mother's chickens were stolen – that was the last straw! We put the two farms up for sale, and Gemma, the biggest official co-operative in the country today, made us an offer we found hard to refuse. They are very rich and already own thousands of acres of land everywhere. They will divide Kikope into small, five-acre holdings and sell them off. I cannot bear the thought that there will soon be tin roofs and huts scattered everywhere, even where my grandfather planted his forest. You see, I like to feel I am living in a country where, if I plant a tree, I can watch it grow, and know that my children will one day be able to sit under it without it being chopped down and turned into charcoal as soon as it is big enough."

OVERLEAF Dawn on Lake Elementeita:
"the flamingoes appeared through the mist".

"Where will you go?" I asked him.

"I really don't know, probably America or Canada. I may become a carpenter. I don't have any regrets. I have had a wonderful childhood and done all the hunting I want – and had some exciting times with buffalo in the forest. Hugh, Richard and I all feel the same. Like my parents, we are quite ready to leave. The only problem will be our two grannies. One is seventy-five and the other is ninety-five. The younger of the two will probably go to England to join my parents. But the other one will have to stay at Hamilton House, the old people's home in Nairobi. She is too old to move now."

Berkeley and I talked way into the night. The fire in the fireplace turned to embers, the moon slipped across the sky, and in the distance somewhere the flamingoes croaked on the lake.

Next morning we rose at dawn and drove down to the lake to watch the sun come up over the Aberdares. A heavy mist, through which the thousands of flamingoes were barely discernible, hung over the silent water. As the sun appeared over the dark mountain range, the mist lifted and mingled with the hot vapour of the steam jets from the lake, revealing one of the most magical spectacles I have ever seen. The flamingoes we had heard in the night emerged from the mist in a cloud of pink.

My visits to Berkeley always left me perplexed and confused. He somehow brought into focus all the things I did not dare face. Like me, he had been deeply attached to the land he had cared for and fought against, and I was surprised at the ease with which he was walking away from it. I could not even imagine myself in his position, yet wondered sometimes if one day I would be.

Sometimes, as thoughts about the future churned through my mind, I would go to Ndabibi and wander round the fifty-thousand-acre neighbouring ranch that had belonged to my father's old friend Gilbert Colville. He had become a legendary figure because of his relationship with the Maasai, and his spirit seemed to linger everywhere.

His solitary grave lies on a small hillock rising above the plain, beside that of his stillborn child and his faithful dog. Before he died, he told the Maasai that he would never leave them and would watch over them and his herd, even after he was gone. The small fever tree planted on the site never rose more than six or seven feet. It never grew, but neither did it die.

One day, when Dorian and I were buying bulls at Ndabibi, we met Raua, the Colvilles' old cook, and three other old retainers, on the road. We had been sitting up near Colville's grave.

"What were you doing at Nyasore's grave?" Raua asked us inquisitively.

"We just went to visit him," we answered.

The four Masai veterans piled into the car and we drove with them back to Colville's wooden house, now empty and silent, but not abandoned. The doors and windows were closed and the wooden slats on the walls had turned a dark brown colour with age. The red paint had peeled off the faded corrugated-iron roof. A gnarled acacia tree spread its leafy branches like an umbrella over the sparse, well-tended space that had once been a garden. Bushes and creepers with great leaves grew in disarray around the house. We peered through the glass panes in the windows. The room was cool and dim. The interior was swept clean, two old armchairs and a faded sofa were still neatly set out around the empty fireplace as it had been on the day he died. A threadbare carpet lay in the same place on the floor in front of the hearth.

"Nyasore was a Maasai like us. There has never been another white man like him," Raua began telling me. "When he first came here his land was covered with many wild animals. There were thousands of Tommy gazelles and impala everywhere. They ate much of the grazing for the cattle and we had to shoot them so that they would move away. Nyasore hunted them on horseback. There were also many lions lying in the bushes during the day and at night they prowled around among the cattle killing the calves and young steers. Nyasore would get very mad because he loved his cattle, just like we do. He hunted the lions with his dogs and guns, accompanied by our warriors with spears. There were all kinds of skins piled up in heaps in his house and many of his clothes were made from lion and Tommy skins. When Nyasore was hunting he could walk all day with only a cup of tea and an egg in his stomach. You would never think he was so strong when you looked at him. We called him 'Nyasore' – the thin man – because he was so lean."

He started with eight Boran cows, two of which were sterile. He added to these with cattle bought from Somalis, or seized in raids, and twenty years later ended up with ten thousand head.

"There was little cattle theft in those days," Raua went on. "If an animal was stolen, we followed it until we found it, and the *mzee* of the *manyatta* would beat the thieves and pay Nyasore back in money or cattle. We never had to call the police like we do now. We just dealt with things ourselves.

"We worked for Nyasore for six shillings a month and he gave us a two-shilling rise when he felt like it. We did not need much money, we had a piece of land where we grew our food and each man was given a coat or blanket and an umbrella and a young heifer now and then. Nyasore knew that we valued cows more than money and we were content like that.

"I too worked for him as a houseboy. I started in the kitchen as a *toto*, and when I grew up I became his cook. I looked after him very well and when he became sick at the end I was there. One morning I brought him up his tea as I did every day and waited for him to call me. But he didn't call me that day. Then I heard him get out of his bed and open the window. He vomited blood. He was taken to the hospital in Nairobi and died there the next day. They put him in the *barafu* (refrigerator) until *memsahib* lady flew out from England.

"We made his coffin on the farm and when it was lowered into the grave she cried a lot and threw some earth on it and went away. Many white men came and did the same and hundreds of Maasai came from all around and stood on the hill for a whole day. It was a sad day. We shall never forget it and our children will know about him. He is up there watching over us, as he said he would. And then *memsahib* lady married *bwana* lord and went to live with him at Elementeita. So now we are left here on our own with the new manager."

Raua fell silent and rubbed his shaven head with his hand. His half-closed eyes gazed into the distance beyond us. He spat onto the ground in front of where he squatted and then rose to his feet, bade us farewell and left.

For a long time, the outlying districts of Kenya had remained as calm as Colville's ranch, but the country was experiencing its inevitable growing pains as it slowly adjusted to independence. Ugly stories were often splashed in bold headlines across the newspapers that arrived on the farm each morning on Wilfred Hopcraft's milk lorry. The present wave of crime and unrest were the inevitable undertow of the country's growth and everyone was a potential target, but for the most part the incidents were confined to the towns and their outskirts.

Then an old lady on the Kinangop, fifty miles from Naivasha, was robbed in her home and brutally beaten up. She died in hospital three weeks later. Not long afterwards, two weekend visitors on their way to the Hopcrafts were stopped, just before sunset, by a tree which had been felled and laid across the road, a few miles from the farm.

Three thugs jumped out from the bush, hit them across the head and demanded their money. A driver from another farm drew up behind them at that moment and saved their lives, but the thugs got away.

As more and more incidents of this sort occurred in the country our parents became an increasing source of anxiety for us. Dorian, Oria and I were often away from the farm and they were left alone, isolated and unprotected.

CHAPTER 17

Among the Elephants

The six months that Oria and I spent running the farm in Naivasha during my father's illness gave us a chance to get close again. In many ways we were very much alike. We did not complement each other; we challenged each other. Oria had inherited my father's Neapolitan gaiety, quick wit and sense of humour. Like me she was quick to anger and like all of us had a voice that in moments of passion rose to alarming heights. She loved an audience and could hold people mesmerised for hours with her stories.

Both of us were fat and ugly in our teens but unlike me she developed her personality to overcome her inhibitions. A friend of mine once said she reminded him of "a sultry native girl whose sensuous body beguiles and bewitches some poor white man". "Unfathomable," he said, "like a character out of Conrad or Maugham." Dressed in turbans, silks winding around her hips, she made striking entrances followed by total silence. She saw evil in nothing and no one, her moments of bad temper lasted a second, old people adored her. She had the gift of making you believe that no one else in the world existed – which was probably just what she did believe while she was with you. She forgave her enemies – when she remembered they *were* her enemies – and usually embraced them simply because she couldn't have cared less. When caught in some terrible lie she'd smile sweetly and say, "You're absolutely right, my darling. How clever you are, I do love you." Nothing was too much trouble for her. When her friends were poor or depressed she promised them the moon. Why not? It cheered them up and a bad moment was avoided.

When she met and married Giugnio, her serious young engineer, she never realised that she had actually cast a spell on him. When the marriage came to an end and they parted she bore him no grudge, but just quickly got involved elsewhere, designing clothes, making movies, or organising tribes to make bizarre jewellery to sell in Europe. Her voice was deep and husky and full of anguish and purpose. She could make "I'm very tired" sound like "At six a.m. tomorrow morning the First National City Bank is going to be blown up." Such was the power of her presence.

One day a Scotsman appeared in her life. He dropped out of the sky and, like Giugnio, took one look and fell irrevocably in love with her. They met at a dinner party in Nairobi where he seemed shy and out of place. From his ill-fitting clothes she could tell at a glance that he lived in the bush.

"City people were packed in a smoky room chattering to one another over cocktails. In this throng was a girl with long, dark hair and slanting, almost oriental eyes that flickered wickedly upon one person after another. On her sunburned forehead silver and golden specks of some curious metallic composition gleamed. Wearing a loose African robe which clung to her lithe figure, she danced with demonic energy, radiating an entirely un-Anglo-Saxon warmth and gaiety, and hanging pieces of silver clashed as she moved. Before the evening was out I worked my way through her many admirers and beguiled her with tales of noble elephants, lions in trees, hair's-breadth escapes and I know not what else, all set on the shores of a far-off enchanted lake called Manyara. She listened, warmly sympathetic, never giving away that she had already been there," wrote Iain Douglas-Hamilton of his first encounter with my sister.

Next day, he flew her to Naivasha in his four-seater plane. She wanted to show him her domain and us her new toy.

It was the first time an aeroplane had ever landed on the farm since my father had descended on the site in 1930. Iain buzzed the house, and came in low over the trees. He dipped a wing to show us Oria sitting beside him. She waved grandly to us poor mortals on the ground and they landed in the bumpy cattle *boma* among the cows. All work on the farm came to a halt as everyone rushed to the landing strip to gawk at the celestial visitor.

When Oria jumped out of the plane a loud murmur rose from everyone on the ground. "Oria, it's Oria, Allah, it's Oria in the plane," they repeated unbelievingly.

Iain leapt out of the plane and walked shyly towards us to be introduced, his hands behind his back like Prince Philip. He wore khaki shorts and an open sleeveless bush jacket. His legs were suntanned and hairy. His blonde curly hair was long and wild and fell over his forehead. He wore horn-rimmed spectacles. There was an appealing, shy, boyish look about him, and he looked much younger than any of us. He looked each of us straight in the eye, and greeted us with an Etonian accent and a barely perceptible Afrikaans twang that he had picked up at Gordonstoun College in South Africa and never completely lost. We took him home to our pink castle for lunch.

"Iain's arrival caused a great commotion," Oria wrote later in her diary. "It was an unforgettable event at Naivasha. Even old Moses, the cook, came to shake hands and welcome him to the farm."

"Tell me, young man, do you always fly like that?" asked an elderly gentleman who had just arrived from Europe and was unused to the kind of life we lead in Africa.

"Only sometimes," Iain answered. "I was hoping to be invited and just wanted to see what I was going to have for lunch before landing." Soon his plate was heaped so full that my father remarked with a laugh: "*Salute*, haven't you been eating lately? . . ."

Before he had finished his pasta we had learned a lot about him. He came from Scotland and, we found out much later, was the nephew of a duke. We bombarded him with questions and hardly gave him a chance to answer them. His northern calm and dignity was quite new to us. He was an Oxford zoology graduate and was collecting material on the life and habits of the African elephant for his thesis. He had been working for almost three years in the Manyara National Park in Tanzania, leading the solitary dedicated life of a scientist. No one in Naivasha knew much about Scotland or elephants, so Iain was quite a novelty. Nor did we yet know what was going on between him and Oria.

Iain stayed the night and at dawn he and Oria filled the aircraft with fruit, vegetables and as much cream, butter, meat and wine as could be fitted in. As the sun rose the heavily laden aircraft took off into the cold, dense morning air and they headed south across the lake.

He took Oria off to his jungle kingdom on Lake Manyara to introduce her to his family of pachyderms.

"It was a beautiful clear African day," she wrote to us later. "We could see the whole Rift Valley cutting down through Kenya. As soon as we were over the mountains that surround Lake Naivasha, we dropped

For four years Iain studied the life of the elephants in the Manyara National Park.

to a couple of hundred feet above the plains. Long lines of cattle and sheep were going out to graze, trailing behind them dust that was swept across the empty land. Here and there was a winding river bed or Maasai *manyatta*, otherwise this vast area was uninhabited. The rainy season was about to break. Massive clouds drifted above us, their shadows moving over the landscape. I had never flown so low before and I gazed spellbound at the beauty of Africa."

Love, marriage, children and success came into Oria's life all at once, when she was thirty-five. She moved in with Iain at Manyara and came back to Naivasha only sporadically. While I was working on *Vanishing Africa* I went to visit them in Manyara with my two daughters and Shaibu. We found them living a fairy-tale existence beneath their spreading fever tree, in a little stone house that Iain had built with the stones from the river below. During those four days together Iain introduced us to his elephant family. He knew each one by name and a few were so familiar he fed them by hand with bread fruit from the trees. We chased monkeys and baboons up trees while lions and leopards looked at us from the long grass or from the curved boughs of the acacias. White egrets perched like ballet dancers on the backs of rhino and buffalo and every kind of antelope galloped away from our Land-Rover, or just stood and stared, indifferent to our presence. African ducks and spur wing geese flew low over our heads and landed on the lake, beside fat snorting hippo.

We went picnicking along the river and swam beneath the waterfalls. In the evenings, with genet cats and mongoose round our necks, we sipped whisky sours and gin fizzes and watched the game come down to the river to drink. The starlit nights were warm and the magic of the African bush enveloped us and silenced our chatter, and we were bathed in bush perfume.

Oria had already completely adapted to her new life in the bush. Lorenzo once said she was like a chameleon, she changed the colour of her life to suit the man she lived with.

"Adjusting to life in Manyara meant that I had to switch over to Iain's way of living and to his work with the elephants. He had a well-established routine: we got up with the sun and stopped working when it set. Meals were at precise hours; the quality of the meal was unimportant but timing was paramount. To me the most amazing of all meals in Iain's camp was breakfast. It was always served at seven. A radio was switched on for the London Stock Exchange Report which came just before the news. Coming from Italo-French parents, but with a British passport to my name, I thought that only the British could live like this. Iain was a perfect example, eating eggs and crisp bacon with a mongoose on his lap, elephants drinking in the river below his house and listening to the Stock Exchange. No one spoke. What an extraordinary people the British are!"

Oria was quick to understand and love Iain's work, just as she had Giunio's. Her vocabulary changed and she started using scientific words appropriate to Iain's wildlife world, she learned to fly and was thrilled by the new perspective it gave her. During one of her lessons she spotted an ostrich from the air, sitting on its nest. A few weeks later she saw the mother march her newly-hatched chicks across the sunburned plain, and later, when she went on her first solo flight, she spotted them again several miles away and subsequently watched them grow a little each week.

Five months after Oria met Iain she triumphantly announced that she was pregnant. She had tried unsuccessfully to have a child for many years and had poured her thwarted Latin motherly instincts on her four nieces. The news had to be broken to my parents, who were still trying to digest Oria's unorthodox relationship with Iain. Now they were going to be presented with an illegitimate grandchild. As Lorenzo had called his father, so Iain in turn called his mother, Prunella, to come and help him out by bolstering his image in my parents' eyes. Prunella landed in Nairobi and he flew her to the farm to meet us. Like Cesarino, she quickly charmed us all and Iain immediately became more acceptable to my parents, although they tried not to show it.

Lorenzo had made a lot of money on the New York Stock Exchange, and with it we bought a lovely old rambling house at the coast on the Kilifi Creek, and a slick fishing yacht. After an unsuccessful year in the congested Mediterranean waters, he loaded his yacht with the best Italian delicacies – parmegiano cheeses, salamis, olives, torrone (an Italian sweet nougat) and several barrels of red and white Tuscan wine – and sent it to Mombasa with Pino, his Italian butler. Lorenzo was a *bon vivant*, but he also loved the sea, and never lost his desire to be near nature.

We spent Christmas *en famille* at Kilifi that year and everyone was invited. Ma and Pa came and were joined later by Dorian, his daughters

Fiametta and Valeria, Oria and Iain, and Lorenzo's father flew out from Italy to celebrate this historic reunion. Shaibu and Lorenzo caught fish and lobster and crabs which Kimuyi and Pino expertly cooked for us. It was an unusual occasion, with many cross-currents. Lorenzo and I were still miles apart; Dorian was adjusting to his new life without Francine and Oria and Iain still had their secret which, sooner or later, had to be disclosed. We resembled an ill-assorted bunch of actors who have walked onto the wrong stage, while our three parents stood in the wings and looked on, silent and perturbed.

One bright and sparkling morning Iain, in his polite, matter-of-fact British manner, told my father that he wanted to talk to him. "Papi," he began (he had already adopted the familiar way of addressing him), "Oria is pregnant."

My father looked up at him, obviously shocked, but controlling his reaction. He knew very well that one day they would have to talk, but he wasn't expecting to hear this. Iain remained composed. He looked my father straight in the eye and awaited his response, but my father said nothing. Oria and I, watching through slits in the shuttered window, held our breath. My father's eyes shifted from Iain's face to the sparkling sea framed in the arches in front of him. The silence between them hung long and heavy.

"Pregnant? That's impossible," exclaimed my father. "How can she be pregnant? She's got no tubes." (Oria had had an operation a year before to remove a cyst from her ovary.)

"But she is, Papi, it's been confirmed." Iain smiled proudly back at him.

"What do you intend to do?" my father challenged him.

"Marry her, of course," Iain retorted with chivalrous determination.

"Marry her?" My father repeated the words with a mocking smile. "You must be crazy, young man. Oria is a girl you have an affair with, she's not the kind you marry." He paused. Ian was baffled by this unexpected reply, and laughed. There was another long silence while we waited for my father to explain himself.

"You want my advice? I'm older than you are and know Oria better than you do. Don't do it, turn around and run while there's still time." Iain's eyes widened, and he said nothing. "You are still a young man and you have your life in front of you. Don't worry about the baby, we will adopt it. It will be a Rocco."

"But, Papi," Ian cried, aghast, "you must be joking. It's my child and I love Oria and I want it."

"Well, Iain, you're an adult," my father said after a long silence. "You do as you want, but don't say I didn't warn you."

The announcement had been made: Iain had won. Slightly embarrassed, the two looked out to sea. Then Ian got up and excused himself, leaving Pa staring fixedly into space. Iain spied us standing behind the open shutters.

"Eavesdropping, you naughty girls," he laughed. "Come on, Oria, now you have to say something. I've done my bit."

Saba, their first daughter, was born four months later. Iain was addressing his first wildlife meeting, speaking to members of the Tanzania National Parks at the Manyara retreat when the first contractions began. Oria went to lie down, but because it was an important occasion for Iain she waited until he had finished speaking before she told him what was happening to her.

"We must let Iain finish his speech," she groaned. "You have no time," one of the wives answered her. "Babies don't wait and it's a two-hour flight back to Nairobi."

"Iain and I drove to the strip," Oria wrote later in her book *Among the Elephants*. "Everyone came to wish us farewell. When we got into the plane each in turn came to kiss me goodbye – all the people, the genet cats and the mongooses. The plane had no self-starter but Hugh Lamprey spun the propeller, the engine roared, wind blew into my face, the doors were locked, we raced down the narrow runway and climbed over the trees and up over the great Rift Wall . . .

"Hanging onto my stomach as the plane dropped and heaved in the empty sky, I felt a great wave of pain pushing through my body, then disappearing only to start again five minutes later. Nairobi was still far away. This, I thought, is where I need that British cool, to pretend that nothing unusual is happening. I needed an image to fix my mind on. Through the light's strange glow, I sighted Lake Natron to the left where long lines of red crusts floated on the water. I loved this desolate lake.

"Suddenly I heard voices crackle above my head. Contact had been made with the outside world. 'This is East Air Centre, your doctor cannot be found, it is Sunday and he is away for the day. We will try and get you an ambulance.' . . .

"This was my first baby and I felt my heart flicker with waves of panic. 'It'll be all my fault,' I thought, 'if anything should go wrong, because of the way I've been living, never giving a damn about the thing that mattered most, our child, and now entirely dependent on the help and competence of others for our survival.'

"An hour later I was on a hospital bed, and Iain was ringing everyone we knew in Nairobi telling them to look for our doctor.

"At six-thirty he arrived – Adriano Landra, my friend, a tough, confident and capable surgeon, with a smiling round face. I knew then I was going to make it . . .

"I heard the doctor say, 'Okay, you can put her out.' And to me: 'Now count up to ten slowly.' I counted till a whirlwind shook my brain.

"Slowly I woke. I heard voices. The room was full of flowers. I could not move for pain. I looked for Iain and found his face, his hair still tousled and covered in dust and sweat from the day before. All my family was there. I heard someone say, 'You've got a daughter, she's fine, she's in the premature unit, she weighs five pounds three ounces.'

"The news was sent to my home and the Africans there named the baby Saba (Swahili for 'seven'), because she was born at the seventh hour on the seventh day of the week, on the seventh day of the month, and she was the seventh grandchild."

Lorenzo and I were in Nairobi at the time staying with Dorian. When we came home from the cinema we found a note stuck in the door announcing the baby's arrival –"A five-pound girl," it read. We went to have a look at her next day. She was snuggled in the arms of a tearful Oria, surrounded by flowers and friends. A victorious, beaming Iain poured champagne into thick hospital glasses while a "Strictly No Visitors" sign hung vainly on the door of the room.

Iain and Oria had thus cemented their union with a child, instead of a gold ring and orange blossom. My parents instantly forgot about the question of legitimacy, and once again became doting grandparents. I had never quite understood what all the fuss had been about, for we had found out that Dorian, Oria and I had all been born out of wedlock.

A month later Iain, Oria and Saba went back to Manyara to finish Iain's work. He taught her what he had learnt from the elephants about the mother–child bond. "Instead of buying the usual Dr Spock's book," she writes in *Among the Elephants*, "I was tutored by Iain. I soon discovered that the elephants showed many of the old-fashioned virtues;

loyalty, protection and affection towards each other . . . For elephants, the unity of a family is one of the most important things in their lives . . . I was deeply moved by the constant affection and care which they showed every day within the families; mothers, daughters, sisters, babies all touching and communicating with each other in a very loving way. Stability seemed to be the key to their security . . . Months of living with and observing these animals taught me something that no text book could ever do. As a result I now felt a great deal more civilised."

Violette, a lovely fat Seychellois lady, joined them to look after Saba and soon after the four left for London. The cold English winters replaced their carefree sun-washed African life. The solemn, grey people hurrying by replaced the smiling black faces and the sounds of the wild were silenced by the falling rain. To keep fit they marched across the English countryside in the rain and mist, wrapped in sweaters and scarves. They grew fat and bored and longed to return to their sinewy African life. Oria hung Kangas on the walls and pasted up their wilderness photographs. Like the Africans, she possesses the gift of joy. It radiates around her and breathes warmth into all the homes she creates.

Strips of film from the movie they had made about their life and Iain's work, before they left Manyara, hung from the nails around the walls of Iain's office. While he worked, Oria sifted through and spliced together the frames from the life they had left behind and put together a pilot film which later led to a one-hour special feature for Anglia Television. She received Iain's university friends and listened far into the night to their scientific jargon. She became pregnant again.

When their spirits sank too low, they fled to their island retreat in Raasay in the Hebrides, where one glorious Scottish morning they decided to get married.

Iain, dressed in kilt and sporran, and Oria, in a long, flowing, flowered dress with heather in her hair, sailed the sound to Skye with some friends, some family and his mother Prunella in the fishing boat of a romantic Russian cousin and his lovely wife Victoria.

Saba, tucked in Violette's strong black arms, waved goodbye to her parents on their wedding day, and when they returned she handed them their first wedding gift, a posy of wild mountain flowers. Next day everyone was talking about the eight-month-pregnant bride. The island people and crofters gathered round the unconventional newly-weds and

OVERLEAF Oria with Saba and Dudu.
"Tactile contact and reassurance . . ."

brought gifts of fresh salmon, heather and home-made bread in hampers. They sat together round a huge bonfire, roasting mutton, drinking wine and beer and singing Highland songs under the northern stars.

Dudu, Oria's second daughter, was born one month later in Oxford, and shortly afterwards Iain became Dr Douglas-Hamilton, Ph.D., with a doctorate *cum laude* by the University of Oxford.

After an all-night party, exhausted, relieved and happy, they began packing again and prepared to return to Naivasha to start writing *Among The Elephants*, a more personal account of their extraordinary experience in Manyara.

The next day, as they left the house, the postman handed them a cable: "PA AND MA HAVE BEEN ATTACKED STOP PA SERIOUSLY ILL IN NAIROBI HOSPITAL."

CHAPTER 18

A Wild Figure Rushed In

The beam of a torch had flashed against the glass-paned entrance door of our home in Naivasha. It was nine o'clock at night. My mother and father were finishing their evening meal beside the fireplace. The servants had long since left, and the house was in darkness. My parents were of the age when unnecessary lights are kept switched off for economy's sake. In the dark and silent room, the tall reading lamp beneath which they sat cast an aureole of light around them. Was it the night-watchman calling to warn them of another Maasai cattle raid, a hippo in the crops, or a woman giving birth? My father looked up, heaved himself out of his deep armchair and crossed the room. He opened the front door and stepped out into the night to switch on the outside light. A heavy blow on the head brought him to his knees. He sank to the floor without a sound. Blood soaked his white hair.

Alarmed by the silence, my mother followed him. Before she reached the door a demented black figure rushed at her and slammed his *rungu* on-to her head. A second blow gashed open her chin. Her spectacles fell to the floor. She could no longer see. (Only a month before she had undergone a double cataract operation and was now totally dependent on her glasses.) Surprise and terror turned to rage. She brandished her walking stick at the intruder. "Get out, you swine," she screamed, "or I'll kill you!" The man lunged forward and caught hold of her stick, endeavouring to pull it from her hand. It had belonged to her father and contained a finely sharpened sword. She pulled back her arm and the sheath remained in his hand. She lunged forward and stuck the sword into his heavy military coat shouting, "I'll kill you, get out!" The bewildered, quivering man faced the diminutive, fierce old lady with the sword in her hand, dropped his *rungu* and ran out of the door into the night.

My mother felt her way to the door and met my father staggering towards her, holding his head.

"My God, Giselle, we've been attacked!" he groaned. "Are you all right?"

She grabbed his arm and felt warm, sticky blood on her fingers. "Where are my glasses, I can't see anything."

My father picked them up from the floor and set them on her face, and suddenly she saw him clearly. His face, his hair and his shoulders were covered in blood. They looked at each other; her lip was swollen from the gash on her chin, blood dripped onto her cotton blouse. Together they moved to the bathroom. My father put his head beneath the tap and tied a towel around it. He filled the sponge with cold water, gently dabbed her wound, and pressed it firmly against her mouth.

"We must call the police," she said, making for the phone on the small table outside the bathroom. She cranked the old-fashioned handle to raise the exchange, There was no reply. She tried again and then again. Finally a voice answered.

"Exchange?" she shouted. "Give me the police."

"What's the matter, Giselle?" the voice answered. "It's me, Wilfred." Wilfred Hopcraft was himself trying to raise the sleepy exchange.

"Wilfred," she said. "Mario and I have just been attacked. We must get hold of the police."

"Are you hurt?" he asked, alarmed.

"Yes. Mario is bleeding profusely."

"I'll get the police and come right over," he answered, alarmed.

She rejoined my father, who was fumbling in a cupboard. The blood seeped in large, red stains through the towel on his head. "What are you doing, Mario?" she asked him.

"I'm looking for the alarm siren."

The siren, dating back to the Mau Mau years, had remained unused in the cluttered medicine cupboard. They found it covered with dust behind a pile of bottles and half-opened, rusty medicine boxes. On the porch they released the catch. The loud wail echoed through the silent, starlit night and bounced off the trees. No one came.

Half an hour later Wilfred raced up the winding stairs followed by two armed guards, and met my parents standing on the blood-spattered porch, holding the wailing siren. He led them gently back into the house and listened with horror to the story they spluttered out to him.

I had just finished dinner with my two daughters in the French Embassy in Nairobi, where we had stopped for the night on our way to Kilifi, when the telephone rang. I picked it up and heard Wilfred's familiar voice. "Mirella, your parents have been attacked. They are badly hurt. You'd better come back immediately."

I looked at my watch. It was ten o'clock. "I'm coming," I told him. I turned to my little girls snuggled on the sofa by the fireplace. "Come on, girls, let's get dressed," I said. "We're going back to the farm. Pa and Ma have been beaten up."

As we stepped out of the front door, the phone rang again. "Don't come. Your father is in a bad way, and must go to hospital, Dr Bunny is here." Wilfred's voice echoed as in a nightmare. "Go and wait for them at the hospital, we'll be there in two hours."

Like a fast slide projection on a screen, gruesome images chased each other through my mind. I put the girls to bed and drove to the hospital in Nairobi.

At one o'clock in the morning, the white Peugeot station-wagon finally pulled up in front of the hospital. I reached the car before the engine had been switched off. My father sat in front, his head thrown back, his face streaked with lines of dried blood, his mouth open. He seemed dead. Pushed aside by the doctor, I moved to the back of the car where my mother was sitting. She looked up at me and tried to smile. Her swollen lip with the great gash on her chin told the ghastly tale.

"Oh, Ma, how are you?" I stammered.

"Oh I'm okay," she answered cheerfully. "Don't worry about me, it's Pa who's bad." She grabbed my arm to steady herself, and we slowly followed the stretcher carrying my prostrate father; his head was monstrously swollen, his white hair caked with dark, drying blood. They wheeled him into the emergency operating theatre.

Surrounded by the shocked, kindly nurses, my mother and I remained in the casualty department. Despite her appearance, she was alert and seemed not to be in excessive pain. Through the gap in the drawn curtains, I watched the doctor cut away the blood-caked hair, which fell around my father's feet. I put my mother to bed, leaving her in the care of the nurses, and returned to the Embassy to join my sleeping children. I swallowed a Valium, and lay back on the soft pillows beside them totally confused.

I called Dorian at his Nairobi office next morning. My mother was already up and dressed when he and I arrived at the hospital. The swelling on her lip had gone down and she looked almost normal again. A large piece of Elastoplast held white gauze over the wound on her chin. She was sitting beside my father's bed. His head had doubled in size, the skin around his eyes was black and blue. He appeared unconscious and was breathing heavily. We held her hand as she held his. The doctor came in with the X-rays.

"He has a fractured skull and the jaw bone is cracked," he told us. "It's not all that serious, but could turn nasty at his age." My father was seventy-eight.

Dorian and I left the same morning for the farm after a lengthy session with the head of the Special Branch of the Rift Valley police. James, Mwangi and Moses, our three faithful house servants, and Kamaru, the old ragged gardener, came down the stairway to meet us. They had all been with us for nearly fifteen years. When we asked them why no one had heard the siren they remained mute, eyes downcast. We summoned every man, woman and child on the farm to the house. They drifted through the trees one by one and, in small groups, silently took up their places on the steps and along the stone wall of the garden. They greeted us with sullen, expressionless faces. No one spoke. In a few clipped sentences Dorian reviewed the previous night's events and asked them to comment or explain. But they just stood there, looking at their feet. The futile interrogation lasted an hour. The blacks and whites stared at each other on a silent stage. Dorian dismissed the gathering, which melted back into the trees. My mind rushed back to the Mau Mau years, when even the most loyal of our African employees succumbed to the fear, superstition and intimidation created by circumstances and I became aware again of the gap that would never be spanned. I began to question the origin of my roots.

We walked back into the sitting-room and dropped into armchairs. Dorian poured himself a stiff drink.

"Now what?" I asked him.

"No use expecting the police to come up with anything."

"What about the witchdoctor?" I suggested.

The witchdoctor still remained all-powerful in Africa and was more feared and respected than the modern, smartly dressed, Western policeman with his heavy boots and insignia cap. The witchdoctor belongs to the realm of the unknown; his powers of suggestion can kill or heal. His sticks and stones, his feathers and bottles, his garbled incantations have proved more effective in Africa than the bullets and guns and high court judges and the modern police force. I had had some extraordinarily successful experiences with witchdoctors in the past and understood the reasons for their pre-eminence. Once when a power-saw disappeared on the farm the witchdoctors were called in. The suspects were lined up and a loaf of bread crumbled on a tray in front of them. Each man had to swallow a handful. One of them was unable to do this without the help of water. He was the culprit; his fear had made his mouth quite dry and we retrieved the saw.

In Kilifi, £200 in cash disappeared from the safe one day. We had long ago given up using the police to help retrieve our missing items so, full of rage, I turned to the witchdoctor.

Three wizened men arrived, looking like a delegation of Snow White's dwarfs, with long white beards, crinkly hair and alert black eyes set in wrinkled faces. We sat with them on the coral wall overlooking the creek and told them our tale.

"We'll come tomorrow at five o'clock. Have everyone in the house present – we'll soon find out who took the money," they assured me.

They returned next day and installed themselves beneath the spreading frangipani tree. Lorenzo and I and his girlfriend Muriel were there with Marina and Amina; the four Africans who worked for us squatted, intrigued and silent, under another tree, a few yards away. We eyed each other; the culprit was among us.

The little men extracted some feathers and small round stones from a well-thumbed leather pouch. With their fingers they traced three lines a few inches deep on the ground in front of them and lay a long stick inside each groove. They placed the rounded stones and some bones in an empty tin and covered them with water. We all lined up and one after the other stepped over to the lines traced on the ground and repeated in Kiswahili after the leader, "If I am guilty of the theft, may I fall dead and the devil tear out my heart and my body be eaten by the hyenas in the bush." We took a sip from the tin and jumped over the sticks avoiding each other's eyes so as to keep a straight face. One by one we went through the little ritual. The wizened men watched the Africans closely. Their eyes darted from us to them.

Mainge, the gardener, was the last in line. He stood slightly to one side, his arms crossed on his chest, a sullen angry expression on his face. When it was his turn he put the tin to his lips but did not drink from it and jumped the line. The ceremony was over, the stones and bones were put away and no one fell dead. When Mainge reported for work, I told him he had been dismissed. He came at me with a large kitchen knife, and was stopped just in time by the horrified houseboys standing by. They disarmed him and led him outside to his house.

Early next morning, the three old men came to see us again. Unruffled and dignified, they told us Mainge had taken the money and asked us for the balance of what we had agreed to pay them. As the money changed hands in the large open sitting-room two African policemen walked in followed by Mainge, and asked angrily what they were doing there. The witchdoctors just stared back with guilty, frightened faces and didn't answer. All their magic powers seemed to drain from them and they began to shake all over.

"I called them," I answered, and proceeded to explain the reason.

"Have you got a permit to use witchcraft?" one of the officers asked aggressively.

"I didn't know you a needed a permit. Since when?"

"It's the law," he answered curtly and nodded to the men he'd brought to take away the three culprits.

Since independence, witchcraft had been officially banned as it was often used for personal vengeance and had been the cause of many deaths. The witchdoctors, we discovered then, were permitted to practise their craft only on their own premises, under special government licence.

The three men were stuffed into the back of the blue police Land-Rover and driven away. Mainge sat triumphantly in front between two uniformed policemen. Surprised and furious at Mainge's victory, I followed them and crossed the ferry to the police station on the other side of the creek. The three witchdoctors had already been locked in the cells and Mainge sat chatting to his friends under a tree. We glared at each other. The inspector and I had a heated exchange. He arrogantly reiterated the words the police officers had spoken earlier. "You can bail them out if you like, but they must spend the night in the cells."

That night, as I was preparing dinner in the kitchen with Kimuyu, a large black cockerel came hurtling through the window from the dark outside and landed on the stove, upsetting my pans. It was Mainge trying to intimidate us with an evil spirit. I went next day to pay the bail and release the poor little fellows. In the car, they told me they had been beaten in the cell and showed me the raw, swollen welts on their backs and knees.

A week later as I was driving home from the little Mnarani village with some fresh bread for breakfast, I saw a body hanging from a tree about fifty yards from the road. I thought I was hallucinating. I stopped the car for a better look. There was no mistaking it: as I approached I recognised Mainge. He was swinging gently in the breeze, the early morning light threw a dappled pattern over him from the leaves and pink flowers above. His feet were only six inches from the ground and a coconut fibre rope attached him firmly by the neck to a thick branch. His eyes were closed, his swollen tongue protruded from his mouth and he had wet his pants. Beyond him the sea sparkled in the strong morning light. Witchcraft can drive a man to confession or suicide through fear.

After the attack on our parents Dorian and I were recommended to another witchdoctor. But when we pressed him for details, he asked for more and more money and his revelations were most unsuccessful and unconvincing. We realised it was a hoax, bade him goodbye and left, wondering if witchdoctors were also losing their powers in the new independent Africa.

We never discovered who had been the perpetrators of this savage attack on my parents or whether the motive was more than mere theft. Had it been a personal vendetta? Or an attempt to drive them from the farm so that some African could buy it cheaply? For a month my father hung between life and death in the Nairobi hospital and spent another convalescing at the Muthiaga Club. I never thought he would recover from the incident. But he did. Two months later he returned to the farm.

Had the attack on our parents signified the death cry of ethnic prejudice? The whites in Kenya were no longer the masters and the relationship between blacks and whites would perforce have to alter. Kenyatta's ambition to bring his country into step with the twentieth century meant a total upheaval of all its traditions.

A new society of black politicians and businessmen had emerged, a class of people outwardly adjusted but inwardly searching for a new identity. Hotels, bars, schools and restaurants were now open to all alike. But the black man, like the white man, would have to adjust.

Gangs were now roaming the town in packs, like hungry wolves, spreading their ugly web of lawlessness and crime across the country, into the villages and along the lonely roads. I had never been afraid to travel unarmed and alone across Kenya's wilder districts during the shooting of *Vanishing Africa*, but in today's Kenya, the danger from man replaces that of the wild beast. Most crimes remain unsolved, gangsters are rarely caught, and their booty is seldom recovered. The police force is young, naive, corrupt and still inexperienced. Fifty years ago, Karen Blixen had already written in her book *Out of Africa*:

> If for a long enough time we continue in this way to dazzle and blind the African we may in the end bring upon him a longing for darkness which will drive him into the gorges of his own unknown mountains and his own unknown mind.

I was dining with a friend one night at the Twilight Café in Nairobi. Several inches of rain had fallen on the city and the streets were feet deep in water. Abandoned cars, helplessly parked, waited in the flooded streets. Few people were around that night, but the restaurant was gay and surprisingly full. White-jacketed African waiters glided between the candle-lit tables and the colourfully dressed diners of all races gave the place a festive look.

A sudden stir at the entrance followed by a hush made me turn my eyes from the face opposite me. Five men dressed in jeans and leather jackets with felt hats pulled down over their eyes stood like tigers, taut and nervous, ready to spring or run. Two held machine guns across their bodies. The room froze.

"Don't move, or we shoot." The heavily accented voice betrayed an excited quiver of suppressed fear. Like the mock-charge of an elephant, the act was designed to frighten. A brief silence allowed the words to sink in.

"All hands on the table, don't move or we shoot," the man repeated as three of the raiders moved slowly into the room. We obeyed like automata. In low, sexy voices the gang told us to empty our bags on the tables, remove watches and jewellery and turn pockets inside out. Gliding from table to table, they calmly and professionally scooped the booty into rough cloth bags.

My mouth went dry. My nails dug into the palms of my hands. I could hear the rain fall outside. Would our table, tucked away in the dark corner to the right of the door, pass unnoticed? A woman struggled with the ring on her finger. She was having difficulty slipping it over her middle knuckle. The impatient gangster glared at her. Would he cut off her finger? The restaurant owner and his wife stood paralysed beside the cashier. The till drawer was locked. "Keys," one of the men demanded. The cashier extracted them from his trouser pocket, the drawer slipped smoothly open and the contents were emptied into a cloth bag. The drawer fell to the stone floor with a clatter and everyone jumped in their seats. The three men moved back swiftly towards our end of the room, the bulging bags clasped firmly to their chests. For one exciting moment I thought they had not seen our table but they stopped in front of us. I unclasped my watch and slipped my silver Persian rings and bracelets onto the table with the wallet from my companion's left breast pocket and the contents from his trouser pockets. A long, sinewy black hand scooped it all into the bag. I heard my bracelets fall. The five men disappeared into the street, the heavy red velvet curtain hanging in the doorway moved slightly behind them and it was over.

The incident at the Twilight Café was just one of many in Nairobi and its outlying districts. Before the Mau Mau years, criminal offences had been confined to petty thieving, and Nairobi had been a peaceful city, safe to live in. But since 1970 almost every day the newspapers have carried front-page headlines of daring robberies with or without violence. "Africa's Chicago," I once heard someone call Nairobi.

There had been several bold, daylight hold-ups in banks. Hundreds of thousands of shillings changed hands at gunpoint and were never recovered. Talk of police and government involvement was never proved. Armed guards, police dogs and bullet-proof window panes appeared but were of little use. The influx of teenage school-leavers failing to find employment in the cities led to bag-snatching; vehicles were stolen and rarely recovered; shops, restaurants and bars were attacked at gunpoint at all hours of the day and night. The inhabitants of Nairobi moved about with caution, avoided travelling after dark, and at night locked themselves in their homes behind heavily barred doors and windows. Alarm systems and Securico *Simba* watchmen became part of every household.

When my parents, now bent and broken, returned to the farm they both carried pistols in their pockets. Each night, as darkness fell, all doors and windows were locked and my mother shuffled through the house on a nightly security check before she went to bed. She never understood how pointless this was. Despite all her efforts the house remained vulnerable and easy to enter. If we came home after dark she would fly at us like an angry wasp, reprimanding us like children and betraying her terrible fear. My father never said anything, but I could always feel his face muscles relax when he saw us appear.

CHAPTER 19

Black Man, White Man

The attack on my parents brought into focus a reality we had been trying for a long time to avoid. We could no longer leave them alone without help. Finally Giovanni Spazzini, a native of Calabria, was hired to help manage the farm.

Spazzini was over sixty when he joined us. A tough, lonely man without family or ambitions, he was a bundle of contradictions. His humble, peasant background had filled him with esteem for his *padrone*. He was always polite and respectful when dealing with his superiors and possessed the inborn gallantry of the Italian male. Painfully shy, he lived a life of almost total solitude; he rarely mixed with others and invariably refused all invitations, even when these were limited to the family. Enveloped in a thick carapace of arrogant aggressiveness, he fended off the world.

He had left southern Italy when he was twenty-three, after his wife had eloped with his best friend. The incident had badly wounded his pride, honour and self-assurance and, unable to face the reactions in his own small town, he left for Africa, "because it was far away". Firmly convinced that all women were whores, he kept well away from any further emotional entanglements, restricting all contact with women to the fulfilment of his physical needs. During the war he was captured in Abyssinia and spent five years in a P.O.W. camp in Kenya. When the farm on which he was working in Rongai was Africanised, he lost his job and had to leave. He came to us.

Working on the land gave him his only real satisfaction, and he had over the years acquired a profound knowledge of farming. He served his *padrone* with the honour and devotion once proffered by soldiers to "king and country". In our case the *padrone* was my father. This of course made life difficult and frustrating for Dorian, who was again attempting to run the farm.

Spazzini had spent forty years in Africa and spoke Swahili like a native though he never learned to speak English. His attitude towards the Africans bordered on contempt; he regarded them as a definitely inferior race, and was totally ruthless in his dealings with them. He used his white skin and his position as manager on the farm to impose his authority, and he expected complete, unconditional and immediate obedience. When he did not get it, which happened frequently, he flew into a terrifying, often comic rage. He swore at the Africans in Italian and Swahili using every dirty name at his command. Why they never slit his throat remains a mystery. He referred to the men as "*bastardi*", to the women as "*bastarde*" and to the girls as "*bastardette*". He was known as "*Makako*" (ugly monkey), a Swahili-sounding Italian word he often used when abusing them.

The Africans, in general, dislike being commanded by someone who, like them, is a salaried employee, and Spazzini's nervous temperament caused much turbulence on the farm. The Africans, with their sloppy disregard towards their work, their lies, their petty thieving and their constant attempts at deceit drove Spazzini to a state of exasperation, which only those who have tried to farm with Africans can understand. He became so paranoid about them I sometimes thought he would end up like Hitler with the Jews.

Under normal conditions he would have been murdered or forced to resign, or would have precipitated a general strike, but an inexplicable love/hate relationship existed between him and the Africans, which we were never able to understand. Like an angry rhino with a thorn in its rump, Spazzini vented his lonely frustrations on them. They seldom retaliated and handled him like a child in a tantrum, forgiving and forgetting without rancour. Twice he nearly died. Margaret, his sweet, long-suffering housemaid, nursed him patiently and tenderly back to health, but as soon as he was back on his feet he began shouting and abusing her again. She sadly complained to me, her large, soulful eyes brimming with tears. But, next day, she seemed to have forgotten the whole trouble, and they were both laughing and joking.

I found his arrogant behaviour towards the Africans impossible to condone, and sometimes told him so in no uncertain terms. Then fifty years of pent-up misogyny would unleash itself on me and our encounters became electric. Spazzini and I could not get on. Why he remained with us often baffled me. I think that, somewhere very deep down, he really liked me, but he could not bear living under my orders.

His profoundly solitary life led him to seek companionship among the Africans. They were ultimately the only people he talked to and they provided the only outlet for his bottled-up emotions. When he wasn't fighting the Africans he was befriending them, both with equal intensity, but familiarity breeds contempt, it leads to loss of respect and ends up with *fitina*, vendetta.

Spazzini was always enveloped in a thick cloud of *fitina*. We were well aware of it, but did not take much notice as the work on the farm progressed. *Fitina* was part of the running of the farm, and we had learned to shrug it off.

As time went by, more and more complaints were brought to us. On my daily horseback rounds of the farm, I would stop and chat to Spazzini in the fields. He always seemed pleased to see me – my little visits broke the monotony of his day, gave him the opportunity to vent his feelings and opinions, and allowed him to show me the fruit of his labour. He stood for hours under the hot sun, the handle of his cane tucked firmly inside the seat of his pants, watching the row of women bent in half weeding the long lines of crops, their buttocks upturned and their short skirts revealing long, naked shining black legs.

"*Buon giorno, Signora*," he would cry in his gruff voice, tipping his grease-stained hat with Italian gallantry.

"*Come va oggi?*" I would answer cheerfully from my horse.

"*Ma potrebbe andare peggio* (things could be worse)," was his invariable answer.

But this friendly tone never lasted. When Spazzini was dissatisfied he vociferated loudly, shaking his cane at me to emphasise what he was saying. The conversation would become heated. The women stopped working, straightened up, stretched their aching backs and wiped the sweat from their brows, their trim young breasts sticking out provocatively at him through their flimsy cotton dresses as they watched our little pantomime with amused giggles. Spazzini would turn and bark at them to get back to work, and I would turn and ride away.

One day I found an envelope in the drawer of my father's desk. In it were a number of allegations of what Spazzini had been up to in the fields, among the maize stalks and in the orange groves, signed and thumb-printed by the women and girls on the farm. My father had dealt

OVERLEAF Spazzini stood for hours under the hot sun watching the row of women at work.

with these accusations without saying anything to us; he understood perhaps more than any of us the man's dilemma. With all his faults and aggressiveness Spazzini was a victim of life, and fundamentally a good, down-to-earth man. The Africans recognised this and established an undeclared truce. *A modus vivendi* was reached.

Despite tensions of this kind on the farm, Dorian and other white Kenyans had been aware for a long time of the African potential for commerce. Dorian represented the new breed of "white Africans", and in Nairobi he was becoming more and more involved with the new African businessmen. He soon recognised the fact that African partners would inevitably become part of successful business in Kenya.

Education, for all its defects, was contributing to a healthy inter-racial understanding which had not been possible before.

Peter Okondo was one of Dorian's business partners in Nairobi. He had travelled extensively and absorbed a great deal from the Western world. Peter was half Jaluo and half Samia from the Lake District bordering Kenya to the south. Through the Catholic mission his father had been one of the first men in his area to come into contact with Europeans. At twenty, Peter himself had entered university in Cape Town, which he left with a degree in economics. Twenty years later he was handling a large sector of Nairobi's property business, to the tune of one million pounds. He remained a close friend of President Kenyatta who had made him the first treasurer of K.A.N.U. (the Kenya African National Union), and was now very much part of Kenya's affluent society.

Joseph Kamau, whose father had been killed by Dorian's patrol in the Aberdares, was another example of Kenya's new face. During the two years that he worked for Dorian in Nairobi he put aside part of his earnings each month, and when he finally left to set up on his own he bought a second-hand Peugeot 504 station-wagon and started a taxi service. Within a few years he owned several vehicles and a large Mercedes lorry and, by African standards, was a rich, successful man. He now spoke fluent English and his smiling good looks, coupled with his drive, his ambition and his will to work, made him a natural winner.

Joseph, like many others on the farm, had become part of our family and he considered Dorian and my father his mentors. My father, always ready to listen and assist whenever possible, was a man they knew they could count on and trust. He created work, helped when babies were born, treated the sick, coached boys for examinations, gave wise advice. The Africans respect age and my father, with his head of white hair and unwavering moral principles, was much revered and feared. When Joseph got married he brought his wife, and then each child that was born, to meet my father, an African gesture of respect for the eldest in the family. In Joseph's case, my father had replaced his own. As he became more independent and successful we saw less of him on the farm, but he kept close touch with Dorian in Nairobi, and always appeared on Christmas Day with a gift for my father.

Joseph was committed to Afro-European friendship and was eager to go into business with us. When we once discussed the situation in Kenya he held up his hand and said, "You see it is like a hand, each finger needs the other in order to function properly. Until we grow up, the white man is the stronger, longer, middle finger. We must not try to run before we have learnt to walk."

Joseph and Peter and many like them represent the hopes of Kenya. A new type of situation has emerged where colour is no longer a factor to be considered, and where a dialogue is possible on equal terms. But the modern-style African constitutes only two per cent of the population. For every successful businessman there are five thousand men and women still struggling for survival, and the birth rate increases each year.

The workers on the farms had progressed least since independence, but the little side benefits that farm life provides made up for the more glamorous but ultimately less beneficial bonuses to be found in the cities. This was well illustrated in the case of John Mugo.

John had been the headman on our farm for almost fifteen years. He was pleased to be in a senior position and was the link between us and the people working for us. Criticisms were vented through him, *fitinas* revealed, thieves caught or dismissed, and union and labour office problems sifted and solved. He had only one defect – he really liked to drink the potent African *pombe*, a brew made from maize flour and honey, I tried to wean him from this habit by suggesting he be promoted to go and work for Dorian in Nairobi, a much sought-after privilege, if he stopped drinking. He did, moved to Nairobi, and at first all went well. His salary was promptly doubled and after six months of apprenticeship he moved up the ladder, but he held his new job for only four months before being dismissed for ineptitude. Unable to find another job he joined the mass of the unemployed, then came back to the farm and accepted a lower salary. He had eight children to educate, and his wife was pregnant for the ninth time. For John and many others like him, the farm represented a sort of haven when all else had failed. Some owned small plots of land in the government settlement schemes but they were unable to make enough to keep and educate their families. The government endeavoured to turn these subsistence schemes into entities which would give a family £100 a year over and above their living necessities. But the aim proved difficult to achieve. Lack of organisation, experience, capital investment and overlarge families forced the men to seek employment on the European-owned farms. The European farmers did what they could for them, but their limited finances did not allow for trimmings and an inevitable condition of natural exploitation arose again. This often led to unrest and the newly formed labour unions, still young and ignorant, fanned the fire. Discontent grew each year, gravely jeopardising Afro-European relations.

However, despite the hardships of adjustment, the majority of Africans have eagerly joined the race for knowledge with its goal of material wealth. They have not all yet realised that education begins at home, and that they must learn to walk before they can run.

To the African, children, like sheep and cattle, are a source of wealth. They are born, if possible one every year, and no thought is given to their future welfare. They are a gift from God and God will provide for them. Tribes grow and multiply in this way, and the presence of a new child is as normal as the urge that produces it. Birth, like death, was in the hands of fate. But education suddenly threw an entirely new light on the previously simple family requirements.

Macharia was the fifth child of Mainge and Hannah. He was two years old when Kenya became independent. His father had worked on our farm for twenty-five years as a simple labourer, was industrious and devoted, but had never learned to read or write. Macharia, by contrast, went to school when he was six. At seventeen he had not yet graduated from the Loldia primary school on the Hopcraft farm a few miles from his home. He wanted to go to university, get a degree, and enter a law school. But there were some three hundred thousand children seeking further education each year and in 1976, for instance, there was room for only a hundred thousand in the schools across the country. The rest remained dissatisfied, uprooted and lost. The crime rate increased alarmingly as thousands of disillusioned, discontented youths poured out of the crowded schools into the cities. Many were gaoled for crimes ranging from petty thieving to murder and assault. An attempt was made in the prisons to set up facilities for technical training. Any person who went to gaol for more than one year was automatically taught a trade. But few were able to get jobs when they were freed.

I tried to convince Macharia to become an apprentice to a technician in order to learn a trade. He listened to me attentively but still hankered for the university. He wrote many letters which betrayed his feelings.

26th February, 1976

Dear Mirella,

As I'm obligated to solve my schooling problems I will write to you tirelessly. I always spend sleepless nights trying to solve these problems but I'm unable. My parents push me time to time with undelicate chains, trying to convince me not to squander time.

I'm not okay as I may say. Well I don't have a good opportunity to come and hold a dialogue with you. Much thanks for the favour you applied on my re-entry. Although I'm still not content. Still suspended, what will be the next stride. But due to the providence's presence things will be okay. Nowadays I possess a burdened head and, in fact it needs to be unloaded before the year get one more month older.

Dear Sister A (he wrote to Amina),

Much greeting read the following statements. Firstly I thank God for giving this chance to write a few words. I just want to tell you that you must work hard in school for future. We are quite well, there is nothing wrong. You must spare a minute of your time and write to me a personal letter. I am going to be very happy. I promised you that I must write a letter to you, I have done it now. How is your school studies. You must work hard to have a highest degree of position (education). "Studies make perfect." I want replies. Until on April we see each other.

And then one day he said to me, "I have decided I want to go on studying until I succeed. I don't care how many years it takes." Knowing my views, he avoided me as much as possible after this, but whenever we met and I asked him how he was, he smiled and said, "I am

busy with my head." Iain and Oria had offered to pay his tuition in exchange for minor holiday services and Macharia remained convinced that if he persevered, he would one day become a lawyer even if it took him fifteen or twenty years.

It broke my heart to watch his hopeless struggle. Even if he succeeded the chances that he would find work afterwards were extremely slim.

Like Macharia, Mweru was born on the farm, the last of seven children. Her parents had been living there when my father arrived in 1930. Her mother nearly died giving birth to one of Mweru's brothers, but my father successfully delivered the baby and saved both their lives, and the child was subsequently named Mario and became the seventh child on the farm with that name.

Mweru grew up with us and when she was of age my mother took her into the house and taught her all that she now knew. She became not only an excellent lady's maid but also our beloved "soul sister". Mweru and I shared a great deal. From her I learned about African emotions, courtship and marriage, and about the ancestral custom of female circumcision. She had a charming habit of always placing a flower on my pillow when some romantic friend came to visit me.

She gave birth to four of her babies in her hut assisted only by her mother, but one of them was born as she was walking to hospital in the Naivasha township twenty miles from the farm. She just lay down beneath a tree, and was picked up by a passing car just after the baby had appeared and taken to the Naivasha hospital to have the umbilical cord cut.

When she gave birth for the sixth time I went to visit her and found her lying weak and exhausted on her wooden bed in the semi-darkness of her hut. Her four other children stood around her, while her wizened old mother stoked the smoky fire in the middle of the floor.

"What is it?" I asked her, as I ducked into her smoky hut.

"A girl," she replied bashfully, covering her face with the bedcover. The little ball of life snuggled in her armpit.

"But it's white," I exclaimed, lifting the sheet. "Whose baby is it? This is a *muzungu* baby."

"Oh no, it's not. Don't you know that all black babies are born white; they turn black when they go into the sun," she replied smiling.

Mweru was an independent girl. She would live with men but never marry them. Her five other children all had different fathers. She cared

Mweru and Millela . . . "Don't you know
all African babies are born white?"

for and educated them on her own, and now one of them was white. She called her "Millela" after me.

Millela lived on Mweru's back or hanging from her breast for a year. Like Mweru she was very pretty. Her skin was pale brown, her head covered in faded amber curls. She was the first person I saw each morning when Mweru brought me my tea in bed. I would take her under the covers with me and she snuggled up soft and brown, cuddly and warm like a little bushbaby. But Mweru never admitted to her baby's paternity and kept her secret well guarded.

Three years later, as Millela grew, we suddenly noticed that her feet resembled those of one of our own children. All hell was let loose when the meaning of this discovery sank in, and a typical Rocco emotional drama ensued. Mweru remained silent, smiling bashfully as all eyes turned towards her. But the pretty little mite now clinging to her long legs was, when all was said and done, a part of the third generation at Naivasha, and as much one of the family as Fiametta, Valeria, Marina, Amina, Saba and Dudu. Each of us reacted differently to the new situation. My parents were never told – I dread to think what would have happened if they had found out. But Millela became one of us, the rest of us had to accept the fact, and so we took our first step towards integration.

CHAPTER 20

Before It Is Too Late

As the years went by our lives in Naivasha were more and more shaped and coloured by Africa, but now the Africanisation of the land threatened our home beside the lake.

A friend visiting me from New York once asked me if I was working on a new project. It was a question close to my heart. As we sat beside the fire in Oria's garden that night listening to the hippos in the lake, I told him the story of Naivasha. We were still talking as dawn crept over the Aberdares, and while I spoke I knew that someone, some day, would have to tell this story. Then he said, "Why don't you do it yourself before it's too late?"

Next day I sat down with my parents and took the first steps into yet another adventure, which, had I known what I was letting myself in for, I would never have undertaken, for writing my African Saga turned out to be much more complex than I had anticipated that night under the stars. As I prodded and dug into my family history I discovered many things: strengths and weaknesses, aspirations and inhibitions as yet unknown to me.

Extracting speech from my father now was like pulling teeth. He had never much liked talking about himself, but when I got him going he was articulate and his mind was still very clear. He delivered his recollections like a Neapolitan stage actor, but he never talked of Irene, his first wife, dismissing all allusion to her with a shrug of detachment, behind which, I later discovered, he hid a painful memory, a memory that he was still unable to talk about sixty years later.

My mother was a spirited talker, but her memory was failing and she faced the empty chasms with distress. She loved to talk of her youth and her famous family. Both she and my father remained unresigned to their old age and my explorations into their past were often painful. We had always taken them so much for granted and had been unaware, until it was too late, of the wealth of experience and knowledge that lay accumulated in the deep lines of their faces.

Dorian was invaluable in his contributions of facts and anecdotes. He and I shared a specially good relationship and he enjoyed our sessions as much as I did. He revealed many things about himself, the family and the farm which I did not yet know. We were both deeply concerned with Africa and Naivasha and followed similar trains of thought.

Oria and Iain were worried. They resented my intrusion into their private lives and were reluctant to talk to me. Lorenzo on the rare occasions that we were together was the most useful critical contributor. His advice, his remarks and his judgements were accurate and ruthless because he was foreign to our clan and the country we lived in, and he really cared about what I was trying to do.

The self-discipline of writing almost destroyed me. I had never yet had to face myself in this way before. I stopped seeing my friends, going to the movies or having any fun. The abstinence I imposed on myself made me feel sometimes that I was ready for Holy Orders, and several times I gave up. The season changed, the rains came and went as did the beginnings and ends of six years. The farm slipped from brown to green and back to brown and I was always writing and rewriting.

With the birth of our six daughters the third generation had now been firmly established. My parents withdrew into the background and Dorian, Oria and I moved forward to take their place.

The growth of our family, like that of the country in which we grew up, was turbulent; most events, however unimportant, inexplicably turned into emotional dramas. Only Naivasha itself seemed to remain unaffected. For my parents it was now all they had left; their European roots had been severed and, too old to move elsewhere, they were now trapped in their "golden cage". Their lives were behind them, the Europe they had known and left, with all the gloss and opulence of *la Belle Epoque*, existed no more and what remained of their lives was now unequivocally linked to Naivasha.

After the war my father's hatred of the British had produced a strong desire to leave Kenya and return to Europe, but my mother had somehow persuaded him to remain and the effort to make such a major move was now too great for them both. Their holidays in Europe became less and less frequent, and my father's desire to travel slowly evaporated, despite my mother's insatiable *wanderlust*. "There is not enough money," was always his excuse, but I felt that the real reason was that he no longer wanted to travel with her any more. Slowly they let go of the strings that attached them to Europe and the few remnants of their families still living there. Dorian, Oria and I came and went and carried news back to them. My parents would always be at the airport to meet us, but with each return the grip of old age was more evident. They seemed to be shrivelling up and became more frail and bent with each year. Always proud and carefully groomed, my mother defiantly kept up her appearance, but my father's efforts were less successful. He no longer seemed to care. His clothes hung on him like the clothes of another man, and he moved slowly, with dragging feet. One day, when I got home, I found that their bathroom mirrors had all been lowered, and the telephone bell replaced by a loud, jangling one of the sort used on station platforms to announce train arrivals. They had slept in different rooms for many years now but kept their doors wide open so they could hear each other call, if either should need help, and as an extra precaution had agreed to bang on the floor with their canes if necessary.

My mother was the stronger of the two and had so enveloped my father that he was no longer able to free himself from her. Quite unconsciously, she had absorbed him into her life and held him captive. Too old and tired now to fight, he capitulated and spent the last ten years of his life silent and resigned, waiting beside her for the end. He never complained or spoke of his conditions to anyone. With this lesson in front of him, Lorenzo always kept me at bay. "I won't end up like your father," he reminded me when he thought I needed it, and I slowly moved away from him, for I too was vividly aware of the similarity.

One day Dorian came to the farm with a new lady. She was Austrian, and her name was Eva. She appeared in Dorian's life when he was at his most vulnerable. Since Francine's departure Oria and I had developed a protective and often oppressive attitude towards our brother, and we were very critical of the women he met. Hardly ever did they seem good enough for him. We took a good look at Eva and dismissed her as nothing more than a passing acquaintance. She was pleasant and polite and spoke English, French and Italian, but she had a broad Austrian accent, a rather loud voice and her surname was Hardegg which was rather unfortunate with two girls like us around.

Our family was like the elephant heirarchy. It had a matriarchal touch

Our third generation. *Top, left to right*: Gigi, Saba, Valeria (*above*) and Fiametta, Marina. *Bottom, left to right*: Mario with Saulia, Dudu and Amina.

OVERLEAF   Mario and Giselle in 1975. "Each year the grip of old age was more evident."

to it, and Dorian had been much affected by this. Eva quickly sensed that Dorian had a pair of overbearing sisters although her behaviour was always outwardly cordial.

On one of Dorian's weekend visits to the farm, he took Oria and me aside and announced to us that Eva was pregnant. We exploded and told him he was crazy. "Don't you have enough on your plate as it is? What do you want another child for?" we exclaimed. He looked at us crestfallen, embarrassed, but also a bit amused. He agreed with all we said but what was he to do? Eva was already over thirty when she met him and desperately wanted his child. He had tried unsuccessfully to persuade her not to have it and now was turning to us for help. "Leave it to us," we replied. "We'll persuade her."

Oria and I spent many hours talking to Eva in Nairobi explaining all our various worries about the pregnancy. She listened sad and bewildered to our ruthless onslaught, and finally agreed to follow our advice for Dorian's sake. But she remained unconvinced.

Poor Eva! Little did we know what agony she was facing. But it was Dorian's welfare, not hers, that we were concerned with at that moment.

She lost the baby – due to stress, the doctor told her. We drew a sigh of relief but she was left with a broken heart. She moved in with Dorian in Nairobi and became pregnant again, but this time wisely kept her secret to herself. She was well into the seventh month of her second pregnancy when Dorian finally broke the news to us. Fiametta and Valeria, now in their early teens, had difficulty in adjusting to the new woman in their father's life and Valeria, in particular, took the news very badly. In August 1973 a seventh girl joined the clan. They named her Giselle and she immediately became known as Gigi. A tearful but victorious Eva presented her first child to the Rocco family.

As for Dorian, he had asserted himself at last. At forty-two he was quietly slipping into my father's position as head of the family and one by one we began to turn towards him for help, guidance and advice. "Ask Dorian," became an almost daily phrase in the family, and Dorian always had something intelligent, interesting or constructive to offer in reply.

But Eva and I got on no better, however, and the ensuing friction affected everyone. Only Dorian remained unmoved. "All these goddamn women!" he would groan, clasping his head, and in order to survive he simply switched off. He heard, said and saw nothing and went stoically

My mother's life-size sculpture was placed on the outside wall of our home and became a traditional prop for family photographs.

about his business, managing by silent indifference and aplomb to overcome and silence the cackling women around him. My father kept silent. He had nothing to say and no longer seemed to care.

Two years after the birth of Gigi, Eva gave us the first male heir to the family. Blond and blue-eyed, like his mother, he had none of the Rocco characteristics. But they named him Mario, and when my father saw him for the first time he turned to my mother and said, "Now I can die in peace." I would sometimes find him at night, sitting beside little Mario's crib in the dark. When I asked him what he was doing there, he would answer, "I'm just listening to him breathe."

Dorian and Eva got married shortly after Mario's birth. Oria, Iain and I were in Europe and only Lorenzo, still in Kenya, joined my parents for the simple wedding ceremony at the registrar's office. With a red carnation in the lapel of his white linen jacket and a bottle of Veuve Clicquot he brought some gaiety to the otherwise solemn occasion.

When we returned from Europe we had a massive family reunion in Naivasha. "Are you burying the hatchet?" a caustic neighbour asked. Mario was held up and the little bundle was passed around like a peace offering. It was the last time we were all to be together in Naivasha. We sat round a cluttered lunch table, finishing the ritual Sunday meal, when Willy, our frisky pet Kikuyu goat, came charging round the corner chased by an angry sow. He took a flying leap and landed like a bomb in the middle of the table, sending our plates flying, upsetting the glasses of wine, and, with screams of delight from the children and indignant exclamations from poor Ma, closed our last family reunion.

* * *

Lorenzo lost almost all of the quick fortune he had made on the Stock Exchange in Rome and like the rest of us returned to Kenya to collect his thoughts and reorganise his life. His return inevitably drew him back to Naivasha and to me. The link that had once joined us had worn thin, but had never been severed. He had been away so much that his children hardly knew him, and their superficial, often indifferent attitude towards him greatly saddened him. He suddenly became painfully aware that filial love comes from togetherness, and that he was deprived of the deep-rooted gut-love that I enjoyed. He always told me it was impossible to live with me for more than a few weeks but some invisible force kept drawing him back to me. He put out his hand to me again and together we started our ascent from the sea bed.

We settled in at Kilifi and found momentary peace again close to nature. We restored and extended the rambling house overlooking the creek, and set up a "sea-safaris" venture from which to earn a living. We went into the tourist business, taking high-paying clients on exclusive fishing expeditions, and after the first season we paid off all our debts. Lorenzo's Mediterranean yacht *Samaki* was sold and shortly after hijacked to South Africa by a political fugitive who was later caught in Durban. *Hydra*, a smaller, simpler boat adapted to the Indian Ocean, replaced the sleek *Samaki* and put out to sea every morning at dawn with Lorenzo at the helm. Lorenzo seemed calm and happy now in his new life with his new-found family, but two seasons later we both got bored with the arrangement and went to the Persian Gulf to fulfil an old ambition to make a documentary film.

When *Vanishing Africa* was published in America, Lorenzo and I had gone to New York where the success of my book brought me an assignment for *Life* magazine. I was asked to do a picture story about the Arabian dhows, the historic sailing vessels that annually ply the Indian Ocean. We had been for many years intrigued by these heavy Arab galleons, romantic vestiges of an ancient civilisation, that sailed across the horizon opposite our house in Kilifi, their great lateen sails filled with the monsoon wind, and we longed to know more of their origins and traditions.

I had begun shooting my story for *Life* in the ancient dhow harbour of Mombasa when Lorenzo suggested we make a documentary film associated with my story. With his girlfriend Muriel, who was living with us at the time, he now, two years later, hopped a cement freighter to Dubai where he bought a small fishing dhow, christened *Mir-el-Lah* after me – the least he could do, he said.

We spent five months sailing from Khorramshahr at the top of the Persian Gulf to Mombasa, with a small film crew. Kimuyu and Matheka, another bright youth from the farm joined us in Dubai. We provided them with seamen's passes in lieu of passports and they became the first and second mate of the *Mir-el-Lah*. Neither of them had left Kenya before and the sea journey was a major event in their lives. Matheka had become quite familiar with the sea in Kilifi and had learned to swim, but Kimuyu had spent his life in the hills, enclosed by land. He was scared stiff of the sea and never learned to swim. Before he stepped aboard he slipped one of Lorenzo's inflatable life-savers into his sleeping bag.

During our five-month journey Kimuyu and Matheka became sailors. They learned to read the compass and the stars, they grasped the rudiments of navigation, and took their turns at the helm. They became such an integral part of the dhow, we often wondered what we would have done without them.

Lorenzo then withdrew to Kilifi with Kimuyu and Matheka to recuperate from the arduous film venture on the *Mir-el-Lah*. He needed some peace and quiet to reorganise his thoughts and dream up some other crazy idea. He loved his rambling home by the sea and the carefree, simple fishermen with whom he roamed the Indian Ocean in his new fishing boat, fittingly named *Next Year* because it had taken four years to launch. He entered the big British Airways fishing competition that year. Competing against a fleet of sixty-five fishing boats he won the first prize with a two-hundred-pound black marlin. The prize was three tickets to the Seychelles Islands. He gave the tickets to me and the girls and, with Kimuyu and Matheka, his friends Barry and Bob, who shared his nomadic sea life, he left once again aboard the *Mir-el-Lah*. We joined him by air and spent a month all together, roaming from island to island on our Arab house-boat, drifting through the hot, sun-swept days, absorbing the light and beauty of the tropics and forgetting everything and everyone. On such occasions we made up for our disjointed life and proved Lorenzo's theory that people must live together for short intense moments to avoid the corrosion of day-to-day rust.

Alas, our film did not turn out as we had hoped and *Life* magazine folded; we had, however, lived yet another great adventure together and had caught a glimpse of a rapidly disappearing world; Lorenzo wrote his first book, *The Voyage of the Mir-el-Lah*, which he illustrated with my photographs. I returned to Naivasha to nurse my wounded pride. I had handed over my little house to Oria and Iain as they had no home of their own when they returned from Oxford and were too large a family to move in with my parents.

From my parent's house I watched the little home I had put together for my own family slowly take on my sister's personality and, within a few months, the Douglas-Hamiltons were well established where my wandering spirit had once roamed. Their two little girls, Saba and Dudu, tough and brown like forest berries, danced and played on the lawn beneath the fever trees, naked and uninhibited. The African children from the village crept towards them curious and shy at first but were soon happily playing with them. There did, however, remain a distinct sense of white superiority, even among the very young. But the overall sense of camaraderie, the mutual sharing and the general feeling of goodwill were apparent and touching and were much encouraged by Oria and Iain.

Three boisterous young dogs, cross-bred from an imported bull-terrier bitch from the Douglas-Hamilton home in Scotland and my mother's Doberman, provided frequent dramas. Fierce and highly strung, they were forever killing or maiming some favourite pet or new acquisition, and one day the three precious peacocks were found strewn in shreds across the lawn, their delicate feathers blowing in the breeze. They were excellent watchdogs, but did not seem able to distinguish between the Africans and would streak across the field in hot pursuit of the women and children on the farm, forcing them to scatter, screaming, in all directions, to scramble up trees, dive to safety in hay sheds or passing tractors, or cling, terrified, to our legs. What started as a game always seemed to turn into a vicious free-for-all which sometimes ended with torn clothes and bleeding limbs.

A tough-looking young Turkana tribesman presented himself at the farm office in search of work one day. One of the dogs was asleep on the floor by my feet. As the man halted at the door, the dog opened one eye and, before anyone could react, flew at him, sinking its fangs into the man's leg. I was so ashamed and upset I hired the man on the spot although I had no work for him. Despite repeated harsh punishment each time this happened, the dogs were never to be cured of their apparently instinctive urge. They fought savagely among themselves, their fangs so deeply embedded in one another's flesh that it often took up to half an hour to separate them, leaving them with tattered ears and torn bleeding paws.

One Christmas we were all gathered around the lunch table guzzling the ritual festive meal. A dog was lying quietly beneath the table picking up the scraps that fell to the floor. None of us noticed his brother wander in through the open door. Without any warning a violent commotion broke out from beneath the embroidered Florentine tablecloth, and the whole table rose off the ground sending plates, glasses, wine, Christmas pudding and turkey flying. Iain grabbed one of

OVERLEAF Saba and Dudu: "they had no inhibitions".

the dogs by the tail and yanked it so hard that it momentarily let go of its opponent and sank its teeth into his right hand, ripping it open so badly between the thumb and forefinger that we had to stitch it.

A few months later they attacked Dorian's dog in the same way. Dorian was by now so exasperated by this constant fighting that he picked up an iron bar and slammed it hard on their heads, inadvertently killing them both, to the despair and fury of the Hamilton family. I often wondered what strange, mad urge sparked off these violent confrontations, for when they were not fighting, the dogs lay together in the sun, sleeping and licking and loving one another.

Oria took over the studio my mother had worked in when we were children and started a small bead industry with the Maasai women on the farm, adapting her creative imagination to their age-old craft. Over a dozen capable and experienced women executed her designs and, together, they created a range of Afro-European necklaces, beaded head-dresses and leather waistcoats, jackets, skirts and coats which sold well in Europe and America.

Soon everyone on the farm was flaunting beads freely purloined from the factory: rings of beads for the fingers, beads sewn into belts or watchstraps: beads hanging from earlobes or necks. They were a much sought-after "perk" for the workers.

This side occupation provided Oria with an outlet for her creative urge. It succeeded so well that people travelled to Naivasha to buy from her, and her little cottage industry grew so big that it finally took up too much of her time and she had to close it down.

Now that, to my regret, I no longer had a home of my own I lived much of the time at "the big house" with my parents. But I soon realised that, despite its size, it was no longer large enough to accommodate me and my ageing, domineering mother. She seemed to occupy every corner of the house, and expected all who lived with her to act according to her own precise wishes. To avoid her unpleasant daily reprimands and bickering, I decided to build a house of my own. All my adult life I had longed for my own home, but somehow fate or my erratic, restless temperament had made me pull up sticks and move on.

I had secretly dreamed of a place where I could relinquish my duties as a wife, mother and daughter; a creative sanctuary void of domesticity. There was a conflict between my feminine self that wanted to conform harmoniously to a patriarchal world, and the individual in me capable of creating a world of my own which no one could share and which satisfied my craving for solitude.

One evening, as I was walking home after a hard day on the farm, I decided on a site. I sat on the grass and gazed at the open space in front of me, visualising my dream home. I saw it standing there elegant and tall, between two towering acacia trees at the bottom of the hill. It was a good position near enough to "the big house" to enable me to keep an eye on my parents, and be close to them in case of need, and yet far enough away to be on my own.

That night I could not sleep. My mind was filled with my vision. Next day I spoke to Dorian about it, and asked him if he thought I was mad.

"Not at all," he answered. "I think it's a very good idea."

I told my parents about my idea. My father just looked at me and smiled – he did not want to be involved. My mother disapproved of both the idea and the site. "It's too near the house, it won't fit into the surroundings, it will mar the contours of the garden and look ridiculous and out of place beside 'the big house'," she announced emphatically. I felt a bit crestfallen but my vision spurred me on.

I did not have much money and decided to build my house from materials available from the farm. So I hired a team of casual workers to cut the tall papyrus stalks by the lake for the roof. My friend Des Bristow on the nearby Colville ranch produced an African builder called Solomon and allowed me to cut twenty blue gum trees from his forest which we trailed ten miles to the farm with a tractor and chains. I bought seven hundred bamboos from an African friend who traded in the bamboo forest on the Kinangop and a week later, when all the materials were at hand, the work commenced. It took them two years to finish the simple A-frame construction which was covered with fifty thousand twisted papyrus stalks. A series of problems plagued my little enterprise, as if fate were putting my perseverance to the test, but I held on, determined to see it through. I finally enlisted Roger's help to complete the house. The huge skylights in the roof and the heavy glass of the hinged windows in the sloping side were tricky to install, and I needed expert assistance. With the help of Chege, a skilful Kikuyu carpenter, the house was at last completed. Between them Roger and Chege did in ten days what Solomon had not done in ten months. Suleman, a Swahili carpenter I brought up from the coast, lined the inside of the house with a split bamboo design, a tricky job requiring precision and patience.

From his bedroom window overlooking the site, my father watched the construction grow a little every day. I think he was rather surprised at and proud of the result and satisfied by my dogged perseverance. When it was ready, with bursting excitement and a sense of great achievement I watched the men gather up the tools and sweep the floor. It was the first time I had undertaken such an operation. I could not wait for the next day when I would move in.

From the cellar in "the big house" I brought up the mass of exotic trimmings gathered during my meanderings across the world in the past ten years; there were hangings from Afghanistan and carpets from Persia; brass trays, camel bags and carved wooden chests from Arabia and antique cushions from India. I unrolled the huge Ethiopian rug which Lorenzo had brought me from Addis Ababa and which had remained for many years covered in fine dust on the cement floor of the cellar. Mwangi, Moses and Macharia, the three house servants, aided by Mweru, traipsed up and down carrying my possessions on their heads. I had removed the heavy, carved Zanzibar door from my mother's studio and placed it at the entrance. The golden brown shades of the different woods and the twisted papyrus stalks of the roof provided a sober, *pain brulé* background to the brightly coloured, exotic designs in the carpets and cushions.

The long, empty interior with its tall, sweeping lines began to fill and come alive. The embroidered Indian cushions with the inlaid mirror chippings were splashed across the king-size bed. The fireplace I had designed and Solomon had so cleverly erected, with the flat, wine-red murram stones from the hill, jutted out into the room from the sloping papyrus roof. All the shavings and bits of remaining wood had been swept into it so we could test its draw, and by dusk all was ready. The faded evening light drifted in long shafts through the three skylight windows in the roof. Dudu and Saba, still only three and four years old, picked flowers from the garden and stuffed them between the papyrus in the walls.

"Go and call Pa, and tell him that my house is ready to receive him," I said to them.

I watched the three return like advancing lights in the dusk, my father's snow-white hair and their golden curls lit from behind by the last rays of the sun. "Well, Pa, what do you think?" I asked him proudly as he stepped through the door.

He nodded several times, letting his eyes wander over everything before he answered in Italian, "*Non ce mal, non ce mal* (not bad, not bad at all)." He was obviously impressed.

My mother was in Nairobi with Oria and Iain. I was looking forward to surprising them on their return next day, and to hearing what she would say; she had been so opposed to the whole plan.

"Let's light the fire to try the fireplace, it's so cold in here, we need a lot of heat to fill such a big room," I suggested excitedly.

"There is too much wood in there. You should take some out," my father said. "Wait till tomorrow, there is no one around now."

But I was impatient. "It's okay, Pa, nothing will happen." I turned to Macharia and told him to get some coals from the kitchen in "the big house".

"You are being stupid," my father said quite angrily. "Why can't you wait till tomorrow when Ma and the others return?" But I couldn't wait for tomorrow; I had waited two years already for this moment.

Macharia poured the coals carefully onto the shavings and we all watched them ignite. A tiny wisp of blue smoke rose into the tall chimney. The draught was good and soon the fire was crackling gaily. Heat began seeping towards us, filling the room with warmth. My creation sprang to life as if God had just breathed over it.

Night fell and it was time for bed.

"Oh, please can we spend the night here with Mirella?" Saba and Dudu begged. "We want to sleep with her in her new house."

But Prunella, who was visiting us from London and had joined us, took the tearful girls by the hand. "You can sleep with her tomorrow when Mummy and Daddy are back," she insisted.

I accompanied them to the car, and explained that I had to stay and look after the fire. "Wouldn't it be awful if my house burned down?" I said to them as I hugged them good night. "Tomorrow when Mummy and Daddy and Granny are back, we'll have a big house-warming party."

"Let's have dinner, here, Pa," I said when I returned. Pa was sitting beside the fireplace in a little armchair I had bought for him.

I went out into the night to check that all was well. I had placed a bucket of water by the door and sent Macharia outside to keep watch, just in case a spark should fall from the chimney onto the highly inflammable dry papyrus stalks. For a while I watched the tiny sparks rise out the chimney pipe into the cold night air and then die before they had time to settle. I sent Macharia home.

Moses brought us dinner on a tray and set it out on the floor in front of the fireplace. I opened a bottle of red wine and flopped down beside my father among the cushions on the floor. It had been a long while since he and I had been alone, and I relished the idea of entertaining him in my very own home. I lay on my back on the floor and gazed up at the towering roof above me and the pattern of twisted payrus supported by the long, blue gum poles painted black with wood preservative. The wind seeped through the roof like a sigh of nature, and the large window panes reflected the flames in the fireplace, making them dance on the hundred-foot fever trees outside. The heat forced us to move back several times from the hearth. I stared at the dancing flames and burning embers for a long while. My eyes moved up the stone fireplace and followed the transparent smoke filtering into the room. I thought of Oria's little girls and what I had said to them about the house catching fire.

Then I saw it – a ring of tiny trembling flames flickering around the neck of the chimney just where the murram stones pushed through the papyrus thatch.

I screamed and shot up as if an electrode had hit my spine, and rushed for the door. It was pitch dark outside. I grabbed hold of the bucket of water, but my foot caught in a rock lying by the trench, I fell on my face and the bucket spilled. The house servants, preparing to leave for the night, heard my screams and within minutes had reached me. The garden hose, with which we had washed the floor, was still lying on the ground beside the protruding chimney. Moses picked up the hose and was up the ladder shouting, "Water, water, turn on the water." He tore at the burning papyrus in an attempt to separate it from the rest of the house. Mwangi turned on the water tap in the bushes but there was no pressure and when I switched on the pump at the bottom of the steps the pressure was suddenly so strong it pushed the hose from the tap nozzle. The wind caught hold of the tiny flames. Within minutes the whole roof was a crackling blaze, and a great spiral of black smoke rose towards the sky.

I stood paralysed for a moment at the bottom of the stairway and watched my house burn. Then I rushed to the small open door at the back. As I entered I caught my last glimpse of the interior. The Indian cushions were still intact on the bed. I scooped them up and shoved them through the door with the Ethiopian rug. As I returned for more, lumps of fire fell all over everything, and then I saw the beams ablaze. They caved in and came crashing to the floor. Then the glass in the windows cracked and exploded. The shattered glass rained all over me and I was suddenly engulfed in thick black smoke. The terrifying scene brough me to my senses and I dived through the door, the soles of my naked feet scorched and raw as I fell on the ground outside.

Cars began arriving; Africans poured in shouting and hooting their jungle danger calls. The peaceful night was suddenly filled with the terrifying cacophony of fire. I picked myself up from the ground and limped down the slope. There was nothing I could do now, but watch my dream on fire, as if God had painted great flat strokes of curling flames around it. The spongy, brittle papyrus incinerated like rice paper. The wooden A-frame and bamboo cross-pieces turned to red-hot bars. The acacia trees on either side caught fire and the tiny, feathery leaves fell in sparks to the ground. The whole outline of my house was drawn with fire against the black night sky. I ran for my camera and for a moment forgot it was my house burning and saw only the picture framed in the viewfinder. As I pressed the release button, I noticed that three fingers of my hand were bent at right angles at the middle knuckle. I looked at them and felt the pain and suddenly became aware of myself in all the commotion. My soaking dress stuck to my body. My hair hung wet and bedraggled down my face. My eyes stung and tears ran down into my mouth. My scorched feet were bleeding and caked with earth and leaves. I fell to my knees and sobbed into my hands, and was picked up by some Africans who carried me up the stairs into "the big house". I heard voices against the crackling fire, all talking at the same time.

A group of men and women and some children stood by the entrance of "the big house". They closed in on me as I approached, gasping at my appearance. "*Kaso Raho, ne Shauri ya Mungu,*" they kept repeating to me. "Tighten your heart, it is the will of God, be thankful that you are alive."

Then I saw my father for the first time. He pushed his way through the group of Africans and came towards me, looking like a little, bent gnome, so fragile and yet so strong. I fell into his outstretched arms. "It's all right, Mirella," he said in his faint, croaky voice, trying to reassure and comfort me. He looked up into my tear-stained face and

OVERLEAF   "I watched my dream on fire . . .
for a moment I forgot it was my house burning."

patted me on the cheek. "We'll rebuild it together, it's only money after all." He was looking for something to say to calm me down.

"Only money, like hell," I thought. "Will anyone ever know?" But he knew; he had watched me all along and had shared my first moments of joy only an hour before. What he did not yet know was that the first hundred pages of this book and the tapes of the talks I had had with him and my mother had gone up in flames with the rest.

PART V

The Tree Withers

CHAPTER 21

His Last Safari . . .

It was dawn on 5th April, 1975. The sun appeared, a ball of fire over the Aberdare Mountains to the east, and once again painted the morning sky with the colours of the sunrise. It crept rapidly upwards, liquefying the brilliant hues and turning them into transparent light. Dawn and dusk in Africa do not last long; the passage from day to night and from night to day is intense and fast and the magic moments that precede them are fleeting.

I stood knee-deep in the thick, cold mud of the papyrus swamp on the edge of the lake that day, armed with my cameras, as I had done so many times before in my endeavour to catch Africa's awakening. Each time the spectacle was different. The lake was still and silent. Only the smothered sounds of the awakening water birds were audible as they moved from their night quarters to begin the daily search for food.

It was the end of the dry season and the rains were late. The farm and its inhabitants waited in breathless anticipation for the first rains to soak the parched, thirsty land and dispel the dust clouds. The early morning air was still, clean and crisp and the moisture of the night spread a transparent web all around.

I returned home to join my parents for breakfast. The smell of strong Italian coffee and freshly baked brioche wafted towards me as I trudged up the stone steps and crossed the lawn. Meal times in our family had become a sort of ritual. They were the only times in the day when we were all together and enabled our parents to keep in touch with our frantic lives. A lot of time and effort was put into meals and we were all expected to be punctual for them. We had to be properly dressed and contribute to the conversation. In exchange my father saw to it that the food was well and tastefully prepared, with many variations. My mother and father sat at either end of the table and there were always at least two

OVERLEAF Lake Naivasha: the sun appeared, a ball
of fire over the Aberdare Mountains to the east.
Dawn and dusk in Africa do not last long.

well-trained Africans in attendance, dressed by my mother in elegant, imaginative uniforms.

My mother never learned to cook but she was adamant about properly laid tables, appropriate crockery and cutlery and scalding plates. My father's natural facility in the kitchen and his love of cooking as an art often turned his dishes into exciting and much applauded creations. The Rocco cuisine was well known in the country and much appreciated and envied by all who came to our home. My father taught Oria and me to cook and several of Kenya's top African chefs started at Naivasha. (My father's star pupil was Kimuyu, whose culinary creations sometimes outshone his own. Even on safari in the bush he managed to produce fresh bread, warm brioches and cheese soufflés in an oven which he dug in the earth and covered with hot coals from the wood he gathered around the camp.) But because of his aversion to dairy products, my father himself never cooked with butter or milk. This infuriated my mother who had been brought up on French cuisine in which both are used prolifically. As a result, over the years she lost all interest in food and my father was never able to hide his dismay each time she refused the dishes he had so carefully and lovingly prepared for her. As he was in command of the kitchen, Italian cuisine prevailed and often led to heated discussions: "That eternal unimaginative tomato sauce and pasta is so boring," my mother would exclaim disdainfully, while my father raised his eyebrows, shrugged his shoulders and pretended to turn a deaf ear.

Coffee egg was one of father's daily indulgences. Two eggs were beaten with sugar to a froth, and strong, black, Neapolitan coffee added. Beaten with a teaspoon, the froth was brought to a particular consistency before the steaming coffee was gently and lovingly poured down the side of the cup, making the pale yellow froth rise to the top. He would then drink it slowly, straining it through his moustache. There is something so decadently delicious about steaming coffee and sugar-egg froth. Any children sitting at the table with him would crowd round his chair like hungry birds and be spoon-fed with chunks of freshly baked home-made bread and brioche dunked in the coffee.

The 5th April was a Sunday. My father was still dressed in his pyjamas and dressing gown, a funny habit that lingered from his childhood days in Naples where Sundays were for getting up late and slowly in order to mark a day of rest. The breakfast things were cleared from the table. My father shuffled slowly to his room on the third floor to begin his routine Sunday preparations. I settled down in the spacious sunny living-room to clean my cameras and sort my films. My mother busied herself with the flowers, one of the few occupations still left to her. The lazy Sunday mood hung about.

"Mirella," I heard my name suddenly echo down the stairs. Mweru ran down to me, an anxious tremor in her voice. "Mirella, come quick." Sensing her alarm, I dropped what I was doing and rushed towards her. I met her on the stairs. "Come," she repeated, "Come quick. *Mzee* has fallen."

I found my father lying on the straw carpet beside his chair. "I missed the chair, I can't get up," he said. I put my arms beneath his armpits and pulled him gently to his feet. He was so frail and light. "I can't feel my leg," he half whispered as he limped to the bed supported on either side by Mweru and myself.

He was covered in perspiration, and was in obvious pain. His face was ashen, and his fists tightly clenched. His left foot lay pointing outwards at right angles, and he groaned when I tried to turn it. Mweru ran to call Iain and Oria at their house. They arrived a few minutes later and raced up the steps two at a time.

"Don't move him," Iain said as soon as he had examined him. "It looks serious, we must call the doctor." But it was Sunday and the doctor was not in his surgery. Iain jumped into his aeroplane and flew to Naivasha to pick up the Indian doctor, Shah. Half an hour later he was back by my father's bedside.

"The leg is broken in the upper femur," Shah told us gravely. "I have given him morphine. He must go to Nairobi. It is serious at his age."

Nairobi was seventy-five miles away on a long and dusty pot-holed road and my father was eighty-two years old. It took Dorian two hours to contact the flying doctor service who sent a plane to fetch him. We watched and listened to the sky. At two o'clock in the afternoon the distant drone of the approaching aircraft finally wafted across the lake and within minutes it roared over the house. Iain lit a smoke signal and cleared the cattle from the runway. The aircraft headed towards the brown hills behind the farm and circled back to the landing strip. It bumped gently towards us and taxied to a halt. Iain and I helped unload the stretcher and accompanied the young pilot and an older gentleman to my father's room.

OVERLEAF   My father had left the farm so many
times before in similar dramatic conditions.

At the bottom of the winding stairway I waited with the servants and the children for my father to appear. Not long after, Iain and the pilot emerged carrying the stretcher with my father's frail body covered by a maroon bedspread, and led the silent little family procession down the stairs to the car. Oria followed with Ma, smartly dressed for town, and behind them James and Mwangi the houseboys with downcast eyes and respectful steps carried a suitcase and some cushions. Lorenzo waited by the car at the bottom of the steps.

"*Forza*, Mario," he said as he bent over the stretcher. My father looked up and patted him on the cheek.

"Lorenzo, I'm glad you're here," he replied. The two men exchanged a look of solidarity reflecting the mutual understanding that had always existed between them, but which neither had ever admitted to.

A bunch of African children had gathered around the plane and watched, wide-eyed and silent, as the stretcher was loaded onto it. My father smiled feebly at each one of us as we tearfully bent to kiss him goodbye. He had left the farm so often before in similar dramatic conditions and we never knew whether he would return. My mother climbed into the cockpit beside the pilot and the plane taxied down the runway towards the brown hills; it turned, halted for a moment and took off in a cloud of dust, passing low over our heads.

Tears spilled down Oria's face and Lorenzo stood, tight-lipped, leaning against the car. All eyes were focused on the disappearing plane. Right arms were outstretched – were we waving or saluting? The dust settled and the little gathering slowly dispersed.

"Let's have tea," Iain said in true British fashion, breaking the hush the aircraft had left behind.

I went for a walk along the lake and lay in the long grass, looking up at the sky and thinking of the way my day had started and how it had so unexpectedly ended. I followed the sun in its descent behind the hills and once again watched the momentary splash of colour streak the sky. The mosquitoes rose and started their incessant hum around me. The water birds settled for the night. Three pelicans flew very low and landed on flat webbed feet in the still water behind me. Suddenly it was night, and I walked home.

*

My father survived the first operation when a steel pin was inserted to join his broken bone. He overcame the bronchitis that set in several days after. But then the stomach ulcer which had almost killed him ten years before began to bleed again. His strength seeped out of him and with it went his will to fight to live. He instructed Oria and Iain who were preparing another European tour for their "Elephant Survival" project to go and do their work and not to hang around the hospital waiting. So they left shortly after for Germany, Holland and Switzerland.

Three weeks after his surgery my father was back on the operating table and I lost the slender hope that I had clung to. After four hours, the surgeon came out. He looked at us and shrugged his shoulders.

"I did what I could. I performed an almost impossible operation. I found a hell of a mess. He should have died ten years ago," he told us gravely. "I'm sorry," he added. "He has had ten years of grace. Now he is in the hands of God." He turned and walked away down the corridor.

My mother sat, bent and sad, on the leather seat staring at the clenched hands in her lap. Dorian, Lorenzo and I waited beside her for our father to be wheeled out of the operating theatre. Two white-clad Africans rolled the stretcher through the door; only my father's white hair, strewn on the pillow, was visible, and on either side of him a black sister held the blood transfusion tubes fixed to his veins.

A month before my father's accident he had presided over a *baraza* and had donated a piece of the farm and a little house for a much-needed dispensary and health care centre. The Sunday following his operation was to be the inauguration date and invitations had been sent out all round.

Unable to attend, my father whispered to Dorian from the intensive care unit, "Go in my place, tell them that I am not well." Dorian and I looked down at his shrunken, hollow face, and we knew he would not live and that he knew it too. Only my mother refused to accept this truth.

"Don't worry, he will pull through," she repeated doggedly. "I know him better than you do."

*

Over seven hundred people gathered from miles around and squatted beside the little, freshly painted dispensary on the farm. Loudspeakers and an amplifier had been installed by our friend and neighbour Roger, who had organised the whole festivity single-handed in his usual meticulous way. The smartly dressed young D.O. was addressing the congregation when we arrived. He spoke forcefully, with ease and conviction, of his aspirations for the country and urged everyone to pull together. At the end of his speech he bowed politely and smilingly returned to his seat. Then Nganga, the six-foot-six newly elected Councillor for the Naivasha district, rose and made his way to the microphone. A big, burly African, he was now a wealthy and important figure in the Naivasha area, and had known us all since we were children.

He grabbed the microphone and barked a greeting to us. He told us of his early days on the farm and sent his greetings to *Mzee* Rocco lying ill in the hospital.

"He is my father too," he said. "He has taught me a lot. We pray for his recovery and his quick return to us. By giving us a part of his farm for our dispensary, he has proved he cares about us. His son Dorian is here today, Dorian is not a *muzungu*, he is an African like us and we are going to treat him like a brother." Loud cheering and clapping broke out. Dorian smiled and nodded and then Nganga invited him to speak.

As I listened to my brother's words, images of our childhood on the farm were interwoven with the dominant figure of my father, the love, respect and reverence he had commanded throughout the forty-five years of his reign, and his slow decline into old age that had now suddenly culminated in the sterile room of an intensive care unit. My eyes moved across the faces of the people listening to my brother, the friendly, tired faces of Africa, resigned and weather-beaten, marked by life. Spazzini stood alone to one side away from the crowd, isolated and severe, his arms crossed in front of him. He was wearing his grey flannel suit and a soft grey hat set slightly at an angle on his head. What was he thinking? His face did not betray his thoughts.

The newly elected M.P. leapt to his feet when Dorian sat down, and urged everyone to work together in a common effort to fight poverty, ignorance and disease. He extracted a wad of hundred-shilling notes from his trouser pocket and counted out fifteen of them in front of his delighted audience, as his personal donation. Then the dancers came on with their drums and feathers, their bells and colobus monkey skins, and cavorted in front of us in a wild jungle dance that covered everyone in dust. The M.P. cut the ceremonial ribbon and the "North Lake Dispensary" was declared open as the schoolchildren, scrubbed clean in their dark blue and white uniforms, sang the Kenya National Anthem.

Kimuyu had prepared a curry lunch which was presided over by Dorian, Eva and myself. It was the first completely African meal served in my parents' home. Perhaps it was just as well that neither of them was present to see the Africans they had kept at bay for almost half a century sitting in their armchairs, sprawled all over the lawn, eating and drinking from their Parisian tableware and glasses.

I left before the last guests and rushed back to Nairobi and my father's hospital bed. I ran down the long, silent antiseptic corridors to the second floor of the St George's Ward. It was 7.30 at night. I slipped on the white robe, muslin mask and plastic shoe coverings, caught my breath and knocked on the door of the intensive care unit.

My father lay on the flat table in the sterile room covered with a white sheet. His eyes were closed. He breathed heavily through the transparent oxygen mask. The blood still dripped at regular intervals into his right arm from a plastic bag, and a saline drip was attached to a needle in his left. My mother sat beside him holding his hand. She had not left his side all day.

"How is he?" I whispered.

"He's much better."

"What do you mean, 'much better' Ma?" I was genuinely surprised.

"Oh yes, we had a little talk together this morning. He asked me why I had not gone to the farm. Had I forgotten that today was 2nd May? He seemed almost angry that I was not there."

"I can't believe it," I whispered, and placed my hand on his forehead. He opened his eyes as he felt the contact of my hand. "Hello, Pa," I said. "How are you?"

"Okay," he mumbled through the mask. There was a twinkle in one of his eyes as if he had wanted to wink at me. "You went to the farm? Tell me, how did it go?"

I tried to tell him in a few concise sentences. He nodded his head slightly and seemed pleased. He looked at me for a long moment and then closed his eyes. I slipped the mask back on his face and sat opposite my mother holding his hand.

For the next three days and three nights my mother and I kept up the long vigil. I began to pray for the end. As I looked at his shrunken body and hollow ashen face, I wondered why we cling to life and try so hard to stretch it beyond its limits. He was a tired old man who had come to the end of his road. On the third day he was moved back to his room from the intensive care unit. That night he opened his eyes wide and spoke quite coherently in a Neapolitan dialect. He spoke of a large family gathering around a dining table, asked all present to be seated and called for more plates and wine to be brought. He stared fixedly ahead of him, looking through us as we stood around him. I tried to answer his questions, to share his "last supper" with him, but he did not see me.

I put my mother to bed. "I want to be with him when he leaves us," she turned and told me, with tears brimming in her eyes as she let go of her last hopes. I remained with her until the sleeping pill took over, and assured her I would stay with him and come and call her if it was necessary. When I returned to my father's room, he was gasping – long, deep, rasping sounds that I had never heard before. The acrid smell of death hung in the room – it was almost unbearable. His eyes were still wide open and still staring at the wall in front of him. I went out and called the sister.

"Is this the end?" I asked.

"I think so," she replied quietly and felt my father's pulse. "Do you want to leave the room?" I looked down at him. I knew he could not see me any more. I shook my head and stayed. The pretty young nurses in their green and white candy-striped uniforms came in and stood beside the sister. The intervals between each gasp got longer, and longer, and then they stopped.

He died at eleven o'clock that night. It was 5th May, exactly one month after he had left the farm. The four weeks in the hospital had been a slow downhill slide into the grave. He knew he would not leave the hospital alive, he had told us all one by one. He had given me his watch and his gold wedding ring, and told me to take over his room in "the big house". I left the bedside and walked down the corridor fighting back a strong emotion. I had never before seen anyone die.

"This is sister Mary speaking, will you come and ascertain death? Colonel Mario Rocco, room No. 8, St George's Ward." The voice followed me down the corridor.

"I want to call my brother," I said. She handed me the receiver and dialled the number for me. "It's over," I said to Dorian on the phone. "He died at eleven."

Dorian arrived shortly after. He put his arm around my waist. He shrugged his shoulders and let out a deep sigh. Together we walked down the corridor to my mother's room. She was fast asleep. I shook her gently.

"Wake up, Ma," I said to her softly. She opened her eyes, a little startled, but could not see me without her glasses. "Pa has left us, Ma." I had difficulty in saying the words. She let out a little gasp like a frightened bird.

"Why didn't you call me?"

"There was no time," I answered. We helped her to her feet, helped her slip on her dressing gown and spectacles, and walked beside her back to my father's room.

I thought I knew what he would look like when he died; he had been so close to death so many times before. But now it was quite different. He seemed to have melted into the bed. His face so white, his hair and a little pointed beard one with the sheets and pillows. The nurse came in and closed his eyes. No emotion crossed her face. She was used to this. She stood with us and said a prayer:

"Almighty God, giver and taker of life, receive the soul of Mario Rocco into your fold. May he rest in peace as he waits for those he has left behind him tonight to join him. Bestow on those who loved him the strength to continue living on this earth without him until such time as you will reunite them. Amen."

She said all the right words, the words we wanted to hear, and then left us alone in the room. After a long silence my mother rose from her chair. "My reason for living has left me," she said feebly. "I too am ready to go now."

Lorenzo arrived at midnight from a dinner party as we were leaving the hospital. He clasped us to him and we stood for a moment in the dark, cold night drawing strength from contact with each other.

Next day we collected Pa's belongings from the hospital – his discarded, misshapen clothes, his hearing aid, his spectacles, and a few loose shillings. I packed his bag in the empty room, then we walked back down the corridor with his suitcase and met an old Italian friend of his coming to visit him. He turned and walked back to the car with us.

Ma and I drove back to Naivasha on the still unfinished Pan-African highway that wound along the high Rift Valley escarpment. It did not matter how long it took to get home. It was like travelling in space, somewhere between heaven and earth. Africa lay sprawled out below us, serene, ageless and forever. On the wide, empty road, there was no need to concentrate on my driving. I let the car roll on. My mother sat beside me, crumpled, dejected and silent, and gazed across the hazy blue Africa which she had crossed with him so many years before.

Images of my father flashed through my head. I had watched him fade for many years, like a powerful engine grinding slowly to a halt. Sitting at his desk, playing his endless games of patience, smoking his endless cigarettes or sleeping in his chair, with his hands crossed behind his head; he was always there, his silent presence everywhere. He had become as much a part of the spacious library in which he spent most of his days as the worn furniture. Resigned to old age, he had long stopped arguing or discussing with us. He hardly seemed to care any more; he rarely spoke and often did not hear what was being said around him. He cut a lonely figure, leaning for long hours on the garden wall staring into space. When I asked him what he was thinking about, he smiled and shrugged me off and just said, "*Alla mia giovinezza, ai bei tempi passati* (Of my youth, of the good times gone by)." He had shut himself off from us and from the world. Occasionally he would come to life when an old friend or a pretty woman came to see him. Then the years would drop from his face, he would straighten his shoulders and the old flicker would return to his hollow ancient eyes, and I thought how old trees just grow stronger, old rivers grow wider every day, but old people just grow lonesome. In the night his cries of "*Mamma Mia*" echoed through the house, like the cries of some already distant soul.

Had the solitary life he led on the farm been of his choice, or had he been so dominated by my mother's overpowering love for him and her unconscious determination to mould his life to hers that he just gave up? Why had he never rebelled against his lot or tried to change it? He never talked to us about his marriage. He never confided or complained, he just kept silent and took his secrets to the grave with him.

A group of Africans standing by the road jolted me from my reveries. There were heavy rubber skid marks on the tarmac and the cement post had been knocked over. A badly smashed white car hung in the bushes of the ravine several hundred feet below.

"Was anyone killed?" I asked the young African who came running up to me.

"No, only the driver broke his leg. I am Mario; I work for Ricky. Don't you remember me? Your father helped my mother when I was born." Of course I remembered him he was Mweru's brother.

"How is the old man?" he continued.

"He died last night."

"Oh, I'm sorry, *Shauri ya Mungu*," he said, and lowered his eyes. We looked at each other and said no more. "Are you going to Naivasha?" he asked me. "Will you ring up Ricky and tell him we have had an accident?" I promised him I would and drove off down the escarpment to the plains below.

The return to the farm was emotional. The house servants, Kimuyu, James, Mwangi and Moses, came down the stairs to greet us and help us out of the car. Sadness shrouded their faces and clouded their moist eyes. They clasped our hands with both of theirs, an African gesture denoting reverence or emotion. Mweru met us by the door with Millela on her back. Tears ran down her face. She had put flowers in little vases all over the house.

"We will never see *bwana Mzee* again," she sobbed as she fell into my arms. Then Spazzini arrived; with downcast eyes he came up the steps holding his greasy hat in his hands. He fell sobbing to his knees in front of my mother and kissed her hand. I was afraid she might reprimand him for losing control of himself but tears rushed to her eyes. She stood erect and put a hand on his shoulder, and gently helped him to his feet. Still clutching his battered farm hat he collapsed into an armchair, buried his face in his folded arms, and let the tears flow unashamedly, years of pent-up feeling finally released. I poured him a stiff drink and let him cry himself dry. He wiped his face with his crumpled handkerchief and loudly blew his nose. Without saying anything he went outside and disappeared among the tall trees in the garden.

In his will my father had expressed the wish to be cremated on the farm and had given Dorian instructions on how to light the bier. But I had been to Benares and seen the Hindus burn their dead on the *ghats* on the banks of the Ganges, and watched a pair of feet swell up and burst in the flames. I found it hard to accept the idea of my father being cremated in front of me.

"I want him to be buried like Napoleon," my mother said to me next day, and, together, we went into the garden to choose a site for his grave beneath a peach tree he had grown from a kernel. I thought his grave should be placed to one side to leave room for Ma's beside him, but she wanted it in the centre. Six old men came to dig his grave and my mother presided over them just as she had presided over my father's life.

OVERLEAF At my father's funeral, the people came from all around to say their last goodbye.

(Photo : Reutie Butler Shober)

The farm lorry had gone to Nairobi the day before with a load of potatoes; it would now return with my father in his coffin. Hundreds of Africans came from miles around carrying branches picked on the hills or in the garden, and lined the road for hours awaiting the lorry. When the coffin was unloaded and placed beneath the trees, they moved with it and squatted silently in the dark shade beside it. The old men and women from the village, the warriors from the hills, the children from the school and everyone working on the farms all around took up their silent vigil together. I placed a large smiling photograph of him on an easel beside his coffin and a copper vase filled with sunflowers. Isaiah, the old tractor driver, placed the ritual sugar-cane branch at his head. He was slightly drunk and started up a long monologue addressed to anyone who cared to listen.

"*Mzee* Rocco was our father, he was a good man, he looked after us, with him we feared nothing, now that he has left us we shall no longer have anyone to help us solve our problems." Tears streamed down his rugged face and trickled into his mouth.

As the afternoon shadows spread across the lawn, the long line of vehicles moved slowly down the drive in a cloud of dust. Friends and neighbours, many of whom we had not seen for years, arrived from everywhere for the funeral. Awkward in their dark suits and ties and their Sunday dresses, they emerged from the dust like ghosts, brushing their clothes and faces with their hands. They carried African flowers from their gardens and placed them on the grass around the coffin. They kissed my mother, dressed in black and looking sad and regal, and her eyes filled with tears each time she recognised a friend she still remembered.

The young African priest came from Naivasha and set up his altar on a wooden table beneath the trees. He read the service in English and Kiswahili. A young black girl in a spotted red dress beat a drum and sang a mournful song. Behind her a choir of Jehovah's Witnesses, dressed in white, accompanied her, and all around her sadness was written on the black faces of the people listening to her song. Dorian, in his dark blue suit, stood with folded arms beside my mother; he suddenly looked more imposing than I had ever seen him before. A single shaft of sunlight broke through the leaves on the trees and fell on him, singling him and my father's photograph out from among the little crowd of white settlers in their outdated, misshapen Sunday clothes.

Dorian and Lorenzo carried the coffin to the grave with Mwangi, James and Kimuyu. As it was lowered into the ground, the sunlight hit the brass handles and for a moment it looked as if it were on fire. John Mugo made a short speech in Kiswahili before the ritual handfuls of earth were thrown.

"*Mzee* Rocco was a warrior, a fearless man. He fought in the war, he walked through the bush in the Congo hunting elephant, and came to Naivasha in his own aeroplane. He has looked after us all for fifty years and now we are taking him on his last safari, as we cover him with the earth of his *shamba* where he has lived and worked with us for half a century." He turned to Dorian and put his hand on his shoulder. "He has left it all to you. You must now lead us, bring us your brains and your money and we will work from our hearts. Show us the way and teach us to follow, for we are but sheep in the wilderness. This is the only road and in front of God we are all one."

My mother kissed Dorian on both cheeks and the gathering slowly dispersed and melted into the trees. When the dust settled we were alone again. I went for a walk with Lorenzo and looked up at the trees my father had planted, towering above us, and suddenly became acutely aware of how many years he had lived here.

Next day I went through his belongings and found a will he had written on 13th February, 1967, almost ten years earlier.

This my will which I am compiling while still *compos mentis* but with full knowledge that I shall not live long – I formally declare that all money deposited in banks belongs to my wife and that my assets are unimportant.

There is an account of my personal money amounting to about two million lire (£1,000) plus one million in *Buoni del Tesoro*, 5% with *Credito di Venezia e di Rio de la Plata*, Naples (Italy). This amount, namely, three million lire, should be shared by my four grand-children: Fiametta, Valeria, Marina and Amina.

Deposited in a joint a/c with *Banco di Roma per la Suizzera* there is a sum of $12,000 (twelve thousand dollars) which I wish to be transferred to Rosetta.

I advise that the farm should be made a limited Private Company in which Dorian would hold 40% and Mirella and Oria 30% each.

I also suggest that the shares kept in safe deposit with Morgan Grenfell & Co. Ltd should, when the time comes, be transferred to Mirella.

All my clothes, after the children have made their selection, should be given to the farm labourers.

Motor cars registered in my name will become the property of my wife.

I bow my head in gratitude to Giselle for all she has done for my welfare. Bless her!

Mario Rocco

"I had watched my father slowly fade."

CHAPTER 22

The Heart of Africa

I distributed my father's clothes, many of them worn and misshapen, a few still quite new and unused, to his four servants. They measured them for shape and size, put on his hats, and tied his neckties and scarves around their necks, giggling like children at Christmas. They thanked me effusively and carried the garments proudly off to their huts. They had never before owned such clothes.

Among his few belongings I found letters from his mother dated 1926, some from Irene, all his correspondence from the internment camp, a few lines he had left behind for my mother and a letter to her, dated many years back, inveighing against the behaviour of Irene and their daughter Rosetta. Its tone was bitter and unforgiving.

Now that he was gone, I began to discover through his letters the man I had lived with all my life and never really got to know. I began to wonder about my father. What had he really been like inside – was he the man we all thought he was, or was he another? The more I thought about it the more I questioned our whole African Saga and the reasons that had pushed my parents to Africa.

Had Irene, the only woman he had ever loved and lost, been the real cause of his flight from Europe? Europeans who turn to Africa and remain there all their lives are often motivated by some strong emotional thrust.

He had allowed himself to be loved by my mother. He had accepted the conditions and had honoured the pact he had made with himself. But what had really been the price he had paid, and had this been the reason for his morose silence in the last ten years of his life? Were these the thoughts that wandered through his mind when he leant for hours each day on the garden wall, smoking his cigarettes, the reason for his cries of "*Mamma Mia*" in the night?

Spazzini on a different level had fled to Africa for the same reason. This perhaps explained the silent *entente* between him and my father and the deep love and respect in which Spazzini held him.

Behind the image of the dazzling cavalry officer whose career had been broken by his exile, whose life had been directed by a powerful and adventurous lady who had taken him to Africa, where he had fallen prisoner in a war he never fought, stood the fragile figure of the true sentimental Neapolitan romantic, ultimately the victim of a life he had not chosen. The hero was in fact a tragic one and the beautiful love story a drama. And my mother, what of her? How had she been affected? What had it been like living with a man who had never loved her as she had loved him? Had she never been able to reach him, and had had to content herself with living for fifty years a life of pretence in a paradise setting? This was perhaps the drama behind the fairy-tale exterior of our African Saga.

*

My mother placed my father's photograph opposite her chair beneath the Botticelli print at the end of the long sitting-room and surrounded it with flowers. She sat all day in her armchair just gazing blankly at it, and every day she leant on the garden wall where he had stood for so many years and looked down at his grave with the fading flowers. All around her the lush green oasis they had planted together enveloped her tiny figure dressed in black, like a picture in which she was the focal point.

I moved into my father's room, emptied his belongings from the cupboards and distributed them among the family. The room had grown old with him. The curtains were stained and faded; the mattress of his silver, carved Zanzibar bed sagged in the middle; the drawers were filled with left-overs from his life – old keys, half-empty medicine bottles, packs of well-thumbed cards, Agricultural Show badges, bits of string and elastic bands, his pilot's licence, an old passport with a photograph of him in 1937 – smiling, handsome and vigorous – and nicotine-stained ashtrays in every corner. The two empty armchairs, with the oxygen cylinder and mask beside them, were faded and worn. His two faithful friends, the African hornbills, still perched on the balcony outside his room, pecked on the window pane. The ceiling was stained and peeling from unattended rain leaks and the art deco lamp was speckled in dust, dead mosquitoes and bat droppings – he had never noticed, or bothered to clean it. The room resembled him – tired, old, worn and in need of repair.

He would never return, so I took over. I moved out every bit of furniture, carpets and hangings and left the room naked and bare to begin its new life with me. Only the antique Zanzibar bed remained. I turned it round, added two feet to each end and fitted it into the alcove. I gathered up the few remaining cushions that never made it to my A-frame house and spread them out on the floor. I worked ruthlessly and, within forty-eight hours, the room was born again. My mother protested half-heartedly at the speed at which I moved, but I explained to her, after having offered her his bed, that if we did not do it now, it would never be done. I believe in drastic surgery.

My father's death seemed to have brought our African Saga to a close. Nothing much changed in our daily lives, but there was a great absence in the house. His memory lingered on. Photographs everywhere of his smiling, tired face with the wicked, laughing eyes, replaced his physical presence. When Dorian and Eva came to Naivasha, Saulia's soft voice would echo through the house calling his name. She was baby Mario's *ayah* and came from Uganda and loved and cared for him as she would her own child. Watching them together always made me feel warm inside. Big, fat, smiling Saulia, with her round arms and bosom, was a living symbol of woman, motherhood and love. Her uninterrupted gaiety and infectious laughter affected all of us, and Mario's days were bathed in it as ours and those of our children had been by others like her when we were his age.

Now that my father was gone, I often caught myself wondering what course Naivasha and our lives would follow. His was the first death in our family and a very definite milestone. The land, Kenya's white highlands; the wildlife, Iain's elephants; the people, our African friends and faithful servants, Kimuyu, Shaibu, Mweru and Macharia, and all the others; and the dream which was made up of all these elements – all these seemed to be slipping from our grip.

He had left us all behind to keep the show on the road, but what was to happen to the show?

Well aware of the therapeutic power of physical exercise, I had suggested to Ma that she plant an avenue of trees and cacti along the drive leading to "the big house", down which my father's body had travelled for the last time. "We'll call it the imperial highway, and it'll commemorate the date of his funeral," I said to encourage her. My mother always saw things in superlatives when it concerned the family and the suggestion worked. Had she not announced on the day of the funeral that she wanted him to be buried like Napoleon? In a last desperate spurt of energy she threw herself and her two gardeners into this new venture. Day by day she slowly advanced down the long driveway. Each afternoon I walked with her, encouraging her, inspecting the progress and praising her.

Her strength was on the wane, but her spirit marched on defiantly. From the terrace at the top of the house I would watch her stride with her canes each morning down the cypress avenue leading to the lake; her tiny shrunken figure with the bright chequered shawl like a drop of paint on the vast canvas of her unruly garden. Standing knee-deep in the long grass, she called out to her gardeners, waving her canes at them like a field-marshal on a battlefield. This same determined spirit had pushed her father through the Panama almost a century before and was now driving us on the farm.

Dorian was in Nairobi, where his business had hit an all-time high, and like the developing nation it was on a steady upward curve. Kenyatta, now an old man of eighty, still held the country in his grip. Despite growing rumours of unrest, capital kept pouring into the country from all over the world. Nairobi became one of the leading modern cities of Africa. High-rise buildings mushroomed everywhere, replacing the single-storeyed ones, and cut an impressive skyline where, hardly sixty years before, Kenya's capital had boasted only a few stone buildings, some canvas tents, some bullock carts and the railway station. Tourism flourished and business boomed. Dorian and his African associates wheeled and dealed and his company divided and formed subsidiaries. Kenya was fast reaching its zenith. But Kenyatta's health was precarious and the nagging question, "What will happen when the *Mzee* dies?" hovered in the air.

No rain fell for two years after my father died and the lake receded to its level of 1963 before Dorian had lost his potato crop. A flat expanse of black soil was again exposed, waiting to be worked and planted. The water was now only visible from the top of the house and once again Naivasha lay beneath a mantle of fine white dust. The trees and mountains quivered in the heat haze like a mirage on the dehydrated, thirsty land. We had long stopped listening to the weather forecast; there was no sign of rain.

Dorian and I began scheming again. We both so desperately wanted to find a viable solution for Naivasha. We could start a small rural industry there which would provide for the many local necessities and give work to far more people than we were able to employ on the farm. We could plant mulberry trees and start a silk industry, or make toys and simple farm implements, or plant avocados and roses for export. Dorian mused out loud to me as we sat on the garden wall or walked through the trees and along the water's edge. I listened to his disconnected sentences. He was a dreamer, an incurable adventurer, always ready to get involved in a new project. And adventurers have been known to turn dreams into reality.

We watched the water recede, our greedy eyes scanning the dark expanse of soil in front of us, tantalising and daring us again. We gazed across the newly uncovered land, both fighting the temptation to move in. We had not yet forgotten the traumatic potato adventure of 1963, and our vows never to plant along the water's edge again. But in Nairobi, the price of everything had soared; food and vegetables were scarce all over the country. Together we calculated the profits that slab of land could bring us and it seemed a crime to let it lie waste.

"Let's take the risk," Dorian said. "The odds are good – six months of dry weather, the crops will be out and we'll have killed all our debts." I listened to him and hesitantly agreed.

Back on the farm I set to work with Spazzini and our team of tractor drivers, many of whom had shared the previous potato battle with us. All day long, the tractors and ploughs broke the soft soil, turning it over, black and fertile. The sharp steel blades sank deep like a knife into chocolate cake. White egrets followed, graceful ladies-in-waiting, picking out the caterpillars and grubs that surfaced from below. Spazzini stood over the works like an angry bulldog, keeping everyone's nose to the grindstone. I watched with growing excitement as the square fields took shape and the long lines of tender green sprouts appeared. Within a month, the hundred and fifty acres were sown with potatoes, beans, carrots, cabbages, capsicum, zucchini and maize. Dorian came at weekends to supervise the progress. The prospects looked good. He began making plans to return to Naivasha, away from the drudgery of city life. The expectation filled him with fresh vigour and enthusiasm.

True to form, the hippo began trudging across the crops again, grazing on the young maize plants and succulent lucerne fields and flattening everything in their way. Undaunted, they broke through the electric wire fences, thorn barriers and ditches, and as the lake receded became ever more insolent. Night guards with guns took up their lonely, mosquito-infested beats again to no avail. But despite the hippo the crops flourished.

A passing horticultural expert from England told us he had never imagined such bountiful yields possible. The blue-grey cabbages, fat and round, weighed up to ten pounds each. Only a few lucky farmers with abundant water could produce such crops in the dry season. Lorries came from everywhere to buy and take them away. Ma would sometimes sit on the bumper of the Land-Rover and look on.

"I wish Pa had lived to see all this, he would have been so proud," she remarked sadly, half to me, half to herself. It was the first time we had started pulling in such a crop.

Then one day the weather changed. The blue sky was spattered with fleecy clouds like snowflakes hanging in the air. The sun rose in an orange haze and tinged the wispy clouds with pink and gold. Longonot was suspended in a misty curtain. For the first time in many months I did not feel the bite of the sun on my back. That night I lay and listened to the sound of distant thunder. My heart began to sink.

Every day the sky began to fill, the fleecy clouds turned grey and pregnant with rain. We were well past the rainy season. But the rhythm had somehow been upset. The wind rose and hurtled through the trees. They bent and sighed and shed their leaves. The dust-devils spiralled once again high into the sky. At noon, heavy silence hung over the farm – the hush before the thunderclap.

Two inches of rain fell that night. The thirsty ground drank its fill and the surplus ran in rivulets along the roads and lay in puddles everywhere. The scent of rain and damp earth filled the air. The flowers smiled with rain drops on their petals, fish eagles screamed as they glided on the wind, cavorting in the sky, giant ibis left the ground with raucous cries and rain birds ululated from every tree. Everything that lived and breathed rejoiced.

It rained every day for a week. The lake began to swell and rise. The joyous feeling of a few days before turned to anxiety. The weather forecast announced heavy rain and storms across the country. Dorian arrived and rushed upstairs to my room.

"We'll lose the crop if it goes on like this," he bellowed with disappointment and rage. "Bloody rain," he muttered, as he moved out onto the terrace and looked down at the sodden world around us. We had been caught again. I tried to find some words with which to console him but I knew it was hopeless. It rained for two months. The lake rose seven feet and our new acres went under. We called in men and women and children from all around. Knee deep in mud and water, they once again pulled up the crops from the gooey ground and fought off the fat black leeches that clung to their legs with engine oil and grease. I had to use my horse for transport, as no vehicle could approach our flooded fields.

Each new day began clear and crisp. In the early mornings, before the work began, I visited the silent fields and momentarily forgot the battle we were fighting. I wondered whether it was not better to let nature take her course, and bow our heads to Africa and gracefully retreat. Pelicans drifted across the fields, catching fish among the cabbages and turnips. Saddle-bill storks, herons, crested cranes and egrets picked their way on delicate legs among the lacy carrot tops and rose, on graceful wings, in front of my chestnut mare, Malaika. Taka-Taka, my Doberman, yapped as he chased after them in a spray of water.

But by midday the fat, white clouds had fused and become dark and menacing. Thunder rolled in the hills and echoed across the lake. At night I listened to the raindrops fall, and in my room the ceiling leaked. Three weeks later, we lost the crop.

Lorenzo's faith in Kenya's future was shaky. He did not want to get involved and was detached from all the goings-on. He was not happy to see me struggling with the farm.

"You're wasting your time and energies, you should be taking pictures," he told me angrily, when he came to visit us in Naivasha.

He was right. I should have been taking photographs instead of fighting Africa. So I went with Amina to join him and Bob in Kilifi and accepted their invitation to another adventure on the *Mir-el-Lah*, this time to Aldabra and Cosmoledo, five hundred miles east into the Indian Ocean.

The archipelago, known as the Galapagos of the Indian Ocean, is still virtually uncorrupted by man and is populated by white booby birds with blue rings around their eyes, frigates with seven-foot wing spans and thousands of egrets, herons and gulls. Giant water turtles carve tracks like railway lines in the sand and wild goats roam in the coconut groves. Bright red crabs live in the jagged lava rocks and in the sea.

Five weeks later, we sailed for home at dusk. The East African coast lay three days' journey to the west. The sky was overcast and black. A storm was rising on the horizon. Lorenzo wanted to wait, but Bob was in a hurry. He had a plane to catch in Nairobi and a deadline to meet in Paris and he persuaded Lorenzo to leave. A few hours into the night, out of sight of land, the storm broke and hit us head on. The sea rose, the waves crashed across our bow and soaked everything. For three days and three nights we fought the storm. Unable to keep our course, we headed south, hoping to outride it. Mombasa was out of the question. We tried for Mafia Island, three hundred miles south of Tanzania, and then Dar-es-Salaam, but each time we turned the bow into the wind the *Mir-el-Lah*, rose so high out of the water that we thought she would disintegrate as she crashed back down again. Four times we set our course for harbours further south and finally, at the end of the second day, Lorenzo announced we had no alternative but to make for the Comore Islands several hundred miles south-west of the Seychelles.

"What happens if we miss them?" I asked.

"We'll end up in Madagascar or South Africa or the Antarctic," he replied, and smiled bravely from beneath the dripping curls on his forehead.

The *Mir-el-Lah* creaked and groaned and rode the waves like a cork, following every contour of the sea. Life on board was reduced to bare essentials; keeping dry, maintaining energy, reducing seasickness and, above all, keeping calm and sane.

Three times the rudder cable snapped. The top-heavy, wooden roof that Lorenzo had erected in Kilifi for shelter began to crack. I lay on my back and watched the cracks widen with every wave. Visions of us capsized in the angry water danced before my eyes. A bang from the engine room brought me to my feet, my heart missed a beat and a cold sweat broke out all over me. I knew, from previous experience in the Persian Gulf, that without the powerful engine propelling us forward the *Mir-el-Lah* could not resist the storm, and would capsize. Matheka dived below deck, while Lorenzo kept the boat's nose pointing into the wind. A leak in the gearbox had completely drained the oil. Matheka grabbed a bottle of our precious olive oil from the reserve kitchen shelf in the hold and emptied it into the overheated cogs. He shifted the gear lever and the engine took up its rhythmic beat again. Lorenzo's face was pale; I saw the muscles in his jaw flex; he did not utter a word, just kept his eyes on the nose of the boat, his fingers tight on the wheel.

"Hoist the main sail," he bellowed, and all hands rushed to man the ropes. But when the sail reached the top of the mast, the wind filled it with such violence that the sixty-foot boom snapped in two. Juma was sent up to untie the ropes jammed in the fragmented pole. He hesitated for a moment and was about to refuse when Lorenzo showed him a pink hundred-shilling note. He grabbed a knife between his teeth and shinned up the dangerously swaying pole like a monkey. Gripping only with his knees and toes, he cut the knot and slithered back to us on deck. The waves were now higher than the dhow; they rolled up behind us in huge banks of dark, blue water and passed beneath the hull carrying us forward as if we were surfing, and the rain kept coming. But we had been soaked for so long it no longer bothered us.

Suddenly, as the third day was nearly ended, Matheka shouted, "Land!" and we all rushed towards him. "Look over there in the mist, it's land, it's land," he repeated, laughing like a clown; and we identified with every sailor who had ever hollared thus.

Lorenzo and Bob and our gallent crew battled through the night waiting for the first light so that they could see their way through the jagged coral reef. Four nights without sleep had put dark circles and deep lines around their eyes and mouths. Soaked through and bedraggled, with a three-day growth of beard on his face, Lorenzo never left the wheel. Bob was gaunt and grey in his yellow oil-skin cape that fell to his knees, his hairy, naked legs and shoeless feet poking out beneath it. He looked like a Walt Disney character. I fed them coffee and boiled rice and wiped their faces with sodden towels, but their adrenalin was flowing and they remained optimistic and in control.

As dawn was breaking, twelve hours later, the anchors were dropped in a lava cove off the northern shores of the *Grande Comore* and we stepped off the dhow onto the steaming, tropical island, alive and safe. We kissed the warm rocks and hugged each other and let the tears flow down our salty faces.

That night, the *Mir-el-Lah* sank. The top-heavy wooden roof could not resist the constant battering of the waves; the sidebeams snapped, and the weight pulled her onto her side. The boards separated and the water poured into the engine room, flooding the hull, and all our belongings floated out to sea.

I stood with Lorenzo next morning on the white beach, surrounded by a large group of curious Comoreans from the nearby village, and together we looked at the *Mir-el-Lah* lying on her side. The waves breaking against her hull swished in and out of the engine room and cabins. The roof floated out to sea together with all her contents, which included the first dummy and the new pages of my ill-fated book.

"Oh God, Lorenzo, what are you going to do now?" I gasped. He waited for a moment before answering, letting his eyes drift over his beloved ship. "Don't worry, I'll refloat her, I'll sail her back to Mombasa and then I'll buy myself a Rolls and drive away from the sea."

I left Lorenzo on the beach in the Comores and returned to Kenya by air with Amina. Dorian, Oria, Iain and my mother were frantic when they discovered that hurricane Emily had swept up the Mozambique Channel and met hurricane Fifi not far from where we were sailing, and that we were somewhere near their point of intersection. Iain was preparing an aerial search, but he would never have found us; we were so small in that big angry ocean.

When Oria and Iain returned they found my father gone. We showed them his grave and they wept when I told them about his last days. Their film project had been accepted and Anglia Television sent a team to Manyara. Eighty thousand copies of *Among the Elephants* went to press, and their elephant odyssey was trumpeted across the world.

Oria and Iain travelled round Europe and America to promote their book and film and then began a massive census of the elephant population of Africa. Africans had been killing animals for food for centuries but now the heavy demand for ivory in the Far East and Europe had created an unprecedented decline in the elephant population. Bands of men, using the latest automatic weapons and sophisticated poison darts, slaughtered the elephants, stripped them of their tusks and buried them in little more than an hour. After several kills, the tusks were scooped up and loaded into large trucks, usually at night, and carried secretly, and with considerable risk, to the illegal traders in Nairobi or along the coast.

At one stage the government made a record five million shillings each year from game trophies, and in 1975 the ivory exported to Hong Kong alone was just over five hundred tons, the product of between twenty-five and thirty thousand elephants. Large areas of the Tsavo National Park, once the classic home of the elephant, became completely cleared of animals.

The government attempted in vain to combat the poaching, but was handicapped by inadequate resources, and I began to understand the importance of the work done by people like Iain. The African's hunting instinct knows only fear and he has no respect for wild animals. It will need generations to bring him to heel and as long as there is financial gain, the efforts of Iain and those who think like him will be like spitting in the wind. I have never been convinced about Iain's struggle to save wildlife. Since independence its destruction has escalated alarmingly. But while, on Africa's dusty trails, man and beast fight for the right of way, Iain will at least have taught his children the wonders of the wild and they will have grown up fearless and will have learned to love the gift of nature's wilderness which man so unthinkingly destroys.

Then, at last, the Ministry of Tourism and Wildlife announced, "All Killing of Game in Whatever Form to be Banned with Immediate Effect." But by eliminating professional hunting the government was also eliminating some of the key eye-witnesses to the ivory-poaching, and thousands of animals died lingering deaths from poachers' snares, like the elephant Iain and I set out to find on one of his expeditions. He had to dart an elephant with a wounded leg on the ninety-thousand acre ranch of an Italian friend of ours in the Laikipia area of northern Kenya. It was one of the last untouched places in the country, still teeming with game. Accompanied by a handful of wild Suk tribesmen, we left at sunrise and tracked through the thick "wait-a-bit" thorn bush for several hours before we came upon the wounded animal dozing beneath a tree. The first dart Iain fired failed to sink deep enough into the flesh; the elephant crashed through the bushes and disappeared from sight. All day we followed in the stifling heat through the undergrowth. Four times Iain fired his darts, but the arrow heads were defective and fell to the ground. Each time the elephant moved deeper into the forest.

Ten hours later, as we were on the point of deciding to give up and return home, we found ourselves dangerously near to the huge beast, which was in obvious distress. Iain had one last dart left. He fired it, and this time it stuck. The aggravated animal turned and, trumpeting with exasperation, bore down on us like an express train. We instantly took off upwind followed by his trackers and leapt through the thorn bushes a few feet from its tusks. Iain's shirt was ripped from his back and he lost his gun and glasses. In my own panic as I too crashed through the thorn bushes, my camera got hooked to a branch and was ripped from my hands. Branches tore at my face and arms and still the elephant's horrific scream kept on. For some unknown reason, it suddenly skidded to a halt, inches from Iain, turned, and charged off in the opposite direction. I stopped to catch my breath, my heart thumping in my ears. I could hear the high-pitched buzz of the insects in the eerie silence.

One by one we returned to the clearing but Iain was nowhere to be seen. Then he suddenly appeared, pale and shaking, his face and arms bleeding. "I could feel its hot breath down my spine," he said with a nervous laugh as he walked towards us.

My bush ramblings with Iain always came as a welcome respite to my self-imposed exile on the farm, for the writing of the family saga was slowly consuming me. Alone with Ma in Naivasha, I turned down invitations, was not at home to visitors, and became bad-tempered and sour. I snapped at anyone who disturbed me and drove Lorenzo and my family wild, pushing them to extreme exasperation and rage, but they never ceased encouraging me for they had a deep faith in me. Whenever Lorenzo felt like striking me, he clenched his fists and walked away, mumbling obscenities, or fell back on his uninhibited sense of humour, and he kept me going. At night, I lay awake, devoured by self-doubt. I longed to give up. The book was interfering with my life and every excuse which drew me from my desk was welcome.

Then one night I read a line in a book: "Writing shows the pains of child-bearing. There is no joy, just pain, sweat, exhaustion. It saps the blood, it is a curse. No one knows this better than the writer. I yearn to be delivered of this book, it is devouring me." I felt better. I identified with other writers and this appealed to my dramatic soul. After that I no longer cared how people reacted to me, the only important thing was to give birth, so that I could be delivered. For six years I had very few joyful moments. The ribbon of my story followed the contours of my growth and all the time things kept happening around me, so in the end my saga was writing itself.

It was vital, I thought, to tell the story as it really was, regardless of repercussions. My encounter with Shaibu had been a particularly important turning point in my African odyssey, for it had banished the malady of racial discrimination which had afflicted almost every European living in Africa. But it was out of the question that I should divulge the facts of this experience while my parents were alive: it would have shattered them.

When Shaibu crossed my life he was sixteen years younger than I. I was a colonial, deeply impregnated with colonial taboos. He was a Muslim whose code of religion and ethics was as refined as my own, if not more so.

One day I caught myself looking at him not as a black man but simply as a man. Something was happening to us, something that had never happened before and neither of us dared to admit this as we played and laughed and hid behind the false pretence of casual camaraderie. The pretence worked as long as we remained each on our own terrain, but when I left for the Bajun Islands with Shaibu and his three brothers on their dhow, I inadvertently trespassed onto his territory. Before leaving I spoke to an Italian friend of mine about the way I was beginning to feel for Shaibu.

"Be careful," he warned me. "You will upset the natural ecology of his life, while you yourself have nothing to lose."

The journey to Kisingitini lasted two and a half days. My new African friends treated me with respectful courtesy and Shaibu was full of tender attention. Each night he unrolled my mattress for me and built a shelter above my head with *kikois* knotted to the ropes. It seemed important to him that I should be comfortable and in need of nothing. His brothers slept some distance from me, but Shaibu curled up on a straw mat at my feet. We never touched, and kept our feelings secret.

A few days after we had settled on the island, I went to sea with Shaibu and his brothers in a canoe. When we were out of sight of land we were caught in heavy rain. The sky became dark and the wind was cold, so we dived into the warm tropical waters with our goggles and flippers.

The current was very strong and I drifted downstream. When Shaibu noticed how far from him I was he swam after me, put out a long, sinewy arm and grabbed hold of my wrist, pulling me to him. He slipped his arm around my waist, and pushed me gently under water beneath him. I looked up at him through my goggles and saw him hovering a few feet above, stretched out dark and powerful in a blaze of bright bubbles. He smiled down at me and I surfaced on the other side of him. With this gesture he had inadvertently taken the first step. He was the man, he took the decision, and the wall that separated us began to crumble. Together we swam back to the boat.

That night in my tent beneath the palms we talked for the first time about the relationship between a man and a woman of different colours. I was very nervous but Shaibu remained calm. The glow from the hurricane lamp played on his face and naked chest and threw our shadows onto the canvas. We sat on the floor and listened to the sea. A pink crab scuttled from under the tarpaulin trailing white sand grains behind it. The jasmine blooms the women in the village had given us that evening lay scattered on the floor and filled the tent with their heady perfume.

I thought of Lorenzo and how I had been brainwashed for so long. I wondered if black men made love in the same way as white men do. I had never had these thoughts before. Excitement and confusion made me shake as if I had a fever.

That night I embarked on the most exciting love adventure of my life. It was to last for two years and was so natural that I wondered what all the fuss had been about. But Kimuyu sulked for days, he went listlessly about his chores and refused to talk to or cook for Shaibu. He glared at us disapprovingly and stared moodily at his fire. Kimuyu had been to school in a Protestant mission and read his Bible each night before retiring. In his view, black girls and white men were acceptable, but he had never yet had to deal with the converse. Whenever I spoke to him now he dropped his eyes in confusion.

When it was time for me to head back home, I tried to explain to Shaibu what it was like in the white man's world – the hostility, the resentment, the prejudice. I spelled it out ruthlessly to him, for it was important he should understand.

It was not possible for him to share my life as I had his. My world was not like his. But he did not listen; perhaps he did not understand; certainly he did not care. Young, impulsive and in love, he wanted only one thing – to be with me, regardless of the consequences. He looked at me imploringly, defiantly, his black eyes on fire and said, "Please take me with you." Aching to say yes, I said no and then capitulated and agreed.

When we reached Naivasha, he faced the first test when I went in by the front door and he went in by the back. I sat in the drawing-room with my parents, he sat in the servants' quarters with the house servants. The situation made me cringe, but there was nothing I could do about it. If we wanted to continue without upsetting the apple cart, these were the conditions, for if my father had found out he would have shot Shaibu, and probably me also and then himself. In Naples, crimes of passion are part of a code of life. Wives and daughters are treated like madonnas, to be revered but never touched – certainly not by a black man – and I had not forgotten how my father had chased Lorenzo out of the house brandishing his duelling sword because he caught him sitting on my bed reading a magazine at two in the afternoon in front of an open door. He was banished for a week from my life.

I had made all this clear to Shaibu before we left Watamu. Officially he was simply my assistant, all else had to remain a secret. He was given a hut in the servants' quarters and after everyone had gone to sleep he used to climb through the window of my bedroom to join me for the night.

I tried to find something for Shaibu to do on the farm, but I was not very successful and I noticed for the first time the class distinction that exists among Africans. Shaibu was half Arab and a Muslim, and there were certain things he just did not do. The privileged position he held as my personal assistant, the friendship that obviously existed between us, and the fact that he talked to me as an equal and called me by my Christian name antagonised the others.

When Lorenzo came to visit me in Naivasha, I told him I had a lover. I needed a reaction from him.

"Good," was all he said.

"But there is something else I don't know how to tell you."

"There is nothing you can't tell me," he smiled back, curiously.

"He is black."

"So what?" he retorted. "Invite him to dinner." Lorenzo did not have my inhibitions.

When I introduced them they struck up an immediate friendship and we all went to Kilifi for two months. They spent the days together, fishing, and Lorenzo did not seem to mind that Shaibu and I stayed together at night. But Shaibu found the situation difficult to accept – it was so entirely against his strict Muslim code of ethics.

At first, I was surprised by Lorenzo's reactions, but I knew it was not indifference. He had for many years tried to free himself from the conventions of his own society and had accepted that others should live as they wished. For him life was like a river where people flowed with the current. If I was happy with Shaibu, why should he interfere? "If I really love you I want you to be happy," he said. I understood then why my union with my husband, even if it was now only spiritual, would stretch into old age.

The time I spent with Shaibu taught me many things. From him I learned the fundamental truths and values of life. Like the lion, the giraffe, the fever tree and the ochre warrior, Shaibu belonged to Africa. At one with him, I was at one with Africa, an experience which has never repeated itself in sheer emotional and physical intensity.

Shaibu stayed with me until I had finished all the photographs for *Vanishing Africa*. When I told him I would be leaving Kenya for a year, while I saw the book through the press, he once more begged me to take him with me, but that, alas, was impossible.

"I can't take you with me," I tried to explain to him. "You are a man of the sea and I live on the land. I travel around and live in a tent and I am white, a *musungu*."

His parents also begged me to keep him with me. "He will die if you leave him here. He is your child now," they said. But it was painfully obvious that this was impossible. Our worlds were too far apart and there was no longer any place for him in mine. Kimuyu went back to my parents in Naivasha and Shaibu returned to his little village beneath the coconut trees.

When I returned to Kenya a year later I went to Watamu to find Shaibu again. His sister led me into his hut. He was lying asleep on a straw mat, a yellow and orange *kikoi* loosely thrown over his hips. His back was turned to the door. I knelt down beside him and put my hand on his shoulder. He turned in his sleep and then I saw his face. It was unrecognisable. I knew immediately he had begun to drink.

He looked as if he had been stung by bees. His eyes and cheeks were swollen, and flies crawled over a nasty cut on his forehead.

When he opened his eyes and saw me, he did not seem surprised. He smiled and yawned, and stretched like a lazy cat. He said nothing, and all that seemed to remain of his old self were the soft eyes and gentle smile.

After a little while we began to talk in the cool dark hut. He had been so totally uprooted by our encounter that he could not adapt to the simple life I had torn him from. He had grown fat and sloppy and shunned his life by the sea, and no longer cared about anything except money. He told me he was moving ivory from the bush to illicit buyers in

Mombasa.

During the next few weeks I tried to reason with him but my words fell on deaf ears. I told him that I would never see him again if he did not stop drinking and pull himself together. He promised he would but he never did.

My Italian friend had been right when he had said: "You will upset the natural ecology of his life". My guilt over his condition was real, but the adventure had drawn me in, as it had him, and now it was too late. During the two years that we had been together I had found myself, but he had lost himself. Unwittingly I had torn him from his world and made him a victim of mine.

CHAPTER 23

Giselle

My mother had her eighty-fifth birthday on 25th April, 1977. We gave her a little birthday lunch at the Bacchus Club in Nairobi and presented her with flowers and a cake with eighty-five candles on it. Some friends came to drink champagne with us. She did not recognise them and put on her little act for them. When they asked her how she felt she answered wistfully, "Very old. I hate being eighty-five, there is still so much I want to do and see."

The lonely constrictions of her life in Naivasha now weighed heavily on her. Her letters, which found their way to us wherever we were, reminded me of somebody hanging onto a rope in the sea and feeling their grip weakening. "I lead a very solitary life in 'the big house', devoid of reason, and wonder why I'm still alive – it all seems so useless now, even if I still attend to the flowers, which seems the last thing left for me to do. I cannot explain anything except that I am so far gone from my normal self that I do not seem able to reform. When are you coming back, I need you to revive my instinct to live – I often, very often, think of you, but I don't remember even where you are so can't address this letter. The children keep in touch so lovingly with their little postcards; they tell me they long to return to Naivasha, so that at least is something accomplished . . . the feeling of a home somewhere always there for them. The weather is superb, the sky is brilliant blue every day, all day."

My mother was a stubborn lady. The frustrations of old age had made her aggressive and difficult to live with. She loved her family and her dogs and believed in discipline. She had rigid principles from which she never strayed, and she tried, not always very successfully, to instil good manners and obedience into her grandchildren and her dogs. So many times we had told her to leave the dogs alone, but she could not stand their insistent show of affection and demand for attention.

Raj, the purebred Alsation puppy, belonged to Amina. I gave him to her when he was six weeks old. My mother protested feebly when Amina triumphantly presented him to her. She was no longer steady on her legs and was terrified of falling or tripping over playful dogs. One Sunday morning, Raj knocked her over as she tried to tie him to a pillar and keep him from the breakfast table. She broke her hip just as Pa had done. She lay confused and in pain for six weeks in the hospital in Nairobi waiting for the bone to heal and then spent another month recuperating with Dorian and Eva. But they were out at work all day and she resented being left alone in the care of the African servants, so I brought her back to Naivasha. I thought she would feel better in her home, surrounded by the things she loved. But her spirit was broken, her mind confused.

I tried to follow the doctor's order and gave her daily physical therapy. But after a month I realised she was getting no better, that she would never walk or even stand again, and that the many pills I gave her were only prolonging the agony. She was so frail and weak, so old and full of sleep, so small in that big armchair. Her mind wandered about, filled with people and images from the past. She talked to me of them and asked me where they were. I sat beside her and held her hand and tried to follow her mental meanderings. We had pathetic, nonsensical conversations – it was like talking to an old child. My stomach contracted each time I entered the vast rooms filled with sunlight and saw her, bent and crushed, struggling to get up from the awful chrome wheelchair. She did not realise that she could no longer stand, and looked at me with dazed, frightened eyes. "What would I do without you?" she kept saying, and I had to fight back my helpless rage and frustration. What could I do but watch and wait and hope it would not last too long?

I had been brought up on a farm where stricken animals were put out of their misery. Was it not possible to do the same for humans? I talked it over with a nurse. I doubled the pain killers and gave Ma sweetened tea laced with marijuana leaves. I filled the vases in the rooms with flowers from her garden and, from the hi-fi set in my room upstairs, played music for her.

Guilty and remorseful, I tried to hide my feelings. Dorian and Oria paid sporadic visits at the weekends and I resented their apparent detachment and the reasons that kept them from Naivasha.

Gentle and devoted, Mweru gave me strength; between her tears and smiles she kept me going. Because of her, I held onto my sagging morale. Together we watched my mother fade. She grew so thin, her silver bracelets slid from her wrist one by one; then I found her wedding ring on the floor beside the bed.

Once as we were dressing her I had a lightning flash of illumination. I saw her young and beautiful again. Her skin was smooth, her neck long and unwrinkled, the light green eyes wide and clear. She looked like a curved lily, momentarily erect and slim in her bed. Then the vision was gone. She was old and worn again.

One day she slept all day. Then I knew that the end was near. The weekend was upon us. I called Dorian in Nairobi and told him to find a coffin. I could not stand the idea of her lying dead in her room while we waited for Monday.

Dorian, Oria and Iain arrived by plane from Nairobi two hours later. I was no longer alone. We stood and watched Ma sleep. She opened her eyes briefly and looked at us and smiled. We thought we heard her say my brother's name. Had she seen us? Had she heard us? Did she know that we were there beside her?

I went upstairs and lit a joint. I was no longer needed. Stretched out on the verandah I watched a fish eagle ride the wind and the daylight fade. Dorian came up to see me. We sat for a long time looking at the sky.

"I wonder what it is that makes people rush to the bedside of the dying?" I finally asked him.

"I suppose it is that invisible link in the great chain that keeps the whole human race together," he answered slowly.

My mother was slipping away from us and was slowly bringing our family saga to an end. She was the last link in our chain. She had kept us together and had always brought us back to Naivasha. Now she was handing over and we would now probably all go our own separate ways.

I went back downstairs to see her. Her eyes were wide open, she stared out of the window in front of her bed at the fever trees and scarlet bougainvillaea she had planted. She looked faded and serene.

"Hello, Mami, can you hear me?" I said as I moved towards her bed. She did not stir. She just kept staring out of the window. "Can you hear me, Mami?" I repeated. Her eyes shifted slowly from the window and froze on my face. We looked at each other for a long moment and then she closed her eyes for the last time. Had she seen me? Had she heard me? We were already in different worlds.

Raj walked in and lay on the carpet beneath the open window, crossing his paws. In the silence of the high-ceilinged room with the blue and white Marco Polo murals my father had painted thirty years before, she still breathed quietly. Her body was slowing down.

The servants sat on a bench in the kitchen and kept another silent vigil. Their chattering had stopped. Mweru stood on the stairway, weeping quietly. A hush filled the house as the night crept in. Unable to sit still, I wandered through the empty rooms so full of her presence, while Dorian, Oria and Iain kept watch beside her bed. I turned off the lights and lit all the candles I could find and carried them to her room. Each time I went to see her, her breathing had slowed down further. I had watched my father die, and the long-drawn-out silences between each breath were the same. She looked like him now. At eleven o'clock she left us, the same hour as my father had two years before.

I lay awake all night on my bed outside and watched the stars cross the sky and listened to the sounds of Africa all around. Confused and relieved I tried to untangle my thoughts. Is there life after death? Someone once told me that energy never dies. Where was she now? And was she taking up as much space there as she had here? I was glad now that I had remained beside her to the end. I listened to Dorian and Iain bringing up the coffin from the garage below and a car drive away into the night.

Next day the grave gaped up at us from beneath the plain casket. We had decided not to have a religious ceremony but just to bury my mother beside my father in the garden. The Maasai women in their ceremonial beads, our faithful old Africans, a few neighbours and some friends from Nairobi stood around us. Saba and Dudu, perched on the mound of fresh earth, clasped each other round the waist. Oria wept beside Iain. Valeria held Amina by the hand. I looked up at Dorian opposite me. Resignation and relief crossed his face. He had been my mother's favourite child; something special had existed between them which we girls had never shared with her. He read some lines from the psalms, and a rainbird called from a tree somewhere.

After my father died I found a verse which he had left for my mother in his diary. With lowered heads and downcast eyes, our friends listened as I read it over her grave from a crumpled paper in my hand.

Toi qui es devant ma tombe
Ne t'étonne pas de mon sort
Il fut un temps ou j'étais comme toi
Viendra le temps où tu seras comme moi.

I walked back into the house and from the covered verandah outside my father's room watched the coffin disappear into the ground beside his grave. Tears rushed to my eyes as the ritual earth was scattered from hands black and white.

Three pelicans circled in the sky, a storm rolled across the lake and, all around, the trees and flowers my father and mother had planted together watched in silence.

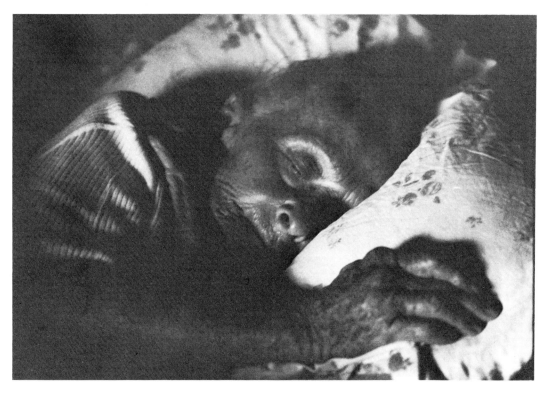

"Each time I went to see her, her breathing had slowed."

Epilogue

I planted a white bougainvillaea on my mother's grave and left Kenya two months after the funeral.

The rains did not subside. Even as I was packing my bags a dark storm rolled towards the farm. I was alone in the house except for Mweru, who waited downstairs in case I needed her. I went for a last walk in the garden. The wind was blowing hard, the trees shed their leaves all around me like tears. I stopped for a moment between my parents' graves and checked that the flowers and shrubs we had planted were in order. I disregarded the momentary tightening in my throat. I could not afford to get emotional. I had to go before the rain stopped me.

As I stepped back into the house a thunderclap followed a flash of lightning and the rain poured down. Within minutes the ground around the house was inches deep in water. Mweru came with a tattered yellow parasol and helped me to carry my bags down the steps into the car. I put my arms around her and held her tight. Was she crying or was it rain running down her face? She looked sad and thin and small. Millela, tucked on her back, blinked the rain drops from her tiny bronze face.

I did not say goodbye to anyone. I just left. It was better that way. I had left many times before but now I was walking away from Naivasha for good. If I returned it would be as a visitor. Sadness and rage tugged at my gut. I needed to get away as fast as possible. The heavy rain made the going slow. The car slithered all over the rutted road. As the farm retreated from me I felt at once both defeated and relieved. It was too soon to know if I was glad or sad to be leaving. Lorenzo had once said to me in Latin, "To try is human, to pursue is folly." The events of the past six months – my mother's death, the rain, the lake which had taken our crops – tumbled through my head. Everything around me was wet and grey, and out of focus. For the first time I was accepting defeat graciously; it was perhaps my first victory.

Longonot, shrouded in rain, loomed up on my right, massive and dark, undisturbed and eternal over the yellow green grass stretching from the lake to her feet. The mountain slipped out of sight as I drove up the steep escarpment past the little church where Dorian and Francine were married, to the top of the Rift Valley. I left the rain below. The sun was shining. A heavy grey curtain hid Naivasha and the lake from me.

That same evening, on the plane to London, I sat beside a friend who was also leaving the country. We talked a long time about Africa and the Africans, exchanging and comparing our emotions, our rages and our joys, and laughed at each other's stories. We talked of Africa as if we had shared a lover who had walked away from both of us. She now lay below us silent and unperturbed, bathed in moonlight. Had we really been beaten by her, or was it just that we had never completely adjusted to her?

"The longer you live in Africa the less you understand it," I said to my companion, and he nodded his head and said nothing.

My mother had once said that the whites in Africa were like an army of occupation, to be tolerated but never accepted. Could uprooted trees grow in foreign soil? Or was there some way of grafting them back onto native stock? Six months later *Dominio de Doriano* was sold to Joseph Kamau, the orphaned boy from the Mau Mau Emergency. We kept the house and eighty acres around it. Dorian telephoned the news to London. I wept and afterwards it felt as if a tumour had been extracted from my chest. All the frustration and anxiety left me and I thought back to my conversation with Berkeley that last evening at Elementeita.

Spazzini moved into a downstairs room in "the big house", to live out the last years of his life. "You don't have to pay me any more, I just ask you to let me stay here till I die, and bury me on the farm beside your father," he had said the day the farm was sold.

A handful of men and women remained with us, the rest were paid off and went elsewhere. There was no longer any work for them.

I had always found it almost impossible to imagine the end of Naivasha – I feared and dreaded the day as much as my own death. But now I felt nothing; no pain, no sorrow, no joy, just relief. My roots were severed and I drifted on a current, waiting for what I do not know, but seeds have blown in the wind and news sometimes comes from Africa.

My darling Ma,
Home at last and it feels so good again. The minute I stepped off the

plane into the African dawn the experience was an emotional one. Iain came to pick me up at the airport, we spent the morning in Langata, saw the children before they went to school, had a wonderful old Kenya breakfast, then went to have lunch at the French Cultural Centre.

Nairobi has changed so much I feel quite a stranger. There are so many Africans in the streets I am overwhelmed. Plenty of smooth young blacks with Rasta hair, tight pants and platform shoes who look at you with suave glances. Everywhere there are scaffolds making progress ever higher as the new Africa surges forth. It is quite astonishing.

We flew to the farm that same evening, keeping low over the watery plains. There has been a lot of rain again and all is green over the crags and steam jets of Hell's Gate, across the lake and down onto the strip. It felt so good to be back, to smell the night-watchman's fire, the damp earth and the trees. Last night I slept in your room.

All the familiar sights and sounds kept me awake, and then I heard a strange new sound I had never heard before. The moon was full and it was very light outside. From the terrace in front of your room at the top of the house, I watched two hippo coming up the winding steps leading to the entrance. Breathing heavily, they crushed the flowers in their path and moved across the elevated terrace lawn, cropping the grass beside the verandah where we ate our meals.

This morning I followed their footprints down the path over Mami and Papi's graves and into the lake. I think this is the first time in nearly fifty years they have come up to the house; it is silent and safe now.

The house and garden have lost nearly all their original pomp and splendour, but like some aged, beautiful queen the bone structure is still good. Slowly it is mellowing down and becoming an integral part of Africa, lovely as ever.

The house is clean and well looked after by Mweru but it feels so big and empty. At every turn Mami and Papi are there vividly haunting yet comforting and laughing. It makes me so sad. I walk around there like a stranger, so full of memories, and no matter how much painting and scrubbing has been done, they are both still present.

It led me to think a lot. About how this was their dream, their house, their time and place, their kingdom. They created it to live and play in, in the way of their ancestors, running away from a world whose changes they could not or did not want to face, to Africa, one of the last strongholds of the patrician spirit of the masters instead of the servants.

And about us, how painful and confusing these last few years have been. We, the children of the future with no futures ahead of us, unsure as to where we belong, eternally hankering to get back to something that is no more, just a beautiful, happy, dreamlike memory that will never leave our hearts – we are strangers wherever we go, because Naivasha is where we belong.

Being back has put many things into perspective for me. I used to think it was Kenya I loved and in Kenya I belonged; that after gruelling years abroad I would come back with all my foreign sophisticated knowledge and to help build up this new nation. But now I realise that it was all a childish dream, born of a need to identify with something. A dream to give me courage as I grope to understand and relate to worlds and civilisations that seem so hard and foreign. Now I know that it is Naivasha I yearned for; this house, this farm, the lake, hills, trees and animals, the love of my family, so proud and strong and gracious. Everything Naivasha ever stood for; a way of life that is no more. All I can do is look at the changes – bushes come down and go up again, it's all part of life and change – in ten years it will be different again.

In a way, we are all victims of our grandparents' flight, for now the modern world where all men are to be equal is closing in around us and there is nowhere left to run. We were Rocco's, and Naivasha made us special. Now the Naivasha we knew is gone but the feeling remains to give us strength as we seek new horizons.

It is painful, yes; all the more painful because we love what we leave behind and have a lot to miss. What is past is past, however, and now we must think of the present and look to the future. Our black neighbours couldn't be more fitting to our thoughts – not one thing is being done on the farm, except grazing all the grass to the roots, and the only income is from *makaa* (charcoal), trees are being cut down everywhere – thank God Ma and Pa never saw that – the Africans have now more money in the banks than all of us put together and not one cent is spent on the farm.

Everyone asks about you and misses you, but don't come back yet, there is really nothing for you now, and for a while you must think of your future.

Love, Marina